*Fifty Years*
*in the City*

# *Fifty Years in the City*

## FINANCING SMALL BUSINESS

John Kinross

John Kinross

To Julian with the authors warmest regards + gratitude for many years of friendship.

29th April 1982

JOHN MURRAY

Typeset by Inforum Ltd, Portsmouth
Printed in Great Britain
by the Pitman Press, Bath

0 7195 3937 4

*To My Present Fourteen Grandchildren . . .*

# CONTENTS

# CONTENTS

# ILLUSTRATIONS



*Illustration credits: 15, The Times*; 16, *The Scotsman*; 17, *Daily Express*; 18, *Glasgow Herald.*

# FOREWORD

A few months ago, John Kinross asked me to read the manuscript of his memoirs and to give him my views. I thus became acquainted with this impressive image of his life, only some aspects of which had been known to me in the course of business contacts over the past thirty-five years, and I told John how much I had enjoyed reading his book. He then asked me whether I would agree to write a short foreword which I am extremely happy to do, for this in my view is an autobiography which is well worth reading.

Most autobiographies contain too large a proportion of personal titbits which may be of significance to the writer but must be boring to the reader. John on the other hand excels in objectivity and has the strength of character to abstain from subjective notions and remarks. He is as factual and precise in describing the important events in which he was involved as he is utterly modest in depicting his own personal role. When noticing so many signs of this modesty on John's part I was reminded of words of advice given by one of the great Americans, Dwight Morrow, to his son when leaving University: 'The world is divided into people who do things and people who get the credit. Try, if you can, to belong to the first class. There's far less competition.' It is evident from John's autobiography that throughout his life he always acted in accordance with that sort of precept. It is also in this spirit that he overstates throughout every chapter of his work the part played by those associated with him and that similarly he understates his own part.

When drawing the picture of his life, John gives a fine survey of the various stages of his career but he also provides a good illustration of the business environment in which he has lived. Those decades between the end of the First World War and the last quarter of this century reflected revolutionary changes in the commercial and social atmosphere of this country: the free-wheeling enterprise characteristic of the Victorian and Edwardian periods underwent a transformation into a climate increasingly circumscribed by regulations and restraints and restrictions. Instead of the former emphasis on daring initiatives, the new endeavours had to be given special impetus towards professional competence and refinement. John embodied, and goes on to embody within himself both of these elements.

What transpires above all from John's recordings and teachings is that he accepted with determination, though gradually and reluctantly, modern requirements of size and technocratic methods. However, the basis of his thoughts and aims has always been, and remains, an unshakeable adherence to the highest standards of discrimination and perfectionism. Indeed, whenever he is faced with a choice between quality and quantity his firm conviction is that quality has to prevail.

The set of values which John not only describes in his clear and simple way but which he practises with powerful determination are inspiring incentives to follow for all those who know him.

*Siegmund Warburg*

# PREFACE

This is the account of a business life in the City of London, and of an upbringing in Scotland during which I acquired my fascination with the world of finance. I am now seventy-seven years old, and my City career alone already spans a period of fifty-two years, but I do not consider it to be over yet.

This account was written in the first instance for my fourteen grandchildren. In the course of preparing it I showed the manuscript to a limited number of people, most of whom are connected with some aspect of the financial world, and nearly all of whom considered that the result would be of interest to a wider range of people than the family for whom it was originally intended. First-hand accounts of City life spanning this period are comparatively rare, and I could never have undertaken the task without the use of the massive amount of papers, letters and diaries I have consistently kept throughout my life.

It is coincidence that this account of a career spent largely in evaluating and backing embryo businesses should appear at a time that small business is once again in vogue. My own experience in the inter-war years, and the considerable success of the Industrial and Commercial Finance Corporation since the end of the last war, prove conclusively to my mind that backing small businesses can be profitable as well as economically desirable.

But there are dangers. Small businesses are like any other type of business. They span the whole range from the truly excellent to the downright disastrous. Unlike established companies whose shares are quoted on the Stock Exchange, they frequently have no record on which their future prospects can be assessed. To sort out the good from the bad requires not only a judgment of men and women. It requires an instinct which comes only with many years of business experience. Increasingly, it also requires the back-up of an organisation with diverse facilities and direct industrial experience in order to evaluate the propositions that are put to it. And the provider of venture capital has to draw a fine balance. He will require a share of the potential rewards in return for the initial risk, but must avoid stifling the embryo business by being over-greedy.

New organisations offering venture capital are springing up almost daily. We are moving into an era where the supply of this type of finance exceeds the supply of entrepreneurs who have the ability to make good use of it. The pressure to back inherently unsound ventures is therefore increasing. For some investing institutions whose experience has hitherto been limited to the financial sphere and the prepackaged industrial investments available on the stockmarket, I foresee storms ahead. Given time, the availability of finance could eventually spawn a whole new generation of entrepreneurs. I hope that in the interim the inevitable failures will not stifle a concept that has always been close to my heart: the finance of small business.

Preparing this account for a wider readership has inevitably meant some departure from the original text which was designed for family eyes alone. Specifically, I have deleted all but the basic detail of my two marriages. My business life is my own, and much of it is a matter of public record. My family life involves others, and it would not be fair to my first or to my second wife to draw them into this account. Neither would they wish it.

The conversion into a published book was only possible thanks to the generous editorial help of my friend Michael Brett (Editor of *The Investors' Chronicle*). My present secretary, Anne Baily, remained sane and cheerful throughout the many drafts she had to type. I am deeply conscious of my debt to both these friends and to many others.

*John Kinross*

## CHAPTER ONE

# *An Edinburgh Childhood*

My parents were married at Helmsley Parish Church on 13 August 1889. In the following four and a half years, three girls were born, but only one survived – Eveleen Mary, born on 24 February 1894. The dates of the two older children speak for themselves: Margaret, born 5 April 1891, died a day later; Kathleen Mabel, born 10 July 1892 died 6 July 1893. My Father was then working on the restoration of Falkland Palace and my Mother, taking the baby with her, had gone to join him there for some weeks in the summer of 1893. Some of the local milk they were given was infected, the baby developed typhoid fever and it proved fatal. I was born at 33 Mortonhall Road, Edinburgh at 2.10 a.m. on Sunday 31 January 1904. My Father, in writing to friends and relatives, told them that the baby was like his Mother, and had the Roman nose of her family.

My Mother was the eldest girl in a family of seven children and had been born on 29 December 1863. She was brought up in a modest house – Birch Farm – near Oswaldkirk, a village about five miles from Helmsley in the lovely North Riding of Yorkshire. She was Margaret Louisa Mary Hall, the daughter of George Blythe Hall.

My Yorkshire Grandfather had been placed in a bank in York by his Father who, I think, was a lawyer in that town. He does not appear to have been interested in business so he retired quite early in life and bought this small property. Among his many friends was the Abbot of Ampleforth and my Grandfather, although a lifelong Anglican, used sometimes to dine at Ampleforth. The food was always excellent, but on one occasion the main course – a casserole of succulent and tender meat – was notable. My Grandfather's curiosity was aroused, and after dinner he asked the Abbot what exactly they had been eating. The answer was – rats! The monks had been threshing corn and had killed many young rats who had been living in the stooks, and were, therefore, thought to have fed themselves on corn.

My Mother's eldest brother was the black sheep of the family. He got into debt more than once, and finally I think my Grandfather could no longer pay his debts and he went to Australia and disappeared. During the lead-up to the final crisis, my Mother, then in her late teens, was so distressed by the effect of the problems on her parents that she herself tackled her wayward brother. Mother possessed great moral courage.

But these problems undermined the family finances, which had never been other than modest. So, as the girls' schooling came to an end, they all sought to use their varied talents in order to earn their living. My Mother, although never able to go to university, was a good English scholar and had read widely. She secured a post as an English mistress in a small girls' school at Thame, near Oxford. From there she went to a school at Totteridge in North London and after what seems to have been a happy time there, she was offered a post, again as an English mistress, in an excellent girls' school in Bellevue Cresent, Edinburgh.

One of my Mother's childhood friends had married a young Edinburgh quantity surveyor – Thomas Fairbairn (the Grandfather of Nicholas Fairbairn, the Tory M.P. for Kinross) and Mother used to go and see her friend Cissy at the Red House, her new home, opposite Morningside Station on the southern outskirts of Edinburgh. One evening at a small dinner party, she sat next to the young architect who had designed the house. He was John Kinross, and as a result of that meeting they later became engaged to be married.

My Father, who was eight and a half years older, had been born in Stirling on 3 July 1855. His Father, who had been twice married, had a large family. He was a coach builder and his firm, William Kinross & Sons was founded in Stirling in 1802 and was one of the leading coach builders in the early part of the nineteenth century. The coaches made in Stirling were exported all over Europe, as far as Russia, and several of them still exist in the Lisbon Coach Museum.

My Father had what would then have been a good education at Stirling High School; but how or why he became an architect I do not know. His forbears had been reasonably successful business men, yet my Father was without question a most talented artist and for nearly a quarter of a century was one of the leading domestic architects in Scotland. After serving apprenticeships in Glasgow with Mr John Hutchison and in Edinburgh with Messrs Wardrop and Reid, he went to Northern Italy for nearly two years, during 1880 and 1881, where he travelled extensively, with Florence as his base. His Mother lent him £250 (all of which he repaid with interest at 5%). One outcome of his travels was the publication in 1882 of *Details From Italian Buildings, Chiefly Renaissance*, dedicated to his Mother, Ann Kinross. He was a natural linguist, and later in his life spoke perfect French and Italian, while his Spanish and German were adequate. This period in Italy permanently influenced his work, and both in his restoration of Falkland Palace and at Manderston, in Berwickshire, one can clearly see the Italian influence.

Back from Italy, he set up practice in Edinburgh on his own account in 1882. The Red House was probably his first commission. Built in red sandstone from Dumfriesshire, it is now a branch of the Royal Bank of Scotland.

*Details From Italian Buildings* had been a scholarly work which had attracted a good deal of attention, not least from the third Marquess of Bute, then one of the largest landowners in the United Kingdom (he owned 117,000 acres and five houses in the UK). An ardent Catholic, and deeply interested in gothic and classical architecture, he invited my Father to become his architect in about 1885 and until the Marquess' premature death in 1900 this resulted in a continuous stream of restorations of historic buildings owned by the Bute family. Although Falkland Palace was the most notable example, the Augustinian Priory, St Andrews, is another fine specimen of his work at this period, while his restoration of the fifteenth-century Franciscan Friary in Elgin (Grey Friars) is considered by connoisseurs to be the most authentic recreation of this period in Northern Britain.

My Father had agreed to devote a fixed proportion of his time to Lord Bute's work but he was still able to accept much outside work, which consisted almost entirely of building country houses and churches. On several occasions, Lord Bute arranged for him to spend several weeks visiting religious buildings on the Continent. If the next restoration was to be a Benedictine Monastery, for example, my Father would visit similar establishments in France, Spain and Italy, living with the monks and not only preparing sketches and plans but learning of the practical reasons which caused the particular religious order to build as it did.

In 1900 work had started on the restoration of Pluscardine Abbey in Morayshire – then a complete ruin – and the main walls were about breast high when Lord Bute suddenly died. His heir was then a nineteen-year-old boy, and the executors had no alternative but to stop all this work, which was of course completely uneconomic. For nearly half a century, Pluscardine remained in this state and then the monks who had previously restored Prinknash Abbey in Gloucestershire moved to Pluscardine. When, in 1960, I saw Pluscardine for the first time, the work was well advanced.

Between about 1885 and 1914, my Father built many lovely houses for a wide variety of people. Some were successful men of business, others members of the aristocracy. The Peel, Clovenfords, near

Galashiels was built for a wealthy flour miller in Leith by the name of Ovens. Then there was Carlekemp in North Berwick for Mr James Craig (now a Catholic boys' school)£ Ardtornish, not far from Oban in Argyllshire, built for Mr Craig Sellers; Thurston at Innerwick near Dunbar for Mr Richard Hunter; and extensive work to Altyre and Gordonstoun for Sir William Gordon Cumming, whom my Father greatly liked. My Father's religious building (apart from Lord Bute's work) included the restoration of the Carmelite Friary Church at South Queensferry in 1889, the Church and Manse of St Peter at Fraserburgh and a new Scottish Episcopal Church (St Peter's) at Torry, Aberdeen, for the English fishermen who came to Aberdeen every year.

In 1894, Sir James Miller Bart, asked my Father to build stables on a grand scale at Manderston near Duns in Berwickshire. The stables were followed by other building and then in 1901 Sir James asked my Father virtually to rebuild the main house.

Sir James' Father, Sir William Miller, the first baronet, had been a Leith merchant trading with Russia and the Baltic countries. When he died in 1887 Sir James inherited Manderston with an estate of some 1200 acres and a fortune of several million pounds. He was a superb judge of horses and when he died in January 1906, aged only forty-two, he had won the Derby in 1890 and again in 1903, when his Rock Sand also won the Triple Crown.

In 1901, back from the Boer War, he wished to transform Manderston into a house where he could entertain on a large scale. He asked my Father to provide about forty bedrooms, and he and Lady Miller wished to have a ballroom modelled on the one at Kedleston in which they had become engaged. When my Father, in accordance with his usual custom, enquired approximately how much he wished to spend he was told: 'It doesn't really matter'.

This work took nearly four years and by the time it was finished in 1905 approximately £250,000 had been spent on the various buildings during the total eleven years. The outcome is a most beautiful mansion house in the style of the eighteenth century, a number of interesting houses for the principal estate workers, a superb dairy where the Italian influence is very marked, and many other buildings. This project, including the design of the formal gardens, was probably my Father's masterpiece. Manderston was occupied by Sir James' nephew, Major Hugh Bailie and his family until 1976, and in 1978 the house and most of the surrounding buildings were 'designated' and so will be preserved. They are now owned by Adrian Palmer, Major Bailie's grandson and are open to the public, who have, not surprisingly, come in large numbers.

It was just before Manderston was built that my Father, in a joint venture with a local builder, acquired a site at the extreme western end of Mortonhall Road in Edinburgh. Here he built four houses in his own version of Scottish baronial style. Three were sold. In 1900 he and my Mother moved into the fourth – Number 33, called Seven Gables, which thus became my birthplace. It was in this beautiful house that I spent the first seven very happy years of my life.

My Father and Mother had travelled widely in Europe and knew many of the international artists of the day, some of whom would stay with them if they were able to come as far as Edinburgh. I can still remember lying in bed before going to sleep and hearing peals of laughter from the floor below when there was a dinner party in progress. I can only dimly remember a grave Frenchman who stayed twice. On his second visit he again came down with my Father to the nursery where, although I was only about six or seven I had some carpenter's tools and liked to try to 'make things'. I remember him taking both my hands in his and counting my fingers – when he reached ten, he said with mock astonishment 'Still ten fingers, and all these *dangerous* tools!' This was Rodin.

My nurse was a Highland girl called Susan, whom I remember with affection. There were three maids, all of whom tended to spoil me but Mother did not let this go too far. She was easily the most important person in my life. I adored her: at the time, and not only in retrospect.

Nearly every year up to the outbreak of war in 1914 we spent a holiday in Keswick, then a quiet little town where we used to stay at a boarding house in 'The Heads', on the way to Derwentwater. Transport was still by horse-drawn coach, and on steep hills most of the passengers would get out and walk. While my Father and sister departed for all-day coach excursions, Mother used to take me to Ashness Bridge, on the way to Watendlath. Here we would spend the day together – she with a book and her knitting, while I dammed the stream that emerges from Watendlath Tarn. I never tired of this and, being strong, I could move quite large pieces of rock to create a fairly deep pool and waterfall. I still enjoyed the same operation when I had children of my own: I enjoyed building dams with my second family when they were young and we had a cottage at the top of Nidderdale in the West Riding from 1951 to 1956.

But my Father's occupation was not impervious to chill economic winds. Lloyd George's budget of 1909 changed many things, and had a traumatic effect on my Father's practice. Many people who had been planning to build large houses cancelled these. Although he still had plenty of work, his clients were no longer spending lavishly. As a result, in 1911 we moved to a much smaller house at 67 Braid Road.

It must have been a sad decision for my Father to part with Seven Gables. Our new home where we lived for the next ten years, was a very ordinary semi-detached, suburban house, built just before the turn of the century.

While we lived in Mortonhall Road I had been going to a mixed kindergarten, Miss Bell's in Lauder Road, quite an institution at that period. When we moved, however, I was sent to the Hill School in Colinton Road. When I left it in 1915 I had an above-average examination record, except in mathematics which was always my weakest subject. And I had made a small number of friends.

Among the companions of my youth was Geoffrey Ransome, a young publisher then in his twenties and the son of an old friend of my parents. When I was about eight he took me to a matinee of Peter Pan. It was the first time I had been inside a theatre, and I was completely carried away. Geoffrey became very much of an elder brother at that period, and often came to spend a Sunday with us and taught me to ride a bicycle. His home was in Yorkshire, and he was then working in Nelson's, the Edinburgh publishers. When he was killed on the Somme in 1916, it brought home the tragedy of the war to me as nothing else had done.

On Saturdays or during school holidays, I would sometimes go with my Father to some building site, and would hold one end of his measuring tape for him. I climbed up scaffolding with him and listened while he discussed details of the job with the builder.

A few other events of my childhood stand out. In 1913 my sister was studying music in Kiel, and I went there with my parents for about ten days in September. I stayed with German friends, while my parents were in a nearby hotel. Kiel was full of naval personnel and one wet morning, on my way to my parents' hotel, I was walking along a narrow pavement behind a middle-aged lady; approaching us was a German naval officer wearing his sword which seemed to be quite usual. There was not room for two people to pass on the pavement, and as he drew level with the lady he used his sword to push her off into the roadway. Seeing this, I skipped off the pavement as he strode by. It was an incident I never forgot. Professor Brandt and his wife, with whom I was staying, were a pleasant couple with one son of about my own age.

Frau Brandt used to invite children of my age to the house, who always wanted to play at Germany versus England with model warships. Germany always had to win; if it didn't, the worst losers of all were the two children of Admiral Von Tirpitz, the head of the navy. It was my first visit to a foreign country and I did not like either Germany or the Germans, apart from the kindly Brandts.

On Sundays at Braid Road, friends of my parents used to come to lunch and then spend the afternoon discussing art and artists. The guests were usually Scottish artists – the painters, F.C.B. Cadell, Robert Hope, Sir James Guthrie, Sam Peploe, John Duncan, Henry Lintott; a brother architect, Washington Browne; and three sculptors, Pittendrigh Macgillivray, Harry Gamley, and Birnie Rhind. Sometimes we went to their homes and I remember Sam Peploe and his wife in India Street as being particularly nice to a small boy – Sam could be very amusing and he never talked down to me. His still-life pictures, which he sold for £10, now fetch over £5,000.

Then there were the artistic connoisseurs like André Raffalovitch and F.W. Deas. Raffalovitch, a wealthy Russian Jewish emigré, lived in a large house in Whitehouse Terrace which was a meeting place for artists of every description. He lived with a most delightful lady – a Miss Gribbell – which was quite an achievement in Edwardian Edinburgh. I was taken to many Sunday morning parties there, for 'Raffy' used to ask a number of children and in the large garden there were plenty of exciting things to do. Years later, reading an article about Aubrey Beardsley, I discovered that Raffy had financed him for quite a long time.

My best friend, who also went to the Hill School, was a boy called Loring McNeill, and during these years we did nearly everything together. On a Saturday morning we would start the day with a round of golf on the nine hole course on the Braid Hills – it cost 6d, and we could have a second round as well for a total of 9d. I did not have any regular pocket money, but apart from my ninepenny golf and my tram fares during the week (the trams were pulled by an underground steel cable which broke not infrequently) I rarely spent anything.

In these pre-war years my father used to go to Europe each summer for two or three weeks on behalf of the Royal Scottish Academy to choose works of art which the Academy borrowed for the next year's exhibition. He had been elected an associate member of the Academy in 1893, becoming an RSA in February, 1905. For years, my father was one of the two Academicians who undertook this selection, partly no doubt because of his fluency in European languages. These visits would always take him to Paris, Rome and Florence and perhaps to The Hague, Berlin, Vienna, Copenhagen or Madrid as well. One year he went to Budapest, which he considered had the most beautiful setting of any European capital city. He knew many of the leading European artists as a result of these trips. My father had an artist's eye for beautiful things and would bring back a dress for Mother, or sometimes a hat from Paris or a piece of jewellery.

Early in 1914 he had been to Berlin, where one of his friends was the Kaiser's architect, who had just built a new State library. Its enormous size struck my Father, for the many thousands of books only filled a small part of the building. To my Father's question as to how it was to be filled the reply was 'The next war will do that'. When the long feared war came in 1914, all that I remember of that hot August was the tremendous surge of patriotic feeling which certainly spread down to my age group. Nearly everyone thought the war would be over by Christmas. From Edinburgh the whole thing was remote, and our daily lives were unaffected. My Father, at 59, was too old for military service. Gradually, his practice virtually dried up and he devoted most of his time to the affairs of the Royal Scottish Academy and the College of Art.

Our two excellent maids went home to the North of Scotland, their place being taken by a young, untrained girl, but she was good-hearted and very willing and Mother appreciated her. Most of the boys at the Hill School went on to Merchiston – which was literally across the road: Loring went there, and soon we lost touch. My parents had intended to send me to Rugby, but the outbreak of war changed that, and in September 1915 after passing the entrance examination, I was accepted for entry to the Classical side of the Senior Department of George Watson's Boys' College.

At that time, the school was housed on the north side of the Meadows, next to the Infirmary. There were about a thousand boys there and it was probably the best of the excellent schools belonging to the Merchant Company. Each class had at least thirty boys, and I was placed in 1A, which was the top form of the first year of the Senior School. Watson's was rough and tough, and very different from the Hill School. There was a good deal of bullying, and the whole school was in a period of transition. The younger members of the staff were leaving to go off to the war, and their places were being taken by women of various capabilities. Homework was set with very little co-ordination between masters, and after I got home, leaving school at three o'clock, it usually took me several hours to get through my prep. Apart from maths, I found the work reasonably easy and in history and geography I usually finished top of my class.

One effect of the war was that it made me read a daily newspaper much earlier than I should otherwise have done. At home, we discussed the latest news from the Front, and a newspaper was then the only source of news. My heroes were Haig and later Allenby. My villain was Lloyd George, a detestable man to Mother with her high standards of behaviour for anyone in public life.

And the war was coming closer to home. On Sunday evening, 2 April 1916, all our lights were gradually dimmed; our neighbours were similarly affected, as were the street lamps. Later, when there was only a dull glow, the front door bell rang, and our neighbour Willie Peploe (Sam's brother) told us that Zeppelins were on their way to bomb Edinburgh and the Forth Bridge. Sure enough, somewhere about 11 p.m. we heard the noise of the engines, and one of the few searchlights picked out a clumsy cigar-shaped object. We all went down to the kitchen, keeping away from the window. Then the bombs started and some seemed to be very loud. But the nearest one was nearly half a mile away in a field near the Braid Burn. Edinburgh had no effective defence, and quite a number of people were killed and injured in the raid. When I got to school next morning, the gates were closed and the west wing facing the Meadows had had a direct hit. The result was that our Easter holiday lasted for more than a month.

Later that year, I remember the gloom when Lord Kitchener was drowned on his way to Russia. That summer too, it gradually became clear that the huge effort on the Somme had failed and all over the country hospitals were filled with wounded soldiers, while after the Battle of Jutland the Naval hospitals were likewise filled. The blue uniforms worn by the convalescent soldiers became a common sight.

My Father was now working from his study at Braid Road, having, as a temporary measure, converted his office in Abercromby Place into a residential flat which he let to a widowed lady, a Mrs Balfour. (Widows were then rapidly increasing.) We ate margarine instead of butter, and practically the only meat we had was mince – though herrings were still fairly cheap and we often had these. Food rationing started, and in time became severe. On a Saturday morning, I used to go to the Maypole Dairy in Morningside Road to buy our weekly rations. There was a long queue and I was often too late for any golf after this.

Games at school were not compulsory and never interested me. I had quite a low handicap in golf and for two or three years I played in school matches, but I never got further than a semi-final. At weekends I spent a lot of time on my bicycle exploring the lovely country to the south of Edinburgh, sometimes with a friend but often alone. I liked the country and felt happy and peaceful there.

In the summer of 1915 Mother went for about ten days as the guest of an old friend to the Gordon Arms Hotel at West Linton. After a week, I missed her so much that on the Saturday I set out on my bicycle to see her. I left home, only saying that I would be back in the late afternoon. West Linton was about fifteen miles away. I had never been there and what with all the hills to walk up and some heavy showers, it took a long time. I found the hotel and Mother was there, having just finished lunch. She was naturally astonished to see me; we went for a walk together and after an early tea I started on the return journey. The thirty-mile ride there and back was well within my resources – the only difficult part had been to leave Mother.

## CHAPTER TWO

# *A New World Discovered*

The seeds of my interests in later life were perhaps sown in mid December 1916. I developed what Dr James Ritchie, our family doctor, called rheumatic fever (though I doubt if this description was accurate). My temperature stayed over 100 degrees for about a month (there were no antibiotics in those days) and when at last it gradually came down, I was kept indoors for several weeks.

I spent a large part of each day in my father's study, where there was always a good fire burning. He would be working at his drawing board and chain-smoking strong Turkish cigarettes – which is the principal reason for my never having wished to smoke. After I had done a little school reading – I was away from school for the whole of the 1917 spring term – I would look at one of the many books with which the room abounded. One day by chance I came across a pile of monthly investment lists issued by a small local firm of stockbrokers, H. Gilmour & Shaw. My Father probably had a couple of small investments and knew nothing about the stock exchange but he regularly received this literature.

I looked through it and soon I was completely absorbed by what I found. When I came to J. & P. Coats I knew this name from Mother's cotton reels. The highest price of the shares was, say, 32 and the lowest 21. In those days Coats were, I think, £10 shares but when I was thirteen it never occurred to me that the prices were not in pence and I imagined myself buying Coats at 21d and selling them at 32d, and at that point I became really interested. I doubt if any of this would have occurred unless I had had all this time on my hands.

For the rest of the time that I was indoors, I spent my days in absorbing the wealth of information obtainable from these monthly investment lists. I made graphs of the monthly fluctuations of some of the shares over the past three years. I began to read the daily financial page in *The Scotsman*, which included a record of all the transactions on the London and Edinburgh stock exchanges of the previous day. I was fascinated by the daily fluctuations in the price of various shares and I wanted to find out why this happened.

My Father was pleased that I had found something which absorbed me so completely, and he got me the monthly lists going back to 1907. One weekend his friend, who was senior partner of Gilmour & Shaw, most kindly came and patiently answered the questions I poured out. What exactly was a preference share, for instance? By then I had chosen a number of shares which I thought were promising and I was keeping a record of their daily price fluctuations. After nearly three years of war, inflation was increasing and prices on the stock exchange were rising. After Easter, when I went back to school, I still looked at the financial pages of *The Scotsman* each day and every month I valued my 'portfolio' which I altered from time to time. In a sense it was just a game, but in fact it was gradually becoming much more than that. The huge German offensive in the spring of 1918 brought the market down sharply, but by 1919 – when I was fifteen – I had a fair profit on my portfolio and I wanted to start investing with real money. I had been preparing for this for some time by building up my Post Office savings account. During the winters of 1917 and 1918, in addition to Christmas presents, I had earned quite a bit by sweeping snow from the pavements of some of the Morningside houses. To top it up, I occasionally went without the hot lunch at school, for which I was given 6d a day.

By the early part of 1919 I had saved fully £10 and one day after school I walked to 18 St Andrew Square to see my friend Mr Morrison at Gilmour & Shaw, whose office stood where the Scottish Life now has its headquarters. I was shown into his room and, having produced my Post Office book as evidence, I asked him to buy me £10 of Mond Nickel ordinary shares. This, of course, was a first rate company but it had never occurred to me that it was not possible to buy a share standing in the market at about £6 – if one only possessed £10! (One cannot deal in one and a half shares.) My friend – which he undoubtedly was – explained this but said he hoped I would continue to be interested in the stock exchange.

After a few days I decided that I could not afford to wait until my £10 had grown sufficiently to invest in Mond Nickel. So I started to look for shares priced at not more than about 2/-. Most of these were rubber shares but by 1919 they had risen substantially and I was not going to buy on top of this rise. After obtaining from Mr Morrison particulars of a great many companies and acquiring a wealth of detailed knowledge about plantation companies, I chose an Edinburgh concern called Hampton Properties Ltd. This had been formed about fifty years earlier and owned extensive mineral rights in Western Australia. Many prospectors had searched for gold on the company's properties but so far nothing of any importance had been discovered. However, the rents received from the grazing rights were sufficient to keep the company alive and I found that the price of the £1 shares, usually around 1/-, had repeatedly risen to anything from 4/6 to 8/- every few years due to rumours of a discovery of gold. However, up to now these discoveries had not been commercial and so the price had gradually declined again until it was once more about the 1/- mark. My plan was to buy 200 shares at 1/-, wait for the next rumour ('due' in about eighteen months' time) and then sell them for 4/- to 5/-. However, before putting this into practice – which I knew depended upon my being able to persuade Mr Morrison to overlook the fact that I was a minor – I decided to take one other step.

The Chairman of Hampton Properties was a Mr W.W. Slater, who I found lived in a large house at the top of Midmar Avenue near where we lived. I thought I would try to find out as much as I could about this William Work Slater before I parted with my precious £10. So the next Sunday morning, I stationed myself on the pavement opposite his house and sure enough, at a little after half past ten an elderly man and a lady emerged, obviously on their way to church. Mr Slater was a small, rather tubby man, immaculately dressed in a morning coat and top hat. The couple set off down the hill and I followed at a discreet distance. After a little, I guessed they were making for a particular church. I followed them in and sat in a pew directly behind them. I went through the service quite mechanically, never taking my eyes off the man in front of me. Afterwards he went into the vestry and when he emerged it was plain that he was a man of some importance in the church. Accordingly, I went again to 18 St Andrew Square, after school, and when I left Mr Morrison had agreed to buy for me 200 Hampton Properties at a limit of 1/-. Within a week or so the shares were purchased, 150 at 10½d and 50 at 1/-. I told no one of this. Only later did I discover that my Father had been consulted before the shares were bought.

About three weeks later, when I opened *The Scotsman* before breakfast, a banner headline on the financial page read: 'Sensational Gold Discovery at Hampton Properties. Shares rise to 35/-'. That morning it was not easy to concentrate on lessons and as soon as lunchtime came I ran up to the top of Archibald Place where there was a paper shop and bought the lunchtime edition of one of the Edinburgh evening papers. Hampton Properties was again headline news, and the shares had risen further. Before long they touched 53/9, which proved to be the top. I had not sold a share, for by constructing a chart by schoolboy methods, I decided the shares were going to £4. Snippets of news from Western

Australia appeared in *The Scotsman* fairly frequently and, while the shares now fluctuated within much narrower limits, they fell on balance. Mr Morrison pressed me to take my profit but I explained to him why I felt the shares would go to £4. Shortly thereafter he came to Braid Road one evening and after he and my father had talked to me I unwillingly agreed to sell. My £10 became about £320 and had I kept the shares I would gradually have lost most of the profit. The gold proved to be only a rich shallow deposit which petered out at depth. Later, I realised that the fall had been accentuated by the directors issuing options to their friends with the right to subscribe at par for new shares ranking pari passu with shares then standing at a considerable premium.

I had a war-time allotment not far from Mr Slater's house. Now that I knew him by sight I found that he often passed by exercising his dog and one day I contrived to get into conversation with him. Later I told him about my Hampton Properties and he was understandably intrigued. After that, he used to stop each time I was there and we would discuss the stock exchange. One day he invited me to tea at his house and gave me an option certificate for a hundred Hampton Properties. By then I had sold my shares but such was my faith in the company that I kept the certificate (which, of course, eventually became valueless). My original profit was simply a case of beginner's luck which in itself taught me very little (never again has anything like this happened to me). The only thing worth noting is the fact that I had persuaded this cautious stockbroker to buy a highly speculative share for a minor: my first successful negotiation. I wish I could add that I brought some present for Mother, but alas I did not. I re-invested every penny. Indeed, I worked and saved and added to the £320, investing it all in Imperial Tobacco, Mond Nickel and a third share which I cannot now remember.

In the summer term of 1919 I passed the Intermediate Certificate of the Scottish Education Department and then had a year in the fifth form. In the summer of that year, when we were having the outside of our house re-painted, the flame from a blow-lamp penetrated a hole in the side of an upstairs window and set fire to the interior of the window frame. In next to no time the whole thing was out of control. I ran to a neighbour who possessed a telephone and very quickly two fire engines arrived. By then the roof was on fire and the house itself was only saved by a fine margin. Firemen and fire hoses were everywhere, and the whole episode lasted fully two hours.

In the sitting room directly below where the fire had started my sister Eveleen was doing her daily piano practice and when all the firemen had left the Beethoven sonata she had been working on was still in full swing: a quite extraordinary example of concentration.

In the summer weekends of 1919 onwards, I often went with one or two friends to camp at Portmore – a lovely small reservoir tucked away in the Moorfoot Hills about three miles from Eddleston on the Peebles Road. Then in 1920, Francis Gamley and I decided to go further afield to the English lakes. He and I had been in the same class at Watson's and though for the past two years he had been at the Academy, we remained firm friends. So early in August we set off on heavily laden bicycles and by that evening we were in Dumfriesshire and camped for the night on a farm near Ecclefechan. The next day we got to Keswick quite early in the afternoon and by chance we ended up at Rakefoot Farm. Castlerigg, overlooking Derwentwater.

Unfortunately, the farmer had caught the money-bug and he charged us rent for the corner of the field where we pitched our small tent – an extraordinary thing to do at that time. We had just enough money to meet our budget and not having reckoned to having to pay rent, we had to be very careful. I kept the money and noted our daily expenditure. One very hot day when we were returning from an all-day expedition and pushing our bicycles up the steep Ambleside road, we saw an Italian selling cones of ice-cream. They were 2d each and Francis wanted one – for that matter so did I – but I knew that we had already spent our 'ration' for that day so I said no.

This resulted in a heated exchange and he very nearly took the money from me by force – not difficult for he was a hefty chap. However, in the end we walked on without the ice cream. Francis was a generous-hearted character and forgave me in due course – indeed, we were both laughing about it before very long. He never forgot this episode and he once told the story to the delight of the assembled company at a business lunch in Edinburgh when he was in his fifties and senior partner of chartered accountants A. & J. Robertson.

After a fortnight, we decided to go home earlier than we had intended. Our money was running out and the weather had changed for the worse. We were quite a sight when loaded up: huge rucksacks and objects tied to every part of our bicycles. On the first part of the ascent to Beattock, a kindly van driver, noticing our loads, offered us a lift and by taking us as far as Carstairs enabled us to get back to Edinburgh by early evening. I had not been in touch with my family and, letting myself in I stole into the house to give them a surprise. I was dumbfounded to hear someone sobbing in the kitchen.

I tiptoed into the room and there saw Mother sitting at the table, her head in her arms. I had never seen her cry in my life and the sight was shattering. She was horrified to see me, thinking that I was more than a hundred miles away. I put my arms round her and hugged her tight, and after a while she told me that my father was very ill and had had a nervous breakdown. He had told her that he was bankrupt.

## CHAPTER THREE

# *In at the Deep End*

My second excursion into the field of finance was about to begin. Our family doctor, Dr Ritchie, had told Mother that complete rest away from home was essential for my father. Sir David and Lady Ochterlony – whose home was then Balmadies, a recently built house in Colinton – had known my father for a great many years (Matthew, their eldest son had been apprenticed to my Father) and when they heard what had happened they at once asked to have my Father at Balmadies.

I went to bed that evening and tried to think what to do. After a while, I got up and went next door to my Father's study. I knew where he kept his business papers and I started to look through these. After four years of war when he had had very little work, the past year had been one of intense activity. Almost every local community wanted to erect a war memorial and amazing amounts of money had been collected to ensure that the memorials would be worthy of the sacrifice made by so many local men. My Father's reputation was such that many local committees had asked him to design their memorial and it had been this sudden swing from one extreme to the other when he was sixty-five, from under-work to over-exertion, that had been the principal cause of his breakdown. Also, in spite of every economy, we had been living much above my Father's small income for the previous six years. To an extent unknown to Mother, debts had piled up.

In my search during that night I found neat bundles of correspondence, each concerning some war memorial, but I also found stacks of unpaid bills, some dating back for several years and many in envelopes which had not been opened. Some of these unopened envelopes contained letters of a type which I had never seen before, all threatening, and some – from solicitors – urgently so.

It was beginning to get light when I went to bed having been up since 6.30 a.m. I had reached a total of several thousand pounds of debt and I did not question Mother's statement that we were ruined. However, our home belonged to my Father, as did his old office, and the former still contained many beautiful objets d'art which were obviously valuable. When I awakened the next morning I realised that the first thing to do was to get at the facts so that I could construct a family balance sheet.

My Father was obviously in no state to talk about this. In any case, the Ochterlonys, who were truly wonderful friends, took him to Colinton the next day. I tried to see everyone who might be able to help. My dealings with Gilmour & Shaw enabled me to go into a strange office and face unknown people. I expected the worst and often thought of some of the characters from Dickens. In fact, most of the people I saw were extremely kind.

The greatest blow on the first day was to find from the Royal Bank of Scotland that there was no money in my Father's account; on the contrary, it was heavily overdrawn. My Father's lawyers were a small firm in Forres Street – Chalmers & Hore – and I saw Harry Hore who knew me quite well. Unfortunately, he knew very little about my Father's affairs. So there I drew a blank – except for one thing. I found that my Father still owned a previous office he had had in York Place, which was not even mortgaged. Harry Hore came with me to see the empty office which had been unlet for some time. There we found many packing cases full of Chinese porcelain, snuff boxes and the like. Mother knew nothing of this and it was like discovering an Aladdin's cave. Up to then, everything I had found had been a liability. Now, suddenly, two assets had appeared from nowhere.

In the evenings, I continued to go through the mass of papers and correspondence in the study. Practically none of my Father's clients knew that he was ill and letters were arriving daily concerning the many war memorials. I consulted Matthew Ochterlony and at once he offered to help me to deal with these. By now I was pretty sure that my Father was not bankrupt by any means. I had seen a Mr Cowie, an art dealer and a friend of my Father's, who advised me very unselfishly how best to sell these treasures. Many were sold in London and fetched more than I had been led to expect.

As soon as the shape of the 'balance sheet' began to emerge, I started on the other tack and went to see the creditors, with bank notes in my pocket from local sales. I had by then learned the value of personal contact, and for that matter many other things, for I was growing up rapidly. I went to see my headmaster, John Alison, told him what had happened and said that I should have to start earning my living and so should have to leave school. He, too, was kind; I was released from paying the next term's fees.

After I had seen two or three of the creditors, it seemed to me that they had not expected to recover the whole debt. From here it was only a short step to trying to reach settlement at a lower figure. At first, I offered them a definite sum, but I soon learned to get them to name the figures they were prepared to accept if I paid immediate cash. Sometimes this proved to be much lower than I had expected. As I worked through the horrific list, the percentage discount rose as my technique improved.

All this time I was seeing Matthew every day and at his suggestion I went to see several of my Father's most important clients. I was invariably received with great kindness and, thanks to Matthew, not one client was lost. Typical of these visits was one to Cupar in Fife where Provost Stark – a local builder and a man who had worked for my Father in pre-war days – received me with great kindness, as did the members of his committee. By then, I was able to assure them that my father would be perfectly well again before long, and I left with a substantial cheque on account. The process was repeated on other visits, though I never asked for any money.

Mrs Balfour had recently left 2 Abercromby Place and Mother and I decided to sell Braid Road and move there. This followed my discovering the copy of a letter which Mother had written in answer to an advertisement for a caretaker and cleaner for an office in central Edinburgh with free accommodation in the basement. Mother had replied to this advertisement when she believed we were ruined. She had been determined to keep us all together.

By the time I read the letter I was reasonably certain that all was not lost, so we decided upon this much less drastic solution and when she next walked over to Colinton to see my father he, too, agreed. He had started to improve rapidly, and his mind had cleared, though he was still physically very weak. However, before long he began to do a little drawing.

Braid Road had cost about £1,000 in 1911. We were fortunate in having three different people who all wanted to buy it, and two of them competed against each other to the very end. The opening bid was £1,500 but on 3 October I sold the house for £2,100 which at that time was a high figure. I had by now sold the York Place Office, all the debts had been discharged and a surplus of several thousands of pounds was in sight. So long as the boom in war memorials lasted, my Father's income was clearly going to cover our living expenses with some margin in hand.

With his agreement, I therefore invested all the surplus capital in stock exchange securities. I still had only one thought for my future, namely to become a stockbroker, and by now I had acquired some genuine knowledge of the market. The early signs of the 1921 slump had by then begun to appear so I proceeded very cautiously. Early in November 1920 I bought for my Father 5% War Loan at 82½. Distillers were making a rights issue and I bought the rights, nil paid, at 41/-. The shares were then £10 par value and had fallen sharply as a result of the issue. These and other purchases proved to be profitable. There were no more money worries thereafter.

At the end of September 1920 a totally unexpected event occurred which changed the course of my life. Our next door neighbours in Mortonhall Road had been the McFarlanes, and Arthur McFarlane was the chairman and managing director of a public company called The United Wire Works Limited, controlled by his family. The company had been formed in 1897 and in 1920 the head office was in Leith, with two other factories in Glasgow and one in Newcastle. They manufactured non-ferrous wire, drawing this to fine gauges and weaving it into a wide variety of wire cloth. The most important department was the manufacture of paper machine wires, the endless bands of wire cloth used on every paper making machine.

The McFarlanes had three children and their only son, Ronald, had been killed in the war. There was thus no one to succeed Mr McFarlane and on 27 September 1920 he had written to my Father proposing that I should be trained in all the ramifications of the business with a view eventually to succeeding him. He wanted to put me in the place which his son would have occupied.

For the first year I was to be in the Bridgeton factory in Glasgow, starting in the engineering shop. I was to be paid 30/- a week, rising to 40/- in the second year when I would probably be in Edinburgh. During the first year I would travel to Glasgow each day, leaving Morningside station (about ten minutes from home) at 8.43 a.m. and returning there at 6. 24 p.m.

This offer posed a difficult problem. The McFarlanes had known me from birth and it was obviously an exceptional opportunity. Yet for the past three years I wanted to be a stockbroker. I went to my good friends at Gilmour & Shaw who advised me to accept Mr McFarlane's offer. I was, naturally, given the same advice by everyone I consulted. I went to see Mr McFarlane who, in his slightly austere way, was encouraging. I accepted his offer because I saw no practical alternative. I told him quite honestly what I had really wanted to do but left it at that. It was agreed that I would start early in December, which I thought would give me just enough time to complete the tidying up of my Father's affairs.

## CHAPTER FOUR

# *The United Wire Works*

So on 6 December 1920 with my new season ticket, I went to Glasgow with Mr McFarlane. The fog was dense, the works looked grim. In Mr McFarlane's office I was introduced to Mr McWatters, the chief engineer in whose care I was to be. I put on dungarees and went for a tour of the factory with him. In each of the weaving shops there were nearly twenty looms, ranging from about eight to nearly twenty feet wide, weaving paper machine wire cloth. The noise was tremendous and it was impossible to hear what anyone was saying. In time, like everyone else, I picked up a crude form of lip reading. Mr McWatters, a fine engineer and a great character, had designed a number of special features for these looms, which were both made and repaired in the engineering shop where I was to work. The looms were manned by women who were naturally curious to know who I was, but the kindliness of the Glasgow character was the thing which impressed me. It was the beginning of a very happy year, when I grew to like Glasgow better than my native Edinburgh.

As there was no canteen, Mr McWatters took me to a restaurant near Bridgeton Cross where for about 1/9d we had an ample two-course meal. Soon I took sandwiches from home and ate these in the factory with my workmates. On that first day when we got back from lunch through the still dense fog, I asked Mr McWatters if the wet marks which I had noticed in parts of the factory were the result of a leaking roof. He looked astonished and then burst out laughing. 'It's not the rain, Jake,' he said, 'it's the chaps spitting out the baccy they chew.'

Many of the people called me Jake, though I was John to some of the girls. One of the foremen engineers – Hughie Ramage – was particularly nice to me. As a boy he had been educated at Heriots in Edinburgh. But he had obviously been somewhat wild and had left home to go first to Australia and then to wander round the world. He served an engineering apprenticeship, married, and when I knew him was probably in his early fifties and very content with his life. Several times I spent a Saturday with him and on one occasion he took me on a pub crawl to some of the tough spots in Glasgow. He was a powerfully built man who could have taken on three average people single-handed.

We started in Bridgeton and ended up in the Gorbals. In each pub he had a whisky and a glass of beer, known as a chaser, and he could go on drinking these without showing any signs of wear. Meantime, I freely consumed an excellent local soft drink known as 'Irn Bru'. We finished up with a late meal in an eating place near the docks. The customers were mainly seamen, including Chinese, Indian, and other races. We carried our hot food to one of a number of rectangular bare wooden tables with benches on each side. Chained to the tables at intervals were a knife, fork and spoon and Hughie wiped these with his large red handkerchief before we ate. I spent the night at his home – it was the autumn of 1921, towards the end of my Glasgow period.

After some months in the engineering shop, I was transferred to one of the weaving shops where after a while I was put on a medium sized loom, about ten feet wide, with one of the experienced girls. I think this was Gracie, and later I worked with Susan – a beautiful girl with dark hair, large sad eyes and fine features. One of the younger girls in the shop was a bit 'simple' and some of the others had bet her that she would not kiss me. So one day she crept up behind me while I was threading up a loom and then literally sprang on me and pulled me to the ground, implanting great smacking kisses. I was the stronger, however, and, disentangling myself, I got up and told her off. There were roars of laughter so I laughed, gave her a playful smack, and went back to my loom. Some of the girls were indignant with their mates who were responsible, but this episode – though embarrassing at the time – cemented my relationship with the weaving shop and the party they organised for my last day at Baltic Works was memorable.

The narrow looms making wirecloth for anything from filtration cloth to window guards were at another factory at Shettleston several miles away from Bridgeton, and further away from the central area, and during the weeks I was there I caught seven trains each day.

Next I was transferred to Edina Works in Leith, leaving Glasgow with real regret. The train journeys had given me plenty of time to read the day's financial news. Now I bicycled down Leith Walk and got to the office in less than ten minutes, so my financial reading was mostly done in an evening. I was in the care of Willie Ballantyne, the Works Manager – a splendid kindly Scot. Again, I worked in practically every department, learning how to draw wire to gauges sometimes finer than human hair. We used diamond dies for the fine wire-drawing and we made and repaired these ourselves, purchasing the diamonds from Hatton Garden.

The man in charge of the diamond die shop was a tremendous gambler and had several friends who worked in training stables from whom he used to get 'inside information'. He would pass this on each day and after I had seen him backing several winners I sometimes had a small bet. Out of nearly twenty bets, I only had one winner. On the last occasion I had a bet, he had received what was clearly genuine information from the stable, and I put a really large sum (£5) on the horse about a week before the race, which was at Chester. I got long odds but when the day came the horse was the favourite and odds on. It was leading the field when, near the finish, it put its foot into an unnoticed rabbit-hole, threw its jockey and finished nowhere.

Coming on top of all the other disappointments, I felt that this was an omen and my friend agreed. I do not think I have had more than two or three bets from that day to this, and that Chester meeting probably saved me thousands of pounds.

After quite a long period in the works, I was moved to the office where I came under John Burnett, the Secretary, to whom I owe a great deal. Mr Burnett was the brother of a well known professional singer in Scotland and he himself had a fine voice. He was also a good business man and a meticulous Company Secretary. When one lunch-time I had sold a piece of wirecloth to an unknown caller who had not quite enough money to pay for it in full, Mr Burnett ticked me off and then, ending on a lighter note, he said 'Just remember the old motto: trust in the Lord – all others, ready cash'.

Our financial year ended on 30 September and for days beforehand we would be working late on stocktaking and then on balancing the books. This usually took several evenings unless we were lucky.

After a time, Mr Burnett gave me some of each day's letters to answer. I dictated the letters, but at that period all of them were signed by Mr Burnett. He always signed first and then read the letter afterwards and, many years later, I realised that I had picked up the same habit.

During these first two years, although I was of course contributing to our home expenses, I managed to save a little. The value of my investments had roughly halved in the 1921 slump but from about 1922 onwards it rose. Every day when I opened *The Scotsman* at the financial page I experienced a sense of excitement. On Saturday afternoon (office hours on a Saturday were 9 a.m. to 12.30 p.m.) I sometimes went to a public library (originally gifted by Andrew Carnegie) to read the *Financial Times* and there I also discovered the *Investors' Chronicle*.

One day I had a letter from Gilmour & Shaw telling me that some

United Wire Works ordinary shares were for sale. Unlike the preference shares, the ordinary were unquoted and none had changed hands for some years. There had been a bid of £4 in the market for some time, and the offered price had just been reduced to £5. The par value of the shares was £10 and the asset value was above that. Regular dividends of 5% were being paid. The shares looked cheap to me to yield a safe 10% and I bid £4.10s, which in a few days was accepted. The purchase had cost several hundred pounds. The shares proved to have come from a deceased estate, but when Mr McFarlane was told who had bought the shares he sent for me. I found him exceedingly angry because, as he told me, he had bid the £4 and but for my interference he would have bought the shares at their 'proper' price. He reverted to the subject of my unnatural interest in the Stock Exchange and said he intended to talk about this to the senior partner of our auditors, Mr A.W. Robertson Durham of A. & J. Robertson.

In due course, I was summoned to 33 Charlotte Square and Mr Robertson Durham told me that Mr McFarlane was concerned that I did not seem to have got rid of my 'Stock Exchange bug'. It would be essential for me to concentrate on United Wire Works' business if I were to succeed. He was Chairman of the Scottish American Investment Company, then the largest of the Edinburgh investment trusts, whose annual reports I always read. I was longing to talk to him about this company, but naturally he gave me no opportunity to do so. I got to know him better in later years, though alas he died while still in the prime of life.

Incidentally, I kept those U.W.W. shares and was a small shareholder in two other local companies. One of these – the Professional and Civil Service Association in George Street – was, I thought, badly managed and in the mid nineteen-twenties I went to two of its Annual General Meetings and spoke against the Board. The company owned a large building (now the Midland Bank) and was clearly worth more dead than alive, so I did what I could to encourage this. It was eventually liquidated.

# CHAPTER FIVE

## *Amateur Theatricals and Polish Seconds*

While the affairs of the United Wire Works occupied my working hours, it was at this period that both my cultural horizons and my personal business interests began to expand.

In the autumn of 1921 a man called Arthur Douglas Elliot came to see me. Arthur was then one of the best light comedy amateur actors in Edinburgh. He was a tubby little man who was completely natural on any stage and who made people laugh and go on laughing. Arthur Elliot was the principal comedian in a series of amateur reviews organised and acted in by a young man named Leycester Anderson, otherwise the amateur Charles B. Cochran of Edinburgh. The purpose of his visit was to ask me to sing a duet with him called 'The Twins' in one of the 1922 productions: *Pot Pourri*.

I could not sing and I had never appeared on any stage. To this day I do not really know why he asked me or why I accepted. The show ran for twenty-one days during January 1922 and drew pretty full houses. Much of it was probably reasonably good, the girls were pretty and some had talent as well. Our duet, while not a 'wow' went reasonably well, thanks to Arthur. But as a result I acquired the confidence one has to possess in order to face an audience and later, in my business life in London, this faculty became a valuable asset.

In 1922, however, it gave me a taste for amateur theatricals and for the next six years they were my principal hobby. After appearing in small parts in further revues, I had a number of straight parts in a variety of plays. Then in 1924, I organised and produced *Little Women*. I had hand-picked the cast and we rehearsed it so thoroughly that we nearly all knew the whole play. John Chiene, later chairman of the Edinburgh Investment Trust and then a young chartered accountant, was a talented amateur actor and played Grandpa Lawrence; Francis Gamley was Professor Baret, and I was John Brooke. The play was a considerable success and from then until I left Edinburgh in 1928 I had more offers of parts than I could accept.

During those years, one of Elsie Fogarty's pupils, Sybil Attwell, was teaching elocution in Edinburgh, and I took part in several plays she produced. In 1926 she entered W.B. Yeats's *The Land of Heart's Desire* for the British Drama League Festival. She herself played Mary Bruin, the heroine, and I played opposite her as Shawn. Father Hart was Alastair Sim, then teaching elocution at the Church of Scotland training college and Naomi Plaskitt (whom Alistair married a few years later) was the Faery Child.

We did not win the competition, which E. Martin Browne came from London to judge, but I got to know Alastair well and later appeared in other plays with him. Later, when he was offered a small West End part, he threw up his safe post with the Church of Scotland and went to London. But although his friends in Edinburgh thought he would succeed, we never expected him to become a comedy actor.

In the summer of 1924 another professional teacher of elocution – Mr R.C. Bell – took the Corn Exchange at Dunbar for one night in August. I played Colonel James Midwinter in Conan Doyle's *Waterloo*. This was the only time I was paid for appearing in what was a commercial venture. It was an old-fashioned theatre with gas footlights, and I was bathed in perspiration by the end of the performance.

In the meantime, because of the difficulty of hiring scenery for amateur productions, I had started a business for hiring out the equipment which I called 'The Players Hiring Company'. I rented a warehouse and stable on two floors in the Dean Village for £12 a year, and there a number of talented young artists worked with me in the evenings. I built up a highly profitable business and we all had a lot of fun. I bought Bolton Sheeting from a Lancashire Mill, had it dyed and fireproofed in Edinburgh, and some of the girls did the rest with a borrowed sewing machine. A complete set of stage curtains about fourteen feet long made in this way cost barely £10 and these I hired at five guineas a night.

During the first season the whole project very nearly came to grief for I booked far too many orders. As the dates approached and much of the scenery was by no means finished, we began to work until 1 a.m. each night and of course all of each weekend. I had undertaken to stage a play in St Cuthbert's Church Hall and this required a large proscenium arch which was built in sections to be erected on the day of the performance. I had an excellent man named Wilson – an ex-naval petty officer – who erected the scenery and on that Monday afternoon he telephoned me to say that we had forgotten the main horizontal 6 inch × 3 inch beam for the proscenium, 22 feet long. I left the office a little early, collected this massive piece of timber from a sawmill in Leith and taking it under my arm and resting it on my handlebars, I bicycled over two miles up Leith

Walk and along Princess Street. How I wasn't stopped by the traffic police I cannot imagine; it at least shows how strong I was then. We screwed the curtain rails to it and got the whole thing up and the curtain working with only a few minutes to spare before the doors opened at 7 p.m.

By the second season, Wilson was working for me whole time. We discovered that a considerable demand for sawdust existed (pubs, fishmongers, etc.) so I made a deal with the same Leith sawmill to buy all their sawdust at 3d a sack and Wilson and I made our own rather large sacks. He possessed a powerful right arm which resulted in our packing enough sawdust into each of these sacks to fill four normal ones, which we sold for 1/- each, a gross profit of 1,500%. I bought a black gelding horse for £8 and a standard four wheel lorry in August 1923 and by this means, we transported both the scenery and the sawdust. By now I had rented the whole building, and Wilson and his wife and family, and also a part-time assistant, were happily living on the top floor which we had converted into two flats. How the local authority allowed this to happen I cannot imagine. I had no influence whatsoever and I suppose I got away with it simply because the standards of hygiene and fire precautions then were very different from today. Mercifully, no trouble ever arose.

In November 1926 one of the Edinburgh doctors who knew me socially took a theatrical friend of his to see an Ibsen play in which I was appearing. This man was then the chief executive of the Wilson Barrett theatrical company and the next morning (Sunday) my doctor friend invited me to meet him that afternoon. He told me that I might be suitable for a small part in a forthcoming West End production and they would pay my expenses to come to London for an audition. While I was momentarily tempted, by the next morning I knew this would be foolish and wrote to London declining the offer. The play he had seen was Ibsen's *Emperor and Galilean* in which I played Basil of Caesarea, an earnest young Christian who has long theological arguments with the Emperor Julian. It was the longest part I ever had to learn – some of the speeches ran to nearly three pages of script – and I scarcely understood anything of the lines I had to put over with such passionate sincerity! Isabelle Pagan, a remarkable woman and a devout Theosophist, had translated the play from the Norwegian. Ibsen said of it 'This will remain as my chief work' and this was only the second performance of the play in English. We had full houses for the three performances, people having come from as far afield as Cambridge and London.

In one of the scenes, Julian calls up the spirits of several people – Judas

Iscariot and Christ among them. The play was staged by the Players Hiring Company and we signified Christ's appearance by a brilliant flash of light – a magnesium flare in the wings. Unfortunately, the draught from an open door backstage blew my fireproofed purple curtains into the flare and they promptly caught fire in full view of the audience. In fact, we had two small fires that night, the other being caused by a flimsy black cloth over the open back of an arc spot lamp which stood on top of a high pair of steps in the wings. Happily, the girl on the steps who was using the arc light kept her head and the fire was quickly extinguished.

The last show I produced was *Five Short Plays* at the St Cuthbert's Hall, for two nights in March 1927 for the Rev Dr J. Harry Miller's New College Settlement. I engaged a professional producer (Robert Dalziel) and the casts were again handpicked. The plays were 'Wow Wow', 'The Bishop's Candlesticks', 'The Grand Cham's Diamond', 'References' and 'Master Wayfarer'. The first four were straightforward but 'Master Wayfarer' was much more ambitious. It was a play by J.E. Harold Terry with music by Howard Carr and the part of the Wayfarer had been created for Haydn Coffin. I had seen this production some years before and had wanted to try my hand at it ever since. There are five songs for the Wayfarer, but I cut out the two most difficult ones, and Mr Burnett took endless trouble to coach me. We had full houses and quite good notices but I now feel the Wayfarer was an over-ambitious project.

That was my swan song. In those six years I had played a wide variety of parts. They included contemporary modern comedy (Lord Stevenage in *The Young Person in Pink* – the old Bishop in *The Naughty Wife* etc); Olangsti in Laurence Housman's and Granville Barker's *The Chinese Lantern*, and comedy parts in a variety of one act plays. At the other end of the scale, I had played Basil in *Emperor and Galilean*. I had also stage-managed other people's productions. *Peer Gynt* at the Music Hall for three nights was a particularly enjoyable experience and at the time I knew most of it by heart. I went to the theatre a great deal at that time and continued to do so during my first years in London. To see a professional actor handle a difficult scene in a play I had read fascinated me.

In the meantime, I developed other business interests. I bought in 1925 a small retail business in the Kirkgate, then one of the main food shopping streets in Leith. It was a dried fish shop – selling kippers, salted herrings, finnan haddock etc. The asking price was £125 and I eventually paid £80 for the lease and the goodwill – which proved to be too much.

The purchase was intended to provide a living for a school friend, Geoffrey Nice. He was an orphan, and several years before this the elderly relative who had brought him up had died. Geoffrey was being trained as a mining engineer; he had been working in a local coal mine and a basic defect in his heart had come to light. After a period of enforced rest, he started to look for a job but could find nothing. He was then living alone in two attic rooms, lit and ventilated only by skylights, four floors up at the top of an office building in North Castle Street. His modest savings were shortly going to be exhausted, but even so it took a lot of persuasion before he agreed to my buying the shop. He had pride and integrity.

The fish was ordered each day from Aberdeen by telegram. Unlike the wet fish trade, there was no early morning market to attend and our prices did not fluctuate nearly so violently. On the Saturday evening after we had obtained possession, I moved in with my Players Hiring team and by late on Sunday evening the shop had been re-painted both inside and out. We changed the name to 'The Service Fisheries' and the outside wall was painted white with bright blue formal waves, intermingled with formal golden fish. This was the work of W.R. (Billy) Lawson, a talented young artist who had just finished the Chinese room for Crawford's restaurant in Hanover Street. After this, no one could ignore our shop, for there was nothing remotely like it in the whole of Leith! But what mattered to our customers were our prices. They knew every price in Kirkgate and if they could buy their fish for 9½d against our 10d nothing else mattered.

After some weeks of uneventful shopkeeping, when it seemed pretty certain that the business could only provide a bare living for Geoffrey, I suggested that we might try selling eggs. A minute share of the trade going on around us would have been worthwhile. So I went to see a friend of mine who was the manager of a large firm of wholesale food merchants.

He told me that we should be able to sell a reasonable number of eggs, and advised 'Chinese Smalls'. Instinctively (and wrongly) I said that we would prefer to handle something rather better. 'Well,' he said, 'if you feel strongly about it, I could fix you up with a case of Polish Seconds, but they may be a bit pricey for Kirkgate.' So I bought a case of sixty dozen 'Polish Seconds', and on the Sunday dressed the window with some hay, in the middle of which I put a clutch of eggs which I hoped would look more or less newly laid. We had a large blackboard, framed with more of Bill's waves and golden fish, and on this I chalked in large letters – 'Great Opening Offer of our own freshly imported boiling eggs. Only 1/3d per dozen while they last.'

On the Monday afternoon I had to go to Manchester on United Wire Works business and it was Friday before I saw Geoffrey again. The eggs in the window were the same – the blackboard also, except that by now it was rather the worse for wear. When the customers in the shop had been served (with fish), he beckoned me into the back room. 'How many of your blasted eggs do you think we've sold all week?' I said, 'Well, not many: I can see that from your face.' Geoffrey glowered – 'The answer is three – three eggs.'

The next morning, when my friend heard that we were charging 1/3d a dozen, he said, 'You'll never get that mark-up in the Kirkgate, and I'm rather afraid these Polish eggs are too classy for your trade – I ought to have kept you to Chinese'. When I asked him how long we could go on selling the eggs, he said 'Quite a time. Cut an egg-shaped hole in a piece of hardboard, put an electric lamp directly underneath it, and if there are no spots visible, the egg is saleable.'

That Sunday, Geoffrey and I washed all the 717 eggs left, and tested them – there were no spots to be seen. I re-dressed the window with a lavish display and wrote on the blackboard – 'Enormous success of our opening offer – now a newly arrived cargo of fresh boiling eggs and the price – *only 1/- per dozen*!' At the end of six weeks, when the price had come down by degrees to $10\frac{1}{2}$d a dozen (we had originally bought them for $9\frac{3}{4}$) we had sold about four dozen eggs. Every Sunday evening we re-washed the eggs and for the last two weeks specks had appeared in increasing numbers; these we had withdrawn, after cracking one open to see – and smell.

On that Saturday I went to every shop in the Kirkgate and noted the price of their eggs. I hadn't the heart to invent a fresh gimmick so I simply wrote on the blackboard: 'Our big, lovely boiling eggs for only $8\frac{1}{2}$d per dozen.' When I got back from another trip to Manchester a couple of days later, there was not an egg in the shop. They had all been sold on the Monday. As I was talking to Geoffrey, an elderly man came in to ask for 'another six of those eggs'. When Geoffrey told him we were sold out, he said, 'Och, that's a pity – they had a grand flavour.'

I had expected Geoffrey to refuse to handle another egg, but, on the contrary, he was quite keen to sell Chinese eggs. Our mark-up was tiny but after a while we used to sell four or five hundred dozen eggs a week without any gimmicks – all that mattered was the price.

After about eighteen months, Geoffrey had the offer of a good job with the Mexican Eagle Oil Company, and I sold the business for £45, with great difficulty. He had drawn about £4 a week from the shop, and there had only been a tiny surplus over and above that. I set off my loss of about £30 against experience gained. The buyer was an extremely tough middle-aged Jewess who invited me to settle the transaction at her home one evening. The address she had given me turned out to be an upper flat in as bad a slum as then existed in Edinburgh. When she opened the door she was totally naked except for a skirt. However, as I was determined to get the money, I followed her into a sitting room which smelt strongly of cats, where she handed me a bundle of dirty notes. I counted these and gave her a receipt. She asked me how I had come to buy the shop, and we talked for a short while. She owned several barrows in Leith selling fish and she was obviously not short of money.

The two Manchester trips I have mentioned were of some importance in shaping the future. Turners Asbestos had for many years asked United Wire Works to tender for all the fine brass wire which they needed for the next twelve months and for years we had retained this business. We had been tipped off that competition for this order was going to be stiffer than usual, so I went to Manchester to investigate. At Turners works in Rochdale, I had a friendly talk with an assistant purchasing officer, who told me there had been a 'shake up' in his department and that we would need to do a lot better on price if we were to retain the business. When I reported this to Mr McFarlane he was sceptical, for he did not believe Turners would risk changing from a supplier whose wire had given them no trouble for many years. Nevertheless, our costs were carefully checked and we quoted a keen price. After a time we received a formal note telling us that the year's order had been placed elsewhere. I was dispatched to Manchester the next day.

I saw the same man who would only tell me that we had lost the contract purely on price, but by how much he would not say. I had been in his office for about ten minutes, and I felt I could not go back to Edinburgh with nothing more than this. I left by a long corridor lined by many offices on which were painted the names of the occupant. On one of these, I noticed 'Mr Jones, Chief Purchasing Officer', and I decided to go back. I listened for a moment outside the door and there was silence so I knocked, and when a voice said 'Come in' I opened the door to find an elderly man sitting behind a large desk looking at a file. I told him without a pause who I was, that I had seen one of his assistants, but that I just had to find out why we had lost their contract after all these years, so that we could try to put right whatever was wrong. And before I ran out of breath I said I knew that I had absolutely no right to be in his room and I apologised for this – but please, would he help me?

Instead of being incensed as I had expected he smiled in a kind way and told me to sit down. He then asked his secretary to bring him the relevant file, looked at it for a moment, and then said: 'I think the best way is to let you see this schedule for yourself'. On the sheet of paper were the names of the firms who had tendered, with the price each had quoted. The winning tender, considerably below our price, was from an excellent Lancashire firm. I told him that I thought this price was below our prime cost, to which he said, 'Well, it looks as though your costs are too high for some reason, don't you think?' He actually pushed over a scribbling pad so that I could note the salient information, remarking, 'Just the highest and lowest tenders . . . and the total number tendering if you like'. I thanked him from my heart when I got up to go.

I told Mr McFarlane and Mr Burnett exactly what had happened. As I had thought, the winning tender was below our basic cost and this made no sense to Mr McFarlane. I had been thinking about this on the way back, and I had unearthed a recent catalogue of the makers of most of our wire-drawing machinery. This catalogue gave details of the speeds of current models, which were much faster than anything our machines, many dating from the late nineteenth century, were capable of. I therefore suggested to Mr McFarlane that this was perhaps the reason for our losing the contract. This made him very angry and he told me that if I ever wanted to have my name on the firm's notepaper, scrapping good plant which made a first rate product was not the way to go about it.

I thought a lot about this episode, for I felt Mr McFarlane was wrong. We undoubtedly produced good quality wire, but unless we could sell it at a competitive price what good was that? The gulf between our thinking seemed very wide and I began to wonder if I ought not to try to get a job in the financial world. And once I started to think of this, I knew it was what I really wanted to do. However, one change had taken place: I no longer wanted to become a stockbroker. I now saw stockbrokers as people whose role was simply to execute orders to the best of their ability and then attend to the mechanics of settlement.

I wanted to manage investment portfolios, as I was already doing in a very small way. I had formed a 'syndicate', whose three members had signed a document in schoolboy legalese in which I undertook to use my best endeavours to invest their capital wisely, but in which they also recognised that risks were inevitable and that I was not liable for any losses. The fund started with about £4,000 in all and I operated it for about five years, liquidating it when I went to London. My remuneration was 10% of net realised profits which were reasonably satisfactory.

During 1926 I consulted Mr Robertson Durham about my chances of getting a job in one of the investment trust companies in Edinburgh. He said he thought this would not be possible, since I had no professional qualifications. The fact that I had by then amassed a great deal of specialised knowledge would not, he thought, be recognised. I would have to become a chartered accountant, which at that time meant paying a substantial premium and then earning little or nothing during a three year apprenticeship, which I could not afford to do. I made other enquiries with much the same result.

Meanwhile, the position had changed at The United Wire Works. Four years before this, the McFarlanes' younger daughter had married a young regular soldier, Captain Theodore Green. Maude (a beautiful and hard-headed young woman) had persuaded her father and Theodore that he should resign from the army and come into the family business. I liked Theodore, who was several years older than me. He was to spend some time at first 'looking around', with a view to seeing where best he might fit in; he started this process in March 1922. At that time we were having a lot of trouble with breakages of the seams of our paper machine wires. Speeds of the paper machines had been increased and the traditional seams were not adequate for the increased strain. Theodore had had no experience of business, but this problem interested him and after much experimental work, he invented a new type of stronger seam which did not mark the paper – assuredly no mean feat. It was successfully patented, became known as the 'GS seam' (Green Special), and went a long way towards solving this problem. I, too, ought to have been trying to solve it, but the truth is that I was not sufficiently interested.

This was in the winter of 1926–27 when I was assistant Secretary of the company and nearly twenty-three. I dealt with the routine correspondence each day, and I now signed these letters. I investigated customer complaints, making a report on each one. I was responsible for some of the book-keeping and costing, and each month I produced the first draft of the monthly accounts. My salary had gradually risen each year and by now was £450. All in all, I was content with my life. I had settled into a comfortable groove at the United Wire Works, while my financial passion was given reasonable scope, thanks to the syndicate, my father's, and my own, investments. On the lighter side, I had become very much part of the flourishing local amateur theatrical fraternity.

In 1926 early on the first day of the General Strike, I went to Waverley Station hoping to be accepted as a stoker. But already they had more volunteers than were needed so I went to Police Headquarters where I was immediately enrolled as a Special Constable. After the strike was over I chose to stay on until I went to London. The Police were a magnificent body of men and I had a very happy period of part-time service.

During the strike, the police were withdrawn from some parts of Glasgow; Edinburgh did not suffer the same experience, but I witnessed one large-scale riot at the East End of Princes Street. I was off duty at the time and I noticed a large number of men standing around the GPO and the Register Office. There was a solitary policeman directing the traffic. Suddenly several whistles were blown and several hundred men – they were miners from East Lothian – surged along Princes Street. When they reached Woolworths they smashed the windows, and some of them then started looting.

I was outside the entrance to the N.B. Station Hotel and had a grandstand view of the whole thing. The surge along Princes Street continued with more broken windows but before very long I could see a squadron of mounted police galloping towards the crowd, with their long batons at the ready. The crowd scattered but the police rode through it, re-formed and then came back. There were quite a lot of bodies lying about in Princes Street and the crowd melted away. But while it lasted it was an extraordinary sight. I spent one night in a distillery warehouse which was expected to be attacked but nothing happened, and my only violent action was a year later when one evening I chased two men who had removed a couple of suitcases from the dickey of a car standing in Heriot Row. I eventually cornered them and kept them there until a police constable arrived, when we arrested them.

I don't think I was aware of the opposite sex until I was nearly eighteen, but then – rather late – it came with a rush. I had some dancing lessons at 'The Palais': virtually the only place of its kind. I would take my current favourite there; a few weeks later, it would be somebody else. Without knowing it, I unconsciously compared every girl I met with Mother, who was still the centre of my world, and the result was that all these young women were wholesome characters. This, and the undoubted truth that there is safety in numbers, enabled me to get through my adolescence harmlessly. As for sex of any description, I can honestly say that the thought never entered my head – any passion within me was reserved for the Stock Exchange! And it was now my thoughts began to turn towards London.

# CHAPTER SIX

## *The City via Leicester*

The first move I made to explore the possibilities of London was in the winter of 1926–27 when I wrote to Geo. J. Holmes, then the Editor and – as I later knew – the co-proprietor with Sidney Lamert of the *Investors' Chronicle*. I told Mr Holmes pretty well everything about my financial experience to date – Hampton Properties, my syndicate and the extent of my financial reading (including the *Investors' Chronicle*) over the previous eight years. I sent him a copy of an imaginary prospectus I had written, which contained everything I felt was necessary for the perfect issue. I had an extremely generous reply – far more encouraging than anything I had encountered in Edinburgh. With this Mr Holmes enclosed the draft of an advertisement he had drawn up in which I offered my services. He said that he would like to put it into his paper for the next six issues, and that it would cost me nothing. But the result was disappointing, for I had only three letters and none of these was much good.

More direct action was needed. So I started to write to the Chairman or Chief Executive of practically every financial institution in London. In every case I wrote an individual letter which I hoped would appeal to the particular man, whose annual address to shareholders I had probably read for the past eight years. I commissioned a good professional photograph of myself, and enclosed a copy with each letter, hoping by this means to ensure that I got a reply. Nearly all the replies were much the same; the writer regretted he had no opening for me and returned the photograph. A few added good wishes. Only one photograph out of over a hundred I sent during the next five months was not returned.

The letters were all so brief that I could only guess why the operation had been a complete flop. I started to write to the non-financial people as well, such as Sir Eric Geddes, then the Chairman of the Dunlop Rubber Company and himself a Watsonian, and Sir Bernhard Baron, the Chairman of Carreras, also Harrisons & Crosfield, Courtaulds, and so on. My letters to these men were quite different from those to the financial companies; I just said that I wanted to come to work in London and enclosed my curriculum vitae.

Suddenly the tide turned. I had encouraging letters from Sir Eric Geddes and also from Harrisons & Crosfield. Much more important, three financial people wanted to see me. So in mid-December 1927, I took two days' holiday leave and, one Wednesday night, sitting up in a third class carriage, went to London to stay with an uncle and aunt in East Sheen and attend my five interviews on Thursday and Friday.

I went first to Dunlops in St James's Street. After a while I was shown into an enormous room at the far side of which sat two men. One I recognised as Sir Eric, who introduced me to Sir George Beharrel, the Managing Director. After that I was directed to a chair standing in splendid isolation in the middle of the room. The interview began with what seemed to me a very long silence, while the two men looked both at me and through me.

At the end of what eventually turned out to be a long interview, the like of which I had never experienced, I was told they might make a place for me in their accounts department. But Sir Eric made it clear that, if they did, I would have to give a written undertaking to give up 'all this Stock Exchange dealing'. When I left, I knew that I now had only four possibilities. Never would I have gone to Dunlops after that interview with Sir Eric, who seemed to me to represent the nineteenth century at its worst.

I liked the two people who interviewed me at Harrisons & Crosfield. They were entirely human. It became pretty clear that I could have a good job if I was prepared to go out East. If not, they might still be able to make me an offer, but that was not certain.

Next to 28–29 St Swithin's Lane, where I was to see Sir Arthur Wheeler, who at that time controlled Charterhouse, of which he was Chairman and founder. At that early period of their existence, Charterhouse were simply an issuing house sponsoring good industrial issues, while Gresham Trust, which Sir Arthur also controlled, was originally intended as a vehicle for the issues which, although also of good quality, were somewhat smaller. Gresham's issues ranged from about £200,000 upwards but later Charterhouse, under Hume, undertook many issues of a very similar size to what had previously been Gresham's speciality. Sir Arthur, then sixty-nine, had established Arthur Wheeler & Co at Leicester in 1899 where he still had his headquarters. It had become by far the largest firm of 'outside' Stockbrokers (i.e. Stockbrokers who were not members of any Stock Exchange). During the war he had sold enormous amounts of 5% War Loan and was given a Baronetcy in 1920 by Lloyd George. By 1928 he was a multi-millionaire. He also controlled a number of industrial companies such as Rolls Razor, Low Temperature Carbonisation (now the Coalite Group), United Drapery Stores, British Hosiery Trust, etc. The interview was brief because, as Sir Arthur explained to me at the outset, an urgent matter had just arisen which necessitated his returning to Leicester by the next train. However, I was with him for about a quarter of an hour. Although there was about forty-five years between us, we got on well from the very start. I liked him greatly. He asked me if I would come to Leicester on Saturday afternoon and spend the night at his home. He would see that I got a train which would get me back to Edinburgh by Sunday evening. Naturally I accepted.

My next interview was with a Mr James Carmichael, the head of a large firm of yarn merchants in Leicester, which bore his name. He had amassed a large personal fortune and wanted to have his own man to manage his Stock Exchange investments. I liked him, too, and the terms of the offer which he outlined were decidedly attractive. But I realised that I should not be able to get the broad experience which I felt was essential.

My last prospect was Mr F.A. Szarvasy, Chief Executive of The British Foreign and Colonial Corporation, whom I saw at BFC House, a large building on the north side of Gresham Street adjoining the Guildhall. In the course of a fascinating interview I recognised that I was being sized up by a very able man. I neither liked nor disliked him, but when he said that he would like to have me in his organisation and would write to me after he had thought it over, I was naturally pleased. Before leaving the City I went to see my kind friend Geo. J. Holmes – a tubby little man, in a small basement office in Drapers Gardens.

The next day, at the barrier of the Midland Station at Leicester, a tall, elderly chauffeur spotted me. He took me to Sir Arthur's home at Woodhouse Eaves and, sitting beside him, I told him it was the first time I had ever been in a Rolls Royce. After being introduced to Lady Wheeler, I had tea with Sir Arthur in his study. He asked me how I had got on in London; his comments were both shrewd and kindly. As part of their enormous business, Arthur Wheeler & Co dealt in the shares of many sound, small, local companies in various parts of England, and he obviously did not expect me to have heard of any of them. But I had not been spending much of my time reading without getting to know the 'form' of many small companies. So the conversation became something of a quiz. With the majority of companies he named I was able to outline the business, the approximate price and yield of the shares and how I rated them.

After dinner, he took me back to his study and said that he would like me to join Gresham as personal assistant to his son Derek, who had just become Managing Director. He asked me what I was being paid; when I told him it was £450 a year, he said he did not think Gresham could pay me more than £500 without upsetting their salary scale, but he would find some way of adding another £100 to this. When he saw me off the next morning he said 'This is a very important decision for you. Take plenty of time to think it over.' What a story I had to tell my parents on that Sunday evening. The next morning I was back at the office as usual; we had now moved to a larger factory in Granton where I had a room of my own.

Quite soon the letters began to arrive. Each of them contained an offer; though the letters from Dunlops and Harrisons had conditions attached. Sir Arthur's letter was kind and fatherly, and he also wrote a charming letter to my Father. Obviously the choice lay between Sir Arthur and Mr Szarvasy. I consulted Mr Robertson Durham, still Chairman of the Scottish American Investment Trust, but he was too careful to be of much practical help.

At this juncture, I also went to see Mr McFarlane at Mortonhall Road and in a long talk I told him everything. He could not have been more understanding, and his basically kind character came to the fore. I had maintained such a degree of interest in the Stock Exchange for the past seven and a half years, that he felt it would probably be right for me to follow it. I readily agreed to stay with United Wire until the end of March to hand over my various duties.

When Mr McFarlane died in 1934 he was succeeded as chairman and managing director by Theodore Green who made a quite outstanding success of enlarging the business during the thirty-five years when he was in charge of it. In 1934, when he took over, the profit before tax was £25,696 while in 1969 it was £1,184,786, having been £1,446,809 the year before. I saw him, with Maude, on many of my visits to Edinburgh during that period and had a warm relationship with both of them. I also have a great regard for Anthony and Michael, his two sons, who succeeded him in 1969.

To return to 1927. I accepted Sir Arthur's offer and politely declined the remainder. Sir Arthur replied with a warm welcome, enclosing an Arthur Wheeler & Co cheque for fifty guineas. At Woodhouse Eaves Sir Arthur said that it might be all to the good if I came to Leicester for a few weeks in order to be shown exactly how A.W. & Co functioned, before going on to London to start my new life at Gresham. The warm personal relationship we had established made this all the more attractive to me, and I readily agreed. The type of letter which he had written to me, quite apart from the generosity of the cheque, was something I had never experienced in Edinburgh, and on the whole I was not sorry to be leaving Scotland. But the parting was not without pain when it came to leaving my Mother and my Father. I am sure that Mother always hoped that I would stay in Edinburgh, but during that year when I was trying to get a job in London she never once uttered a word against it, and now her principal concern was that I should be safely housed. As a result of her enquiries I spent my first months in London in a boarding house at 21 Collingham Road, SW7, in the care of a Miss Gillies, the owner.

On Sunday morning 6 May 1928 when I left for Leicester, I said goodbye to Mother at Abercromby Place. This was the really awful part. My Father came to Waverley Station, and waiting for us there was dear John Burnett who, as the Secretary of United Wire Works, had done so much for me. I still have a happy snapshot of him and my Father on the platform just before the train left.

At Leicester I found a handwritten note of greeting from Sir Arthur at the Grand Hotel where I was to stay until I found suitable quarters. Sir Arthur had left instructions for the whole of my hotel bill to be charged to A.W. & Co.

A.W. & Co's office occupied a large part of the side of Town Hall Square opposite the Town Hall, where each morning Sir Arthur arrived punctually at 7.30 a.m. Next morning I was there a little before nine and was met by George Victor Smith. G.V., as I came to call him, I would rate as the better type of professional man, the son of a Leicestershire doctor. He had joined A.W. & Co after leaving school; he was now Sir Arthur's partner.

Soon Sir Arthur bustled in, taking my hand in both of his and greeting me most warmly. He told me that he had had a desk for me installed beside his own. There was an ear-piece for me connected with his own telephone. If I listened to all his telephone conversations (and he spent most of each day on the telephone), he thought this would be the best way for me to get the hang of things. He would signal to me if he did not want me to listen. Apart from this, I was to spend my time reading each day's prospectuses of which there were several and writing a review of them, which he would read over the weekend. He would usually be in London two days of each week and advantage would be taken of these two days to show me every aspect of the firm's operations.

After this introduction, we went into an enormous dealing room, in one corner of which Sir Arthur sat. Mr Smith's desk was some distance away and beyond were three of the dealers. Near Sir Arthur was his personal secretary, Miss Orchard, a superbly efficient, middle-aged woman with an incredibly quick and accurate mind who had been with him for many years. Sir Arthur had not nearly finished reading his large post when his telephone rang. Seeing no wave from him, I picked up my ear-piece. The caller was Philip Hill, and the subject of the conversation was the original flotation of Beecham Pills Ltd by Charterhouse two months earlier. Philip Hill, together with his partner, Louis Nicholas FCA (an able Liverpool chartered accountant) had been appointed to the board of Beechams, with Hill as Chairman.

Control of Beechams had been acquired several years before by a syndicate headed by Sir Arthur. The telephone conversation brought home to me the complex nature of the recent flotation. At that time Hill possessed no issuing house of his own. It was only in March 1932 that Philip Hill & Partners, the embryo merchant bank, was formed as a private company, becoming a public company in October 1936.

During the days which followed, Sir Arthur's telephone was rarely silent. The next call that morning came from Ernest Savory, senior partner of E.B. Savory & Co, who were Gresham's official stockbrokers. Later Mossy Myers of Myers & Co, with whose firm A.W. & Co did an enormous business, came on the line. At the end of the day several jobbers spoke to Sir Arthur, telling him of deals they hoped to negotiate and ascertaining the degree of his interest in these. One particular jobber had a near monopoly of all out-of-the-way shares on the London market. He depended on A.W. & Co to place these and although the business had to be passed through a broker most of it was actually settled by direct contact between A.W. & Co and the jobbers. When a large deceased estate was being sold, the selling broker would leave the shares in the smaller companies 'firm' with A.W. & Co for about ten days. In other words, A.W. & Co had exclusive rights to offer them for sale over this period. A.W. & Co then sent out letters to selected lists of people, offering these shares in small parcels which were usually sold well within the option period. As the days went by other telephone callers were the heads of most of the issuing houses, some of the general managers of the clearing banks, and many professional men in London and throughout the provinces.

Sir Arthur had started his business life in the accounts department of Simon May & Co, a much respected firm of wholesale textile merchants in Nottingham. But stockbroking attracted him and after a brief period when he and Arthur Blake were in partnership as Blake & Wheeler, he had established Arthur Wheeler & Co as his own business in Leicester in 1899, independently of the Stock Exchange.

A member of the Stock Exchange was not allowed to advertise but as an 'outside' broker Sir Arthur was free to do so. He started by offering shares in sound local companies to people in the same locality who possessed other investments. He invariably offered to settle through the buyer's bank; the technique proved very successful.

The business had grown apace and become a unique organisation for placing large blocks of shares in good quality companies with private investors throughout the country. By the nineteen-twenties it was by far the largest, and easily the best, business of its kind and during the first thirty years of this century it was a pioneer in making a fundamental contribution to financing small businesses by maintaining a market in this type of share – something which the Stock Exchange was not able to do, even in those days before some of the excellent local exchanges were closed, when federation centralised all real power in London. (In my view a terrible mistake which sooner or later will have to be rescinded if the Stock Exchange is ever to play an effective part in the finance of small businesses.)

The tremendous volume of A.W. & Co's daily mail entailed unprecedented co-operation with the postal services. A.W. & Co did their own primary sorting and then despatched their post from three main-line centres: Leicester, Derby and Nuneaton. None of these could handle the volume on its own. There were arrangements with many company registrars to notify A.W. & Co of all changes to their register of shareholders at frequent intervals, and from HM Registrar of Companies they purchased the names and addresses of shareholders of the best of the newly quoted companies

In April 1928 the mailing list totalled about 750,000 names, of which more than a quarter had at some time dealt with A.W. & Co. A set of envelopes could be run off to everyone on the entire list, or, more selectively, to anyone who lived in any particular county or city or who was mainly interested in some particular section of the market, be it property or beer. This unique and complex operation was superbly controlled by The Reader Printing Co Ltd of which Sir Arthur's younger son, John, was joint managing director.

After the 1914–18 war there had been a boom in new issues, which had added further grist to A.W. & Co's already large business. If they were prepared to recommend an issue (and a great many of these post-war issues did not come up to the standard they required), its success was virtually assured. A small local issue might require the circulation of no more than 50,000 prospectuses, while something on the scale of the Beecham issue (£1,075,000) needed the whole of the 750,000 names. At that period many of the larger underwriters – the people or organisations who agreed to take up shares the public failed to buy – would enquire whether A.W. & Co were 'sending out the prospectuses' and, if they were, this became a major factor in arranging the underwriting. A.W. & Co charged a substantial fee and in addition they were paid brokerage on every accepted application form which bore their code mark.

The vital aspect of A.W. & Co's approach was the covering letter enclosed with the prospectus, giving its salient points in an easily readable fashion, and recommending the issue. This was usually written by G.V. Smith. During the 1920s, except for a bad year in the post-war slump of 1921, I think A.W. & Co were making at least £200,000 net profit at the lower end of the scale and often very considerably more.

When Sir Arthur went to London during that first week, G.V. Smith talked to me for a time and then I listened to Walter Dewhurst, the senior dealer, speaking to brokers all over the country.

About this time I first met Clarence Sadd, then manager of the main Leicester branch of the Midland Bank, and clearly an exceedingly ambitious man. Later Sadd had a meteoric career and eventually became Chief Executive and Vice Chairman of the Midland, collecting a knighthood in the process. But he overplayed his hand and was forced to resign from the bank in 1948. The precise circumstances were never disclosed. He died in 1962.

I met him at a dinner of the Framework Knitters Guild when Sir Arthur was Master. He opened the conversation by enquiring if I read the Bible, to which I replied 'not very often'. 'That's a pity' he said 'I get all my best business phrases from it.' During the next twenty years I saw a certain amount of Sadd and for a time I had a differently worded letter from him on my birthday each year – a typical Sadd gimmick. Much later when I joined Industrial and Commercial Finance Corporation (ICFC) in 1945, I had a fulsome letter from him and later I was bidden to lunch at the bank. He was obviously cultivating Lord Piercy (then Chairman of ICFC) because of the latter's close connection with the then Prime Minister, Clement Attlee. Sadd's objective was clearly a Peerage.

During my two and a half months in Leicester I listened to practically every business conversation of Sir Arthur's. It was a wonderful education and I learned a great deal which, by more conventional means, it would have taken me years to acquire. Because of all my background knowledge most of what I heard was readily understandable – had this not been so, the idea would probably have misfired. At a weekend, I would usually be invited to Woodhouse Eaves, where Sir Arthur would go over my comments on the week's batch of prospectuses. He often told me about his experiences in past years, and treated me very much as if I were his own son. I was conscious of the unique relationship we enjoyed, and I found it easy to talk to him without reserve.

In June I left Leicester for Gresham in London, with very real regret. Gresham's office had just moved from St Swithin's Lane, and was now on the ground and first floors of Basildon House, Moorgate. I had a small room on the first floor looking on to Coleman Street with a connecting door to the large room which Sir Arthur and Derek used. Derek came on most days, Sir Arthur at least twice a week. One of the semi-executive Directors, Major J.S. Ruttle (an Irishman with a temper if provoked) also had a desk in Sir Arthur's room. The staff, which was all housed on the ground floor and basement, numbered about thirty in all.

When I arrived on my first Monday, I was greeted by Edward Hill, the Secretary, who introduced me to Cecil Greenfield, the Assistant Secretary, C.W. Finch, head of the registration department, and Charles P. Heselden, the Secretary of many of Sir Arthur's companies, and R.E.G. Thompson, a young accountant.

Edward Hill was very much the senior member of the staff, a chartered accountant, and an outstandingly able man. I grew to like him greatly and respected his high intelligence and absolute integrity. Heselden was an able man who eventually left Gresham to go to Philip Hill, where he became a director of Quadrant Trust and the original Secretary of Philip Hill & Partners Ltd. Greenfield, a sensible unpretentious man, was a chartered secretary. All in all it was a pleasant office in which to work. Derek Wheeler asked me to start by reading the files of cases then in the pipeline for possible flotation. I was doing this when, at about eleven o'clock, Thompson came to say that as usual at this time several of them were going out for coffee, and they hoped I would join them. I was quite unused to this, regarding it as a waste of precious time, but thought it best to respond, and for several days went with them, until I could tactfully drop it. When Derek was in London, I went with him to practically all his meetings, in or out of the office, and took notes from which I dictated a precis of what had occurred.

A fortnight's holiday with my parents then provided a brief interlude, and when I returned to London it was arranged that I was to handle a small Offer for Sale of the Ordinary shares of The Embassy Club in Bond Street. This was not large enough for Gresham, so was to be carried out under the label of Moorgate Issues Ltd, a Gresham subsidiary. This first assignment came my way mainly thanks to Sir Arthur, who – on the basis of my reviews of prospectuses – had decided that I was now ready for it. The Embassy was then a unique establishment, its presiding genius a remarkable man called Luigi Naintre. The Prince of Wales was a member and often took a party there. Everyone knew Luigi, and the membership was a cross between Debrett and the wealthier names in the Directory of Directors.

I made an early appointment to see Luigi at the club: itself a revelation to a twenty-four year old Scot whose experience of social life was limited to the Palais de Dance in Fountainbridge. We had an over-rich lunch with which I drank orange juice. Luigi's eye never left the room and when two beautifully dressed young women arrived, he rapidly excused himself and went over to their adjacent table. 'Now!' he said, 'you are both very very naughty. You told me you would come to my party last night, and you did not come. I am hurt.' 'Oh, we're terribly, terribly sorry, Luigi,' they said. 'Everything went wrong last night, and in the end we just couldn't come.' 'We-ll' taking his time, 'I forgive you – this time. But please – never, never do this to me again. . . . But I show you how I feel about you both; I keep the last two prizes for you. Wait – I go and get them.' In a minute he emerged from his private office with two enormous comic teddy bears. The effect was extraordinary. They poured out their thanks in unnecessary superlatives.

When we had finished lunch he led me to the same private office, and the first thing I saw in one corner was an enormous heap of identical teddy bears! I had no difficulty in getting the information I needed from him. He was obviously a complete master of his craft, and as soon as he stopped playing the prima donna, what emerged was an extremely shrewd and conservative business man.

I duly wrote the prospectus, drafted the third page legal requirements (the 'small print') and in due course took it all to Clifford-Turner Hopton & Lawrence, as they were then, an up and coming firm of solicitors in Gresham Street. Sir Arthur had spoken about me to Mr Harry Clifford-Turner (the founder of the firm) and after he had received me very courteously, I was passed on to his managing clerk, a remarkable man named H.W. Hill. During the next five years I saw a great deal of Hill, who, though unqualified as a solicitor, knew more about issue techniques than most people in the City at that time. He vetted the Embassy Offer for Sale and many others in the succeeding years, and I never remember him being at a loss for a solution, however awkward the technical problem.

The Embassy Offer which did not appear until 2 January 1929 was duly oversubscribed, the list of allottees including many members of the club. But the backbone of the operation was the response from that section of A.W. & Co clients to whom the offer had been sent. It brought home to me the power which A.W. & Co possessed. The new issue boom was in full progress in 1928 and our next issue was Pye Radio. In the autumn of 1928 Derek had reached agreement with Mr Charles Orr Stanley the promoter of the company, and I took over at that stage. Stanley owned an advertising agency – Arks Publicity Ltd – one of whose clients was Mr W.G. Pye, a maker of scientific instruments in Cambridge. In 1922 Pye had started a new department to manufacture radio sets. With their scientific background, Pye's produced reliable sets and this department was soon making larger profits than the original business. But William Pye was more interested in his instruments and the links with academic life in Cambridge which these provided. Stanley was therefore able to persuade Pye to give him an option to buy the radio department on bargain basement terms.

Pye was a likeable man but I didn't take to Stanley and the many meetings I had with him were nearly always difficult. He was often accompanied by his friend, R. Milward Ellis, who became joint Managing Director of the new company – a sardonic character; the first left wing type I had met.

To extract the last ounce in terms of total market capitalisation – in other words, to obtain the best possible price for the capital on offer – I plumped for a two-tier capitalisation for the Pye issue. In order to obtain a 1/- deferred share at par one had to subscribe for £1 of 8% preferred shares at par. If the issue was oversubscribed, the premium on the equity ought to be greater than the discount on the preferred. On 19 February 1929, the Pye issue was heavily oversubscribed with many obvious 'stags' among the applications. This is the stockmarket term for buyers of newly issued shares who hope to sell them immediately at a profit.

I felt that Pye was a growth business, and so I asked Derek if it was all right for me to make a personal application – telling him that I would want to sell the preferred within a few weeks. He just grinned from ear to ear and told me to go ahead. Then, just before the issue, he told me that in view of the way I had handled the issue, Gresham would sell me a few of their 80,000 deferred shares (without the preferred shares) at the issue price. I cannot now remember how many of these shares I bought, but, as in everything else with the Wheelers, it was generous. During the succeeding months, the deferred shares rose to high levels and I made a substantial profit.

Shortly after the Pye issue Derek told me that he and Sir Arthur had decided I was now to be regarded as Head of the Issue Department at Gresham, and not long afterwards my salary from Gresham was increased from £500 to £750. My confidence, which had gradually grown during my eight months in London, now blossomed. I felt on top of all that I was doing.

When I had first come to Gresham I sometimes had my lunch in the ABC Cafeteria in Throgmorton Street in order to absorb the atmosphere. It was full of sharp young men from the Stock Exchange. Their talk made it clear that their main object was simply to outsmart the next man. I knew that I should never be able to compete with them, and I often felt depressed. But, on further thought, I arrived at a totally different philosophy for my own business dealings. I decided that the essential ingredient for success in financial life was to build up a justified reputation for absolute reliability, earning the confidence of everyone with whom one dealt. Confidence in fact was the basic essential of success in the financial world. After that I stopped worrying about the 'clever' people.

By that time I had been to lunch at St Swithin's Lane with our 'elder brother' Charterhouse (the name was chosen because Derek had been at school there). It was clear that Nut Hume, the Managing Director appointed by Sir Arthur, was determined to free Charterhouse from Sir Arthur's (or anyone else's) control as soon as possible and by whatever means. Hume had had a difficult time in the 1921 slump, and he was driving a bus when Sir Arthur originally met him. The meeting led to an offer to Hume when Wheeler formed Charterhouse and over many years Hume undoubtedly proved a competent Chief Executive. Whether Hume ever subsequently recognised his tremendous debt to Sir Arthur is another question.

Following the Pye Radio issue, Gresham made issues in 1929 for L. Rose & Co Ltd, (Rose's Lime Juice), Public Benefit Boot Co Ltd and J. Hepworth Co Ltd, all of which I handled. The Roses were a particularly nice Scottish family, and I went more than once to see Lachlan Rose, the Chief Executive, at his home near Bishops Stortford. A high price had been put on their existing shares, and I tried many permutations before I arrived at a capitalisation which I felt would succeed and at the same time make a profit for us. Inevitably, the capital structure was very highly geared – the original equity was divided into a preferred share, with the fixed dividend thinly covered by the profits the company was then earning, and a highly priced deferred share. But with the help of the well known name, the issue succeeded.

In those days the issuing house controlled the sub-underwriting, which they sent to their own list of underwriters. The issuing Brokers were only given what was left over – usually very little. Nowadays the solicitors draft the whole of the 'small print' and the brokers allocate the underwriting, a thoroughly retrograde step in my opinion.

Another Gresham client was Odhams Press, then under the energetic direction of J. S. Elias (later Lord Southwood); they published the *Daily Herald* which supported the Labour Party. Odhams was continually making further acquisitions during that period and as it was highly geared, much ingenuity was called for each time a new loan issue was being arranged. In spite of a good deal of competition, principally from Investment Registry, Gresham secured a fair share of the many Odhams issues during the late twenties and early thirties principally because Ruttle was a member of their board. Madame Tussaud's was another company with which we had a close connection and one of the Gresham staff spent nearly the whole of his time dealing with their affairs. Ruttle was also a member of this board.

Office hours at Gresham were 9.30 to 5.30, and on Saturday 9.30 to 1.00. But I seldom left at 5.30 and not infrequently the caretaker would come to tell me that he was locking up the building. I dealt with all the new business enquiries which Gresham received, rejecting anything below £200,000, which was then uneconomic. At that time every issue was extensively advertised in the national press, which was expensive, and apart from the underwriting and brokerage there would have been little difference in the cost of an issue to raise £200,000 and one to raise £100,000. Not infrequently people with small businesses which appeared to be perfectly sound would come to see me, and when I had to tell them that we could not help, they invariably asked who could: there was no one.

The point was brought home to me when a would-be customer asked if we had any objection to his trying to find another firm to merge with in order to exceed the £200,000 barrier. I told him that, provided he bought a good business which genuinely fitted in with his own (which, I suggested would not be easy) there would be no objection. This pointed to the fact that if one could find some means of making small issues economically there would be many potential customers. The germ of an idea was sown.

I always tried to make the people who came to Gresham feel at ease in a friendly relaxed atmosphere. To come to the City was an ordeal to many, and to talk openly to a stranger about their private business affairs was far from easy. I had already developed a bald patch and I used deliberately to encourage this by vigorous combing! To appear to be older than my age often helped to win the confidence of the people who came to see me, and thereafter anything that made good sense became possible.

Only once in those years did anyone try to bribe me. Two men – both intermediaries – were describing an obviously third-rate business. They must have realised they were making no progress and after a while, one said to the other: 'Now, before we go any further, let's relax for a moment and have a bit of fun. I'd like to bet Mr Kinross that although I don't think we've put our case very well so far, by the time we've given him all the facts he's going to be able to help us. And I'll back that with odds of 100 to 1 in fivers.' So I was being offered £500 to 'help' them to sell their third rate shares to the public. I treated it as a joke, ended the interview, and a few minutes later they were back in Moorgate.

As time went on, Sir Arthur increasingly asked me to see people on his behalf when he was detained in Leicester. It was marvellous experience for me, and when I succeeded in winning the confidence of some unknown man who then told me what he had wanted to discuss with Sir Arthur I found it very rewarding. Sometimes, I would have to explain Sir Arthur's point of view on his behalf. I saw Sir Arthur Marshall, Harry Clifford-Turner, Philip Hill, and Sir Harry Peat amongst others. Philip Hill I saw fairly often, going to his office at the Quadrant Trust in Pall Mall. He had a very bad skin rash on his face at that time, so that the curtains of his room were drawn and he sat in the shade, while his visitor was in a pool of artificial light.

Once, as I was leaving, he unbent (as I then thought) and said 'If you want to do yourself a bit of good, buy a few Taylors Drug shares. They're such and such a price.' I thanked him, and promptly took his advice, for they were one of his companies. After a little while the shares went down, and I bought more. I eventually sold them at a loss of nearly £1,000. Later the shares went much lower. He never referred to the incident again and I decided not to ask him. When I bought the shares, I assumed that he was going to sell the business, and years later this did happen. Perhaps at the last moment the deal went sour. Whatever the explanation, it taught me never again to act blindly on a tip, however eminent the source.

One day in the early part of my time at Gresham I had a surprise visit from James Ivory, head of Ivory & Sime, then an elderly man. I had known him only slightly in Edinburgh where his firm was one of the leading Investment Managers in Charlotte Square. He undoubtedly came out of sheer goodness of heart in order to satisfy himself that I was all right and with good people. I cannot imagine two more completely different men than Philip Hill and James Ivory.

From time to time I used to do a variety of odd jobs for Derek or Sir Arthur, three of which remain vividly in my mind. The first concerned a cousin of Derek's – Colin Kingham. Colin was managing director of Rolls Razor and a wealthy man. On this occasion he had agreed to finance a young chemist who had convinced him that he had produced a liquid self-sealant for the inner tube of a motor tyre.

Colin had secured an interview with Sir William Morris (later Lord Nuffield), the creator of Morris Motors and asked me to go with him to 'hold his hand'. We went in Colin's Bentley to the works near Oxford where Sir William had his unpretentious small office. My recollection is of a lean pleasant man getting up from a desk littered with papers. Dispensing with any preliminaries he asked Colin to show him an inner tube containing the fluid. When Colin produced this Sir William said 'This tube will seal itself if punctured?' to which Colin assented. So after a moment Sir William took a pen knife from his pocket and jabbed the point of the small blade into the tube – a perfectly fair test. There was a loud hiss of escaping air and fluid and the tube went completely flat. Sir William handed it to Colin, wiped his hands and said 'Well I think there's nothing more to say,' and sheepishly we withdrew. Later I found that while Colin had conducted all sorts of 'tests' he had never got down to the basic simplicity of Sir William's method.

The second episode was in 1929 when I went to see Eugen Spier, then one of the contemporary 'financial wizards'. He had bought Claremont House near Esher from Sir Arthur, the last instalment of the purchase price was much overdue and he had become very elusive. At that time Spier had a very large interest in Combined Pulp and Paper Mills Ltd, which his Lothbury Trust had floated in October 1927, and which was then one of the most active speculative counters on the London Stock Exchange. On paper Spier was a very wealthy man.

Calling one week-end without prior notice I was shown into a beautifully furnished sitting room by the man-servant who had answered the door. The house itself was a superb period piece which Spier had filled with eighteenth century furniture in excellent taste. He offered me a hand made cigarette from what I think was a Fabergé box. Spier treated me with exaggerated courtesy and waved aside the unanswered letters. His object, he said, was to settle the debt using Combined Pulp shares 'at a suitable price'. I decided that my best line was a direct frontal attack so I told him that I didn't want any Combined Pulp shares – just a cheque that wouldn't bounce. After an exchange of unpleasantries I came away with a cheque on account, and within the time I had stipulated we had another one for the balance. Both were honoured.

About a year after this incident Combined Pulp went bankrupt, and in the subsequent liquidation shareholders got nothing and creditors very little. My close friend, Henry Drysdale CA (of whom more later) went to the company's Mill in Koslin, in East Prussia on behalf of the Committee of Shareholders. Henry, who was one of the shrewdest 'business doctors' I ever knew, told me that in his opinion the Company was fraudulent, with the mill only a shell of what had been described in the prospectus. Henry always regretted that a charge of criminal fraud was not brought by the Director of Public Prosecutions against Spier and Bruno Philipp of 63/64 Mohrenstrasse, Berlin, the Vendor, who had received £232,500 largely in Combined Pulp shares which would almost certainly have been sold at enormous premiums (the 1/- deferred issued at par went to over £4). However, the bankrupt company had not got the money to meet the preliminary costs of starting such an action, though later in his life Henry would undoubtedly have paid these out of his own pocket.

The only amusing episode in the whole sordid affair was Henry's adventure in Berlin en route for Koslin. As it was not possible to do the whole journey in one day he had booked a room in the Hotel Bristol, Berlin. After dining, he went up to his room and was just in bed reading his papers for the next day's business, when a door connecting his room with the adjoining one was opened and a very beautiful girl walked over to the foot of Henry's bed and smiled at him.

Henry's instant reaction was that this had probably been organised by Bruno Philipp as a last ditch attempt to prevent him seeing the mill, and at least to give Philipp enough material to blackmail him. It could have worked with the majority of men but all that happened was that Henry leapt out of bed, frog-marched the girl into her room and then shut and bolted the door. Looking quickly around as he did this, he saw no one else in the girl's room but I know that next day he was very careful in checking that his taxi was a genuine one and then travelling in a carriage containing several other people. Incidentally, Henry never again settled into any hotel bedroom without checking that any interconnecting door was bolted on his side.

I never met Spier again, but after a long interval he emerged as a minor City character who possessed an encyclopaedic knowledge of Foreign Bonds and wrote about these for the *Investors' Chronicle*.

The third episode that remains particularly vivid in my mind concerned the action in March 1930 by United Diamond Fields of British Guiana Ltd, claiming damages for 'conspiracy to cheat and defraud' against the two constituent members of the Diamond Syndicate (Barnato Brothers and A. Dunkelsbuhler & Co), the six individual partners of those firms and a number of other people including Ernest Oppenheimer and other men of international repute.

United Diamond Fields whose issued capital was £500,000 had been Gresham's first issue in October 1926 when Nut Hume was in charge. The essence of the prospectus was a five-year contract with the Diamond Syndicate under which the Syndicate bought the whole output of diamonds at fixed prices plus a small percentage of the profits on resale.

The diamonds were there all right but United Diamond Fields made heavy losses, largely because the grading was slanted heavily in favour of the Diamond Syndicate. One of its directors was Victor Coen, a wholesale tobacconist, and in March 1927 he became managing director though he had no experience of diamonds and had never visited Guiana. By October 1927 Coen realised that there was something seriously wrong. A meeting of shareholders in March 1928 appointed a shareholders' committee, all the Directors of United Diamond Fields except Coen and Pires, the resident director in Guiana, resigned, but Coen thereafter received the full support of the Committee, and was appointed Chairman of the company.

Owing to the failure of the 1926 issue, 94% of which was left with the underwriters, Sir Arthur was deeply involved in the case. Victor Coen convinced him that, by devious means, the Diamond Syndicate (which was a fabulously wealthy organisation) had systematically cheated the company. Sir Arthur consulted the firm of solicitors Theodore Goddard & Co and Bertram Ogle, then the second partner, went out to British Guiana to investigate.

The heavy costs of preparing for the action were originally financed by Sir Arthur but in April 1929 the company sold its assets in Guiana (but not its claim against the Diamond Syndicate) to the Bartica Co Ltd, a newly created wholly-owned subsidiary. The Bartica Company raised £90,000 by an issue of £100,000 7% ten year secured notes issued at ninety and Sir Arthur asked me to write the prospectus for this issue which indirectly financed the action. It was an extremely difficult task. I worked closely with Bertram Ogle and we eventually produced a document which, while making it perfectly clear that the stock was highly speculative, resulted in the full subscription of the issue by private placement. All this resulted in my establishing an intimate contact with Theodore Goddard & Co which lasts to this day.

In March 1930 United Diamond Fields of British Guiana v Joel and others came before Mr Justice McCardie and a City of London Special Jury. A few months previously the company had succeeded in obtaining a strong judgment in the Court of Appeal, dismissing an application from the defence which sought security for its costs. Lord Justice Scrutton, in particular, was very critical of the inequity of allowing a wealthy group, charged with fraud, to strangle the victim by getting an order against him which he could not pay.

The case lasted for eleven-and-a-half days during much of which I was in Court. Victor Coen spent ten of these in the witness box; none of the other witnesses being called. A van-load of papers was carried into court each day, but Victor seldom had to refer to these, and he remained unshaken when cross-examined for nine days by three of the foremost advocates of the day, who asked him nearly 6,000 questions.

Sir Patrick Hastings assisted by Theodore Matthew and H.C. Marks appeared for the company and Stuart Bevan, Norman Birkett and Gilbert Beyfus for various members of the defence, which collapsed before the cross-examination of Victor was completed. The full claim of £325,000 plus costs was paid and 12/4d per £1 share of United Diamond Fields was returned to shareholders. The charge of fraud was withdrawn. I had tremendous confidence in Victor and so had bought a good many thousand of the shares at about a third of this price before the case ended. Later, Victor was given a dinner at one of the Inns of Court by the barristers concerned in this remarkable case. He was urged to read for the Bar and this he did; giving up his tobacco business. For the next twenty-five years he had a most successful company law practice.

Suggestions of business malpractice were not infrequent at this time. In the mid-Thirties I was asked to act as an expert witness on two occasions in cases concerning doubtful company promotion. In one of these the defendant was represented by Victor (although until I was in the witness box I did not know this). The defendant lost the case, but my scrupulously fair but searching cross-examination by Victor was quite an experience.

A mission which had nothing to do with the Wheelers occurred when Melville Smith, the Technical Director of Rolls Razor, asked me to meet an extraordinary individual who interested him. This man – I have forgotten his name – was a well qualified metallurgist who claimed to have discovered a process of converting lead into tin. If this could have been done it would have been highly profitable and Melville Smith, an intelligent and thoroughly rational character, was by now convinced that the whole thing was genuine.

I agreed to see the man and after an inconclusive talk during which he said Melville Smith could help him on a technical level and that the amount of money needed was quite small, I agreed to go to see the process in operation. We were a party of four the last one being this man's 'partner'. When this was being arranged we were told that because they had no patent protection they could not show us absolutely everything and they also said they would not take us by the direct route so that we should not know the location of the premises which they said was a dockside warehouse.

This didn't quite add up to me and when the four of us set off I had a rubber truncheon which I'd kept from the general strike in 1926 inside the coat I was wearing. I was fit and strong and confident I could deal with any trouble.

Eventually we stopped at a very sleazy warehouse in a deserted dead-end street on the north bank of the Thames, which I judged to be in the Wapping area. The door was unlocked, some lights turned on and I walked deliberately behind the other three. At the end of a long passage another door was unlocked and we entered a large room perhaps 50 feet × 25 feet. An iron walkway ran around it about 6 feet above the concrete floor and we walked round this. The whole floor was covered with tons of fairly fresh horse manure about 6 feet deep and in this being 'cured', were the lead ingots, connected by a series of electric cables. The atmosphere was appalling. Apart from the difficulty of breathing I remember having difficulty in keeping a straight face – we were shown the 'finished product' and Melville Smith was allowed to take a very small piece of it for analysis (naturally it was tin).

To my mind the whole thing was a load of rubbish but the extraordinary sequel was that in spite of my plea not to touch it Melville Smith paid about £1,200 for a share in the project. In due course he lost the lot.

During my Gresham period, I dealt in the Stock Exchange for my own account pretty frequently. Sir Arthur had no objection to my doing this, provided I referred to him before dealing in any shares related to Gresham's business. This, of course, I did. The first real 'killing' I made was when J. Sears (Tru-Form) Ltd bid for Freeman Hardy & Willis. By then Charterhouse had become a completely independent entity ruled by Nut Hume, who had got rid of Sir Arthur – pretty shabbily, as I saw it. I now went to St Swithin's Lane only very occasionally for I despised Nut who had become exceedingly pompous. On one occasion when I was with him in his room, a telephone call interrupted our conversation. Although no names were mentioned, it was clear to me that the purpose of the call had been to instruct Nut to bid £7 a share for some company and that he would do this shortly. There was some reference to the market, so that I knew the shares were quoted on some UK stock exchange. Nut had also given his caller the precise amount of the total cost, which I memorised.

That evening I went through every share in the London official list but by about 3 a.m. I had failed to find anything which produced the exact figure. Next evening I worked through the supplementary London list and when I reached the 'Fs' I found that Freeman Hardy & Willis deferred shares of £1, if valued at £7, produced the magic figure. I thought it over, and came to the conclusion that Nut was fair game. There were a number of marks in the shares at around 90/–, and next day I had no difficulty in buying several hundred. By then I had opened an account with Barclays City Office and they agreed overdraft facilities of up to £4,000 in addition to which I sold several shares to raise further cash. The shares kept rising and I was paying nearly 110/- when suddenly they jumped, and late on the same day a bid on behalf of J. Sears & Co Ltd at £7 was announced. In all I made about £2,500 and my Father about £600. At no point would my small buying have influenced the market price, though under today's stricter attitudes I would not have taken the risk of dealing.

Ernest Savory (senior partner of E.B. Savory & Co – Gresham's official brokers) had asked me to dine at his club when I came to Gresham in the early summer of 1928 and I met several of his partners that evening. I did not take to them, but Ernest himself I liked very much and for many years thereafter he was unfailingly kind to me. On several occasions, he told me what he knew of some stockmarket situation or other and then left it to me to decide what, if anything, to do. Practically all the transactions which I chose were profitable, and my capital was now increasing rapidly.

I used to reckon my total net worth each weekend, and sometime during the latter half of 1929 I had passed the £10,000 mark. By then I had moved to a cheaper boarding house in Belsize Square, NW3, and when I left the office that Monday evening I was determined to walk to Hampstead. This was a peculiar way of celebrating, but I was imbued with the idea that if I allowed my new found £10,000 to go to my head it would become a liability. So instead of taking my 3d tube from Moorgate to Belsize Park, I set off up City Road, the Angel, then down to Kings Cross, and on to Camden Town, Chalk Farm, and then to Belsize Square. During that walk I determined to go on saving everything I could create until I had achieved financial independence. The traumatic events of my Father's financial problems in August 1920 were still a potent influence.

Early in August 1929 Clarence Hatry telephoned Derek Wheeler one Thursday and then, being told he was not in London, asked to be put through to me. Hatry was then one of the leading personalities in the City and his Corporation and General Securities Ltd had succeeded to a remarkable degree in making public issues for local authorities. For many years this market had been in the hands of a small number of leading brokers, and Hatry had inevitably made some enemies in high places as the consequence of his success. On this occasion Hatry wished to talk to us about Steel Industries of Great Britain Ltd. This company had been registered by Hatry in June 1929, yet the issue – already postponed a number of times – had still not appeared. As a result of the delay, Austin Friars Trust were in the market to borrow £250,000 of three months' money. Was this likely to interest us? I said it could do so and we arranged that he would come to Gresham at five the next afternoon when Derek was to be there. Hatry duly arrived with two of his senior colleagues at Austin Friars Trust – Daniels and Gialdini. Hatry had a magnetic personality, quick, alert and likeable. At that time the forthcoming steel issue had every prospect of success, and furthermore it was an industrial merger which was genuinely needed by a fragmented steel industry. Derek enquired what the collateral would be, and Hatry suggested a block of Photomaton shares – one of the string of companies which he had floated. Derek turned to me, saying 'He's the expert – would Photomaton suit us?' This company had booths in many parts of the UK, where by putting a coin in a slot you had a series of photographs of yourself taken automatically. So far it had been successful but I did not feel it was suitable collateral.

So Hatry said to me 'Which of our shares would you like?' My answer was Associated Automatic Machine Corporation, which unlike most of the other Hatry companies, was a well established concern with a good profit record. Their vending machines were to be seen on most railway platforms. Hatry smiled and said to Derek 'Well he's picked a share I would never sell – but for this purpose that's immaterial. You can have it.' I have forgotten the interest rate, but it was satisfactory, as was the margin of collateral.

We parted most amicably, and Derek promised Hatry a definite answer on Monday after he had spoken to his father. However, on Saturday Derek Wheeler rang me to say that Sir Arthur, unbeknown to him, had agreed to a large A.W. & Co deal also on that Friday afternoon and wanted most of Gresham's spare cash for about six weeks. Derek had at once told Hatry, saying that, if it were to suit him, we would be glad to talk again in about six weeks.

Had it not been for this unexpected turn of events, Gresham would have lost the £250,000, for our security would have consisted of forged share certificates. Although everything appeared to be perfectly normal when we saw Hatry, the shares of his companies began to fall barely a month after this and, on Thursday, September 19 1929, their weakness was the feature of the day's trading. On that day Hatry and three of his associates went to Sir Gilbert Garnsey, then senior partner of accountants Price Waterhouse & Co and told him that they had forged share certificates on a massive scale and that these were now held by some of the joint stock banks as collateral. On September 20, they visited the Deputy Director of Public Prosecutions and later went to Cannon Row Police Station, where they were detained.

On the same day Sir Gilbert Garnsey was instructed by a number of the banks principally involved to investigate the Hatry group, and the London Stock Exchange suspended dealings in the shares of six of his companies. On Monday, September 23 petitions were presented for the compulsory winding up of four of the Hatry companies, including Austin Friars Trust. The following day the Official Receiver was appointed Provisional Liquidator of Austin Friars.

Price Waterhouse sent me a ticket for the final day of the Hatry trial. When the jury returned their verdict of guilty and Mr Justice Avory, an impassive man with a face the colour of faded parchment, addressed the defendants in the dock, I was spellbound. When the sentences came, there was an audible gasp from the public benches, while Hatry – who had behaved with dignity throughout the day – visibly reeled. His sentence of fourteen years was considered very severe at that time, but of course the wholesale forging of share certificates, including some for local authority loans, had struck a major blow at the machinery of the City. Daniels and Gialdini were sentenced to shorter terms of imprisonment, but one never heard of them again.

The fall in the various Hatry shares, culminating in their suspension on September 20, was the start of the financial slump which eventually brought share prices down to unbelievably low levels both here and in the USA, and which continued during the next two years. Because of my contact with Hatry, the fall in his shares made a profound impact on me and during the week beginning September 23 I sold the majority of my own and my Father's shares. They were nearly all 'blue chips' but had already started to fall. As it turned out, this proved to be one of the rare occasions where drastic action taken off the cuff paid handsomely. It was not until May 25 1934 – over four and a half years later – that the position of the various steel firms involved in the frustrated merger was resolved.

By 1930, it was again possible to make a limited number of issues. We successfully floated the Ingersoll Watch Company Ltd; J. Darnell & Son then one of the leading London wholesale boot and shoe manufacturers; and Sun Electrical Co Ltd the wholesale electrical firm controlled by the Tweedie Smith and Rawlings families. But, with nervous markets, these were all difficult issues. Darnell made the bulk of its profit of about £60,000 by paying its trade creditors weekly, in exchange for high cash discounts.

The Sun Electrical flotation brought me into contact with Leslie Tweedie Smith, an unusually interesting man. He had intended to become a barrister, but when he was demobilised his uncle, Mr Rawlings, showed him the Rawlplug which he had just patented. He offered it to Leslie, who had the imagination to see its possibilities and built it up to be a world-wide and extremely profitable business. For about six years, until the Second World War, we met every month; usually at his home in Putney. After I left Gresham in 1933 I was his investment adviser for several years.

In March 1930 in St Giles Cathedral Edinburgh I was married to Mary Dolores Sang (known as Dolly), the only child of George Sang WS. Our first home was a top floor flat at 8 Belsize Square, NW3 where we lived happily for several years. We shared a love of the country and spent most week-ends out of London. My Father came to stay with us during the summer of 1930 for what proved to be his last visit to London, which he loved. One week-end, he and I re-visited some of the buildings which interested him. Britannic House, then BP's headquarters in Finsbury Circus, was very much to his taste as was Frascati's Restaurant in Oxford Street. Taking out a pocket knife he demonstrated to me how the brickwork at Frascati's was so 'tight' that it was impossible to insert a blade between the bricks.

By the autumn of 1930, my Father was able to do less and less, and had become rather withdrawn, though he went frequently to the RSA where he was still Honorary Treasurer. On 4 January 1931 he wrote a first-rate letter about Academy policy in reply to a long letter from the President dated two days earlier, but on 7 January he died suddenly and peacefully. He was seventy-five-and-a-half years old and the cause of his death was arterial sclerosis. After a service at St Paul's Episcopal Church in York Place in Edinburgh, he was buried in the family grave at the Grange Cemetery, beside his two infant daughters. Many friends came to the cemetery, and the Academy was represented by twenty-one of its members. Mother wisely went home with Eveleen after the church service.

I acquired for her a memento of my Father at this time. During the previous summer, David Alison RSA had painted a group which he called 'The President and Council of the Royal Scottish Academy'. In the picture, the President, Sir George Washington Browne, was sitting a little apart and with him were John Duncan, the Librarian, James Paterson, the Secretary, and my Father, the Treasurer. Alison had caught my Father exactly, as he had all of them for that matter.

After my Father's death I asked him if I might buy it for Mother. 'But can a young chap like you afford to buy pictures?' he asked: I replied that I could afford to buy this one. After a moment he took a large jack-knife from his pocket and suddenly slit the canvas in two. The smaller part contained the President, the larger showed the three Academicians, with Henry Hastings the Assistant Secretary in the background. He said that he would tidy it up for me and find a frame, and could I afford £5. When I enquired if that was fair he said 'Perfectly fair. When Washy dies, I'll probably have a market for the other half.'

My Father had undoubtedly effected a transformation in the Academy's investments during his long term as Treasurer. The sale of fixed interest stocks at high prices and their re-investment in the ordinary shares of the Royal Bank of Scotland and the Bank of Scotland in October 1926 was entirely his doing and, as with the planning of Manderston, was years ahead of its time. After his death, the Council of the Academy – entirely on its own initiative – went to considerable lengths to care for Mother. They used various funds and this income was paid to her during the four and three-quarter years that she survived my Father.

# CHAPTER SEVEN

## *The Wheeler Crash*

By 1930 the prospect in the City was darkening, very few new issues were being made, credit was becoming tighter and confidence was low. The cash requirements of the companies Sir Arthur had launched and which were still in the development stage had increased. This applied especially to Low Temperature Carbonisation where the Chief Executive was Colonel Whiston A. Bristow, a sound engineer with an original mind. That however was the limit of his ability and much more was really required. At an enormous cost, he had made considerable technical improvements in the process of producing 'Coalite' smokeless fuel and treating the valuable chemical by-products; but a number of fundamental technical defects remained. In later years, these troubles were overcome but what Bristow believed could be done in months took as many years: a process I was to see repeated many times in my subsequent business life.

A number of other companies in Sir Arthur's empire, such as Rolls Razor Ltd, were struggling with the same basic problems and Sir Arthur was now having to pump in very large amounts of money each month to keep them all alive. Nearly all of them possessed genuine merit; the essence of the problem was one of timing. Could Sir Arthur afford to go on pumping in money until these businesses turned the corner and became self-supporting and then profitable in their own right? (As they nearly all eventually did.)

Alas, the answer proved to be 'no'. The problem was exacerbated by Sir Arthur's accepting too readily the over-optimistic budgets which nearly all these companies were giving him. The crunch came at 5 p.m. on Friday 26 February 1931. Edward Hill – who had just returned from Leicester – came up to my room to tell me that Sir Arthur would file his petition in bankruptcy on the following Tuesday 3 March. Edward had had no prior warning. For me also, it was a complete shock. Neither of us had had any knowledge of the overall position of A.W. & Co. The much lower volume of A.W. & Co's stock exchange business since the Hatry crash was only a minor factor. The root of the trouble lay in all these businesses which Sir Arthur had backed on the eve of what developed into a major trade recession.

The shortfall was likely to be well into seven figures. Many of the 'Wheeler' shares had been rather weak during the previous few days. But they were not alone in this and I had not been unduly concerned. A.W. & Co had pledged these shares as security for large bank overdrafts and during February the fall in prices had reached a point where the security no longer covered the level of the bank overdrafts. Gresham had a daily trading account with Arthur Wheeler & Co; they had temporarily 'warehoused' some of the shares of the Wheeler companies. This had been profitable for Gresham and the shares purchased for A.W. & Co were in Gresham's possession. With Greenfield, we checked the documents of title that evening and all were in order. We came in as usual the next day (Saturday) but there was not a great deal we could do. Derek Wheeler spoke to me from Leicester.

I told Dolly of the crisis that afternoon for she was the soul of discretion, and on Sunday we sat for a long time on Hampstead Heath talking over the situation. On the whole, I thought Gresham would survive, although it was clearly going to be a fine run thing. I was fortunate in having a substantial amount of money in the bank, but if the worst happened I knew it would be extremely difficult to find another job. On 23 February, the number of registered unemployed persons stood at 2,617,658: this was 1,078,393 more than a year before. Among City firms, staff cuts were still the order of the day and I was fortunate not to have had to take any salary cut. Dolly, who was always courageous, took it all very calmly.

Monday was a most difficult day, for by now three of us at Gresham knew far too much of what was going on. I contrived diplomatic 'engagements' covering that day and most of the next. But on Tuesday afternoon an announcement was made, whereupon dealings ceased in most of the Wheeler company shares. I had holdings in three of these, including Gresham itself, but I had not dealt in any for many months.

On that Tuesday afternoon, and for the rest of the week, my telephone rarely stopped. It was a quick lesson in who my real friends were. In the months which followed, Edward Hill was a tower of strength and it was largely due to him that a number of the Wheeler companies survived in their original form. Rolls Razor, for instance, in which Derek Wheeler held a controlling interest, had been losing money. But suddenly Colin Kingham's constructive work over previous years and the large advertising campaigns which Sir Arthur had financed started to pay off and before very long the company was making substantial profits, which formed the basis of Derek's future personal fortune.

A year or two after I had left Gresham Savory reported that 800 Rolls Razor deferred shares were on offer at 1/3d. I bought them on the second day of the Stock Exchange account and about a week later the annual report appeared. It was far better than anything I had anticipated and what came as a complete surprise was a recommendation for a maiden dividend of 300% on the deferred shares in spite of a considerable debit balance carried forward from previous years. In accordance with the Stock Exchange rules the shares went ex-dividend at the end of the account. The outcome was that instead of my sending a cheque to the Brokers I received one from them for the amount by which the net dividend exceeded the whole of the purchase price. I wonder if this extraordinary freak has ever been repeated!

One of the Wheeler companies with which I had been concerned was The British Corosit Button Co Ltd, formerly The Turret Button Co Ltd. Turret was a small, old established, manufacturer of buttons in Hackney, which had acquired the rights for the manufacture of a new plastic button. Sir Arthur had financed the new plant and had a controlling interest in the company. I represented him on the Board and within a few days, the Chairman resigned and I perforce succeeded him. With the source of our finance suddenly cut off, we had to appoint a Receiver before the Writs multiplied. I presided at the first meeting of the creditors. I was only twenty-nine but I was no longer young for my age. I found I had no difficulty in taking the somewhat stormy meeting.

As March 1931 progressed, however, things worsened. One day Cyril Osborne (a senior member of the A.W. & Co staff at Leicester) telephoned to tell me that a man closely associated with us had poisoned himself that morning. This was W.H. Yates ACA, the senior partner of a small firm of Leicester chartered accountants and a Director of Gresham and two other 'Wheeler' companies. His death came as a tremendous shock to us all. Speculation as to the cause of his suicide was rife.

In fact there had been no irregularities and Yates had simply been the victim of the pressures to which, in varying degrees, we were all subject. Before long, we were told that the Director of Public Prosecutions had decided to bring criminal proceedings against Sir Arthur and his partner, G.V. Smith, alleging misappropriation of clients' money.

The facts were these: many clients when buying shares sent a cheque as soon as they received the contract note. Therefore, given the fortnightly Stock Exchange settlement system, there was a delay before A.W. & Co was due to pay the broker providing the shares. The sudden cessation of A.W. & Co's business was thus bound to leave some clients without their stock, which had not yet been delivered by the brokers.

These clients thus ranked as unsecured creditors. Although there was nothing new in this type of failure, the size of the funds and the number of clients involved were unprecedented. Until a few weeks before the failure, the firm was issuing about 5,000 contracts a month (there were over 50,000 regular clients and the staff at Town Hall Square in Leicester, who worked in two shifts from 9 a.m. to 9 p.m., totalled 240).

The case lasted for three days in the autumn of 1931 at the Leicester Assizes. The jury returned a verdict of guilty and Sir Arthur was sentenced to a year's imprisonment. G.V. Smith was bound over and conditionally discharged, thanks to Sir Arthur's insistence on accepting full responsibility for everything – a typically generous act.

Following the traumatic events of 3 March 1931, I had been in Leicester on a number of occasions and remained in close touch with Sir Arthur. After the Court rose on the second day of the trial he asked me to come to Leicester overnight to see him. I caught the first available train and late that evening I was with him at Woodhouse Eaves. He told me that he felt the jury were likely to return a verdict of guilty the next day, and if so, he would probably have to face a spell in prison. He was then seventy, but his spirit was that of a much younger man, and just as soon as he was able, he was determined to start in business again in order to pay his creditors in full. But meantime, there was probably a gap of unknown dimensions to be bridged. He told me that he had decided to ask me if I would take charge of a successor business in his absence, with Walter Dewhurst, the senior dealer, continuing in his previous role. I could write my own ticket for, he said, 'I trust you completely'.

I have never, either before or since, been faced with quite such a difficult situation. On the one hand, I dearly wanted to help this man who had done so much for me and whom I deeply respected; on the other, I wanted eventually to end up with one of the premier jobs in the City, and if I now became an outside broker – even for only a year or two – I felt certain this would prove fatal to my future career.

Nearly three years earlier, on 23 August 1928 when I had been at Gresham for just over a month, Sir Arthur had told me that Arthur E. Blake & Co, probably the leading Nottingham stockbrokers and members of the local Stock Exchange, was 'for sale'. He would like to have bought the business and installed me in Sir Arthur Blake's place, with the promise of massive support from A.W. & Co. I should have been a member of the Stock Exchange and, later on, I could have gone to London having been senior partner of one of the best of the smaller provincial firms at a very early age. Though I was tempted at the time, I had decided to stay in London and Sir Arthur didn't buy the business. I now reminded him of this episode. I said that while this would have delayed my future career for perhaps two or three years, to become an 'outside' broker would probably have put an end to what I eventually hoped to do. I suggested that Walter Dewhurst take charge and if he, Sir Arthur, wished, I would keep in daily touch with the new business, for at least the first year. I said that under no circumstances would I accept any remuneration for it would be a genuine labour of love. Sir Arthur and I talked till nearly four in the morning and by then the formation of Walter Dewhurst & Co Ltd had been agreed, and the warm relationship between us remained intact.

Had I done what he wanted I have little doubt that we could have held on to a considerable part of the old A.W. & Co business. If so, both of us would have made very substantial fortunes. The fact was that A.W. & Co had provided an essential service between the Stock Exchange and the small investor. Had A.W. & Co been left alone there would have been no failure, but it had been used to finance companies requiring cash injections with increasing frequency. This was an entirely different business for which Sir Arthur's judgment at his age was not sufficiently critical. His liquid wealth in the 1920s was a positive disadvantage for, if he was attracted by a situation, he simply wrote a cheque. Had Derek been a few years older, things might have been very different, for Derek could smell trouble; within a fairly short period I think I also could have helped. As it was, Sir Arthur was being advised by people many of whom were not really good enough. And as with so many wealthy men he was continually exposed to flattery.

That night was Sir Arthur's last at Woodhouse Eaves. He served six months of his twelve-month sentence at Wormwood Scrubs, working in the library with Lord Kylsant, the shipping magnate. I had written more or less regularly to him while he was in prison, and had sent him *Leaves from My Life*, by the Victorian company promoter O'Hagan, together with other books. But he rarely knew who had sent these. His only complaint about the life was that the underwear was infernally tickly! On his release he went to Holme-next-the-Sea, near King's Lynn, where his daughter Nancie took every care of him for the next eleven years. On 6 May 1932 he wrote me a brave letter which ended 'I'll be seeing you very soon – fifty-one not seventy-one years old'. Five weeks later I had a long letter in reply to one from me. He was 'in the doctor's hands, a bit more than I expected when I wrote last'.

By now the new firm, Walter Dewhurst, was going reasonably well. The board consisted of three of the old staff at Town Hall Square –

Walter himself, A.C. Sharman a senior clerk and Miss Orchard, Sir Arthur's superb personal secretary. At the outset, I had been fairly active in the business, but once Walter found his feet he naturally wanted to steer his own ship. By nature, he was a cautious man and the business never really took off, though it was sound and profitable. It had been financed by loans from a number of friends of the family; all repaid before Sir Arthur's death.

By Easter 1933, however, Sir Arthur's health had improved to the point where he wanted to start again. As an undischarged bankrupt, he could not do this in his own name, but a thirty-six year old chartered accountant who was advertising for a job attracted his attention. He asked me to vet the applicant with a view to his opening an office in either King's Lynn or Norwich. I gladly did this, but the practical difficulties of starting up were very great and, a fortnight later, I had a letter from Sir Arthur in which he acknowledged these problems.

I went to see him at that time, and later we met in London whenever possible. We also corresponded until the end of his life. Sir Arthur died on 20 May 1943 and is buried with his wife Mary in the churchyard at Holme. I shall always think of him, with affection and gratitude, as a fine and lovable character incapable of any mean action; essentially a straightforward and most generously minded man who helped many lesser people with great unselfishness. He was an entrepreneur of genius. Only his timing was wrong.

After his bankruptcy my Mother, unknown to me, had written to him. I never saw her letter but, in spite of the pressures on him at that time, he replied about a week later in his beautiful copperplate handwriting which I found among her papers when she died:

> My dear Mrs Kinross,
>
> I am indeed grateful for the very kind letter you wrote me.
>
> Your son is a man you have every reason to be proud of and I am hopeful that we may yet be associated together for a number of years to his advantage and mine.
>
> I sincerely hope the great loss you recently sustained* will be somewhat mitigated ere long by the knowledge that your son is, or will be, one of the most successful and respected men in the City of London.
>
> He has all the qualifications necessary.
>
> Yours sincerely,
> Arthur Wheeler

* my Father's death

Following the events of 3 March 1931, Gresham shares were quoted nominally at 'nothing to 1/-', and for the rest of 1931 we had a long-drawn-out daily struggle for survival. Edward Hill, Cecil Greenfield, and I formed the hard core of Gresham during that memorable period and, while we made an effective team, the guiding hand was Edward's. By early 1932, Gresham's financial position had been restored but the mauling we had received had substantially reduced our size, so that, while I now had no doubt about my monthly salary cheque, the question which I asked myself was: with our reduced financial base could I earn my keep for Gresham?

It was a difficult question to answer. No issues were possible and following Sun Electrical on 10 December 1930, there was a gap until 3 May 1933 when we made another issue for Odham's Press, owing to Ruttle being a member of their board. For the first time since coming to Gresham, I had time on my hands. I used some of it to go to some annual or extraordinary general meeting which was obviously going to be controversial. I was very seldom a shareholder but this never stopped me and undoubtedly I learned a great deal from many of these meetings. Some of them consisted of the first or second AGMs of what had been semi-fraudulent public issues of new and highly speculative companies. Some of the worst of these companies never had any genuine mass production manufacturing capacity and were really 'shells' promoted in order to cash in on the public appetite for some new product – gramophone records and artificial silk were two fashionable examples at that time. These meetings were usually very stormy. The halls were packed and on one occasion, realising that the over-eloquent chairman had convinced most of his large audience that all was well in spite of some dreadful figures, I slipped out just before the meeting ended (I was standing near the exit) ran to the nearest telephone and bought all the shares I could at practically rubbish prices. By the end of the same afternoon I had sold them at a profit of some hundreds of pounds, a caper which I did not repeat.

One interesting and packed meeting of an entirely different type which I attended was the EGM of the General Electric Co Ltd early in 1929. Sir Hugo Hirst Bart was in the chair and after a lot of discussion it was agreed to create the 1,500,000 'British' ordinary shares of £1 offered for sale on 21 March 1929 at 42/- per share. This action probably saved the company from a foreign take-over bid. On this occasion I did not deal in the shares but I learned a great deal from watching Sir Hugo's able conduct of the meeting.

By this time, I knew two or three of the leading men in the life of the

City. One of these was Charles Dalziel, a partner of Higginson & Co, the old-established Merchant Bankers now part of Hill Samuel & Co Ltd. A few weeks after the Wheeler crash, he told me that the Royal Exchange Assurance were going to recruit an investment manager to work under the general manager, Mr E. de M. Rudolf, and he suggested that I should apply. I did so and although Dalziel supported the application, I did not get the job. In retrospect I regarded this as a most fortunate outcome for had I joined the Royal Exchange in this capacity (and remained there) I would gradually have become a conventional establishment figure, condemned to a comparatively unenterprising business life.

In March 1931, I decided I needed something by way of an insurance policy. Edward Hill's brother, a practising chartered accountant who had been appointed as Receiver of the British Corosit Button Co Ltd, was finding it difficult to dispose of the business. The new plant was still having teething troubles, but the old Turret business had always been profitable. So, after talking it over with the Green family who controlled Buttons Ltd, then the largest UK manufacturer of buttons, I made an offer to the Receiver for the old Turret part of the business and after a while this was accepted.

Through mutual friends in Edinburgh, I had got to know Edward and Evelyn Carter who lived nearby in Hampstead. Edward owned a small building firm which was then the leading constructor of squash courts in the UK, with extensive premises at Green Lanes, N16. One weekend I moved the plant which I had bought to an empty building there. I formed a small company – Liley & Co Ltd – of which Edward and Evelyn were the two directors, Edward subscribing a minority of the capital. I had Derek Wheeler's blessing before doing this, of course, and my colleagues also knew of it.

The office manager who had been with the old business was a capable chap and Edward Carter was on the spot. Once a week, I went by bus from Moorgate to Green Lanes, eating my sandwich lunch on the way, and spent perhaps forty minutes at the little workshop. I also spent Saturday afternoons there. We made buttons for the dress trade, stamped from sheet metal and then covered with the customer's material to match the dress to which they were attached. Edward and I together had an investment in the share capital of rather more than £2,000, in addition to which we made use of bank facilities. During 1933, when any possibility of my becoming unemployed had receded, I sold the business to Buttons Ltd. They certainly did not pay a high price but Liley had by then served its purposes, all the employees' security was greatly strengthened and Edward and I had made a reasonable capital profit.

During these years, my daily interest in the Stock Exchange had, of course, never flagged although I dealt only occasionally and sometimes as a 'bear' (that is, I sold stock I did not possess with the expectation of re-purchasing it at a lower price, if possible, before the end of the account). This, of course, laid one open to unlimited liability, but at this time with careful judgment and a good measure of luck, it was sometimes very profitable.

In October 1932 I bought our first real family home – a delightful neo-Georgian freehold house called Orchard Way in Edgehill Road, Ealing, then an unmade road on top of Castlebar Hill, about ten minutes walk from Ealing Broadway station. The house, which had been built some years before by W.S. Grice FRIBA for his own occupation, was a real beauty and the garden and immediate surroundings were lovely. We moved early in 1933, and it cost about £5,000 which was quite expensive for those times. In retrospect it seems extraordinary that only eighteen months after the Wheeler crash I bought such a house, but even during the Stock Exchange slump it was possible to make the occasional profit when the fall in a particular share had been over-done. Nothing that survives falls for ever nor does anything, however successful, rise indefinitely.

# CHAPTER EIGHT

## *The Cheviot Trust*

It was towards the end of 1932 that I had begun to think of setting up in business full-time on my own account. But Gresham remained a most pleasant place in which to work and the critical months of 1931 had forged a deep bond between all those connected with it. By early 1933, I was once more working on an issue (Odhams). The number of enquiries was rising and once again I was having to refuse on Gresham's behalf what appeared to be good business, simply because it was too small to handle by conventional means.

I had kept in touch with G.V. Smith, Sir Arthur Wheeler's partner, who was then about fifty years of age. He was, of course, a bankrupt, and possessed none of Sir Arthur's genius, but his business experience was unique; no opening for him, however, had cropped up. One day I discovered that Price Waterhouse, who were liquidating Arthur Wheeler & Co, still had the addressograph plates of all the A.W. & Co clients, or potential clients. When, after several talks with Derek Wheeler, he and I were convinced that Sir Arthur's age and state of health ruled out any possibility of his starting again himself, I told G.V. about this.

Just occasionally in one's lifetime one gets the timing right. This now happened to me. G.V. badly wanted to get cracking and at the same time, I heard that a respectable firm of 'outside' brokers, George Brodie & Co, was for sale; the owner, Charles E. Gardner wished to retire. George Brodie & Co dealt principally in insurance shares, and carried on their small business from the upper floors of 35 Moorgate, in the City of London. Gardner proved to be a decent man and I agreed to buy the business. At the same time, Price Waterhouse, as liquidators, agreed to sell me the 750,000 Wheeler 'names', with their elaborate indexing systems, for £1,000. These systems had not been touched for two years and so were somewhat out-dated.

I think my total outlay was rather less than £5,000. The arrangement which I made with G.V. was this: when he was able to obtain his discharge from bankruptcy, he would buy two thirds of the George Brodie & Co business from me at cost. The business had made only enough profit to provide Gardner with a modest living. Its future depended entirely on G.V., and so I felt it was right that he should eventually have the controlling interest. In the meantime, I had put at risk a sizeable part of my precious capital, on what were frankly very generous terms. At that time my total net assets would be in the region of between £20,000 and £25,000.

Meantime, having become aware of a gap in the system that needed to be filled, I had been searching for some means of floating soundly based, smaller businesses. And one morning while I was negotiating the purchase of Brodie's, I awoke with an entirely new idea. It occurred to me that I could advertise my small company prospectus in just one daily paper (which was the minimum Stock Exchange requirement in order to obtain a quotation) and I could rely on direct mail, using the best parts of the Wheeler list of potential investors (a cheaper and surer method than haphazard press advertising). Operating on these lines, I thought I should be able to make an issue to raise as little as £100,000 at a cost of under £10,000, and yet contrive to produce a modest profit. A covering letter to potential subscribers, summarising in simple terms the salient points of the issue, was a vital ingredient of the formula and if I could buy George Brodie & Co they would be able to do this.

I let these ideas simmer during that exciting day early in 1933. Soon I began to feel that the plan had the makings of a major break-through. The more I thought about it, the more all the details seemed to fall into place. For example, I believed that in order to make small issues successfully, it was necessary to maintain a reasonably active market in the shares thereafter. Again Brodie's, as an 'outside' broker, could provide this; even in those days with all the provincial exchanges the Stock Exchange could not. At that time, G.V.'s knowledge of the broking side was unique. I, in turn, was familiar with the issuing technique, and I had developed the necessary sixth sense to a point where I felt I could distinguish a sound business from a doubtful one. With a little luck, our combined knowledge would cover the field.

What now followed was one of the most active and exciting periods of my life. I had considerable family responsibilities, a pleasant, and by now a safe, job at Gresham with a salary of £750, plus a bonus of £100 for the previous year. The obvious thing was to stay at Gresham. But in the end I decided to follow my instinct. I bought Brodie's and the A.W. list. I felt sure that it would become a profitable business in its own right, even if the issuing house idea never got off the ground.

G.V. Smith moved into the George Brodie & Co offices at 35 Moorgate in the spring of 1933. I went there at least twice a day, and usually we had a sandwich lunch together in his room. I maintained a high degree of secrecy about this association during the whole period of my involvement with Brodie's, which lasted for six years. It was only known to very few people. It is remarkable that such a degree of discretion is possible in a place like the City, where the gossip is endless (as in any village). But if one is prepared to take sufficient care I have proved at several periods of my life that secrecy can be maintained, even over a long period.

By late August, my detailed plans were complete and I told Derek Wheeler what was in my mind. A few days later, when Sir Arthur was making one of his rare visits to London, we had a three-cornered discussion. Sir Arthur felt that I was taking a gamble at a time when it was unnecessary. Derek said that he thought I had made up my mind and it would be wrong to stop me. 'If that's correct, you go ahead old son, and the best of luck to you', said Sir Arthur. And with that, the die was cast.

On 1 September, I registered my embryo issuing house, the Cheviot Trust Ltd. My friend John Davie CA had agreed that his firm Davie Parsons & Co would house it and act as secretaries, so I invited him to subscribe for 10% of the initial £1,000 capital. I also reserved one third of Cheviot for G.V. at par, in order to give him the same degree of participation as I had in Brodie's. I held a 57% interest in Cheviot Trust and at the first board meeting I became Managing Director. At that stage everything depended on my earning a profit; £1,000 of capital was not going to last very long!

My office was a room on the third floor of 6 Bishopsgate occupied by Davie Parsons, and in this way I was able to draw upon this firm's staff. When it came to the choice of lawyers, I decided against becoming a minor client of one of the leading firms of City solicitors. Instead, I would ask Theodore Goddard & Co, who up to then had done very little issue work, if Bertram Ogle who was then the second partner, would personally undertake our future work. He and Theodore readily agreed, and so I had the immense benefit of a first class legal mind throughout the whole of the next five years. Bertram and I had decided we would have every prospectus vetted by Counsel and for this purpose we chose Montagu Gedge KC, then probably the leading company law barrister and a considerable character.

On 30 September 1933 I left Gresham and said goodbye to Basildon House. There followed a busy ten days. I tried to ensure that every eventuality was provided for. Then I asked St James's Advertising which I knew well, to release the following press announcement on 11

October: 'Mr J.B. Kinross has resigned his position with the Gresham Trust in order to take up an appointment as Managing Director of the Cheviot Trust Ltd of 6 Bishopsgate, London, EC2, which has been formed primarily to handle small issues ranging from approximately £25,000 to £100,000.'

I spent the next days writing many letters (typed at Brodie's on Cheviot paper) to everyone I then knew who might bring us acceptable business. And almost at once the 'phone began to ring. Within the first ten days I had 315 enquiries, and I realised that I had crossed a frontier into unexplored territory.

The rest of that year was a period of continuous high pressure. Writing to my Mother before Christmas, G.V. said: 'I wish you could see your son here (at 35 Moorgate). He positively exudes happiness – his eyes are shining as I look across to him. (He is speaking on the telephone.) He is very well and the fact that he never stops working seems to contribute to this.'

My routine was to see everyone at the 6 Bishopsgate office which I kept as the shop window, but my base was Brodie's at 35 Moorgate where G.V. and I shared the front room on the first floor. His capable secretary, Doris Knight, had come back to him and to a large extent, she looked after us both. The volume of business being offered to Cheviot was tremendous, and apart from a first-rate telephone operator and typing facilities I did everything myself. My method was to eliminate all proposals which I regarded as impractical, giving myself five or six minutes at the outside for any one case. This disposed of about seventy-five per cent of the inflow, and I rejected none of the rest without a second look on the following day. I was then left with less than ten per cent of the whole: but to these I devoted a great deal of time.

As the weeks went by the pressure to launch the first issue mounted. I had to make a profit to pay my own salary – it was as simple as that. I drew no salary from Brodie's, although their business was by then rapidly increasing and showing a good profit each month. When G.V. had a short holiday in the late autumn, I took over from him and thoroughly enjoyed the dealing, though the circulars I produced lacked his concise presentation.

One of the most able of the young dealers from Leicester – Victor Cowdell – had by then joined Brodie's, and in G.V.'s absence it was he who kept the whole machine running smoothly. I liked and respected Cowdell, who was the essence of reliability. Very sadly, he died quite young in the early nineteen-forties.

Once Cheviot and George Brodie were established, we reverted to

Arthur Wheeler & Co's practice of buying from the Companies Registration office the names and addresses of the allottees of all the good current new issues. When this office was at Bush House, I used to go myself whenever possible for there was much to be learned by looking through the lists of these names. A good local issue supplied invaluable additions to our records of solid local investors who knew a good thing when they saw one. If any one person already possessed as many as three good quality local shares, the chances of his buying a fourth, if offered to him at a fair price, were high. Occasionally, I would look through the register of some second or third-rate issue, which despite its lack of quality had very likely been heavily over-subscribed. The overall pattern of the names never changed; clergymen and doctors of medicine usually led the list, closely followed by members of the armed forces, especially the army. The other 'regulars' were civil servants, widows, and in fact anyone who obviously could not afford to lose money but needed badly to maximise what he had.

Such a list was always a saddening experience for the tragedies which it contained must have been appalling. Very few of the original allottees of this type would have been quick enough to take their initial, fleeting profit and even some of the heavily over-subscribed ones were already at an appreciable discount by the end of the first day's trading. If anyone had succeeded in snatching a profit in the first few hours, it would have been an allottee described as a 'stock jobber', 'broker's clerk' or the like. Although 'spinster' appeared to some extent, women as a whole were more sensible and it was the men who were undoubtedly the bigger fools. Their naivety was only exceeded by their greed. Of course, we never bought any of these lists, for the names they contained were the last people we wanted as clients.

In the 1928 boom, new issuing houses had been formed at a tremendous rate and it was astonishing to see the number of broker-members of the Stock Exchange who courted them. During this period practically any rubbish could be sold and the brokerages paid out on these issues were substantial.

One day in the autumn of 1928, Ernest Savory told me that he would like to introduce me to a man who had recently formed the Beaconsfield Trust Ltd, Mr Louis Jackson. He had just made a successful issue: Wireless Pictures (1928) Ltd. On the day I accompanied Ernest to Jackson's offices in Bishopsgate, almost opposite the Banque Belge, his second issue – Colour Snapshots Ltd – was opening. We were shown into a very long, rather narrow room at the back of the building which was almost entirely taken up by an enormous oak refectory table which

I assumed had probably been supplied by Drages Ltd on hire purchase. There were some beautiful and extremely expensive flowers in the room and the huge table was piled high with applications for the new issue. Mr Jackson was a slightly built man of average height, perhaps in his mid-thirties. He was sitting at the top of the table, flanked on one side by a distinctly over-decorative young secretary whose natural habitat was, at best, a film studio. On the other side were piles of telegrams – certainly several hundred – confirming late posted applications and the like.

Having been introduced, he seized my hand and indicating the contents of the table he said, if memory serves me right, 'Seventy times over-subscribed, Mr Kinross – what price Rothschilds?' I got out as quickly as I could and took care never to see him again. Why the excellent Savory had introduced me I never understood. I suppose it shows the extent to which the Stock Exchange boom in 1928 had infected even experienced people; for Savory was certainly experienced.

One of the current tricks of this type of issue was to exclude most of the overseas rights from the original company. If the public lapped up the original issue on these terms, another flotation for the foreign rights quickly appeared. In the case of Colour Snapshots, the prospectus of Colour Snapshots (Foreign) Ltd appeared exactly twenty-one days later; I think that this issue, too, was over-subscribed. Two years later, having made six issues of this type, the Beaconsfield Trust itself went into voluntary liquidation. Unfortunately for the City, this story was typical of many at the time.

Five years later, when I formed Cheviot, I was determined that it should only handle issues of first rate quality. The fact that they were to be small in size had nothing to do with their quality. On the other hand, I was under considerable pressure to launch our first issue, for by then I had considerable family responsibilities. Our eldest daughter, Mary Eve had been born on 26 March 1932 and John Sang arrived on 29 December 1933. In spite of these pressures I kept rejecting businesses which though they would almost certainly have made successful issues, did not fully come up to the standard I had set for Cheviot.

This exciting but worrying period lasted for eight and a half months, and it was not until 8 June 1934 that Cheviot's first issue appeared. This was A. Jones & Sons (Bootmakers) Ltd, which I chose from over 500 businesses. I had eventually rejected every one of the early applications. In itself, Jones was a small, unglamorous business of multiple shoe shops with a pedestrian profit record. (It is now part of the Church group.) Nevertheless, it contained all the elements necessary for a successful first issue. Jones was a leader in the top end of the retail shoe trade and its twenty-one shops were in prime positions throughout the south of England – an area in which the cream of the small investors were concentrated in 1934. The issue was for only £65,625 – an entirely new departure in terms of size.

I started to write the prospectus during March 1934. My friend Ernest Braithwaite Savory, having read one of the early proofs, said that if I would like his firm to act as brokers to the issue he would be glad for them to do so. This surprised me, for E.B. Savory & Co were one of the leading brokers in the insurance sector of the market, and had just acted for two first-class large issues. It was a warm-hearted gesture which I naturally accepted. There was, however, an extraordinary outcome to this.

The procedure at that time was that one's broker dealt entirely with the Share and Loan Department of the Stock Exchange and passed on any comments they might have about the prospectus. When the final proof of the Jones prospectus, as settled by leading Counsel, had been sent by Savory's to the Share and Loan Department, Ernest asked me if I would mind if he went to Shropshire for a fortnight's fishing. Everything was now already set for a successful issue. He made it clear that if I would like him to stay until the issue was over he would cancel his holiday. Naturally, I said no, though I took the precaution of getting the telephone number of the friends with whom he was staying.

The completion meeting was to be at 10.30 a.m. on Monday 4 June 1934. The issue was to be advertised on Wednesday 6 and the list was to open on Friday 8 June. Ernest had come to see me on Monday 28 May and the final routine information which the Share and Loan Department had asked for had been supplied that afternoon. The advertising space had been booked and, subject to formal confirmation from the Share and Loan Department, we were all set to go. On Thursday morning, in the absence of any news, I spoke to the Managing Clerk of Savory's and asked him to see the Share and Loan Department urgently. During that afternoon I had heard nothing and I again telephoned. The Managing Clerk said they had not been able to get a reply from the Department, which was very heavily engaged with other prospectuses.

First thing on Friday morning 1 June, I spoke to the second partner, W.R. Rhodes, and told him that, although I could not conceive of any hitch, it was essential to have the formal approval of the Department during that day. Mr Rhodes promised to let me know as soon as possible. But time went on and I heard nothing from Savory's. I began to get increasingly apprehensive. Before lunch I again telephoned, and again at about 4 o'clock I spoke to the Office Manager who said once again that they had 'no news'.

I then decided to take the law into my own hands and go round to the Share and Loan Department, which I did shortly before 4.30 p.m., seeing a Mr Howlett. I said that we had given the information they had asked for. Was everything in order? At that moment his telephone rang and it was obvious that E.B. Savory & Co were the callers. He did not disclose that he had me with him and merely said over the telephone that the Department had no comment on the Jones prospectus. When he had put down the telephone I said 'Am I to understand that everything is in order?' He replied: 'Yes, certainly.'

In a few minutes, back in my office, I telephoned St Clements Press telling them to print the first twenty-five copies of the prospectus for Monday's meeting. Just about 5 p.m., a letter addressed to the Managing Director of the Cheviot Trust Ltd was delivered by hand. It was a short formal letter from E.B. Savory & Co and it said that the Stock Exchange were still not satisfied with the prospectus. Savory's therefore regretted to inform me that they were withdrawing their name as Brokers to the Issue. Just that.

I seized the telephone and rang the Share and Loan Department. No reply. Then I rang Savory's. I asked for one partner after another. Everyone had left; even the Office Manager had 'gone home'. It appeared as if they had all arranged their departures so as to be cut off from me until the Monday morning. But thanks to my irregular visit to the Share and Loan Department I knew everything was in order.

The key was Ernest Savory and after a ghastly few moments when I was afraid I had mislaid the Shropshire telephone number, I found it. A butler answered. Mr Savory was out but would be back for dinner at 8 p.m. I said I would telephone at 9 p.m.

The three hours lasted an eternity. I spent part of the time writing a careful account of exactly what had happened, and at exactly 9 p.m. I was speaking to Ernest. I read him his firm's letter and then told him of my visit to the Share and Loan. He replied: 'I am very sorry that you should have had this experience. You must ignore my firm's letter, and carry on in the normal way. I will come back to London on Sunday and will come to your office at 9 o'clock on Monday morning.' It was an enormous relief, though it was many hours before I got to sleep that night.

Savory arrived a little before 9 a.m. He looked very serious. I gave him his firm's letter and my note. He read both very carefully. After a while he said he would like us both to go over to the Share and Loan Department. We saw Mr Howlett and Ernest asked him what had occurred during Friday in connection with the Jones prospectus. To my relief, Howlett related in his own words what I had written in my note.

Ernest asked Howlett whether he thought his 'no comment' could have misled Savory's Office Manager (who, it appeared, had been the caller). But Mr Howlett said that if the Department had any points to raise it left the Broker in no doubt as to what these were. We then left – Ernest to go to his office while I went to prepare for my 10.30 meeting. Ernest again emphasised that I was to ignore his firm's letter; he said he would telephone me before my 10.30 meeting. He took with him my note and his firm's letter.

When he telephoned he said that he wished to apologise on behalf of his firm. He then asked if I would come to his office at some time convenient to me, as he had arranged for each partner who had been in any way concerned with the Jones issue to apologise to me individually. I told him this was the last thing I wanted, but he said 'I know that, but I want you to do it for me'. Late that afternoon I went to Basildon House where, one by one, the partners concerned came into Ernest's room and in varying ways offered their personal apology, after which I made a point of shaking hands with each of them. When it was over Ernest picked up his firm's letter and my handwritten note and said that he had one more favour to ask, which was that I would agree that he should destroy both of these. I did not ask him either on this occasion or at any later time for the explanation of this extraordinary episode. My own belief was that the other partners were bitterly opposed to acting as brokers for such a small issue by a new and unknown issuing house. My unorthodox visit to the Share and Loan Department must have come as a complete surprise to them. But how they had proposed to deal with the situation on the Monday morning I never knew.

The lists for the Jones issue opened at 9 a.m. on Friday 8 June and were closed at 9.05 a.m., the issue having been nearly twice covered. The 6½% preference shares opened in the market at 20/6d and the 1/- ordinary shares at 1/3d: prices which were fully maintained thereafter.

After this first success I dealt almost single-handed for the next five years with a continuous stream of issues. While I judged all of these to be good businesses, I only used the Cheviot name for the best. I had another company which I shared with G.V. Smith (John Davie was merely a Cheviot shareholder, not an active partner, and eventually I bought his Cheviot shares). It was called The Covenant Trust Ltd, and I used it for small issues for which we sometimes did not even seek a Stock Exchange quotation. This made no difference in the case of a small issue, because Brodie's handled virtually every subsequent transaction in this type of share; there was therefore little advantage in having a quotation. In addition to the Covenant issues, I managed a good many issues during those five years where the name of the broker appeared as the main underwriter, although in practice it was I who had written the prospectus.

This type of 'own label' operation was very profitable. Most of this business I did with F.S. Lewis, senior partner of Sidney J. Lovell & Co, members of the London Stock Exchange, who did not have the organisation necessary to process a small issue. My relationship with Lewis became an unwritten partnership. During a period of four years, seventy-two issues went out under the Lovell banner. Names of the companies launched included George Wimpey, Marley Tile, Curry's, Ilford, Richard Costain and British Tyre and Rubber (BTR): now among the leaders in their respective fields. However, these were all quite large when floated and, as my association with Lewis was entirely concerned with smaller businesses, I was not involved with them.

I made twenty-nine issues under the Cheviot label and about a dozen for Covenant, and altogether undertook rather more than a hundred issues during the five years from 1934 to 1938. Among these there were two which with hindsight we should never have made: Ismay Industries (Electric Lamps), in July 1935 and Old Gate Estates (a property company) in February 1936.

Ismay Industries was, in retrospect, a classic case of a company run by a man who, having made a success of a small business, proceeded to expand it beyond his natural capacity. In the case of Old Gate Estates, I made the fundamental mistake of disregarding my original instinct and allowing myself to be persuaded to sponsor the issue, which I had originally declined. Although the company was floated to acquire only one property (Dudley Court in Upper Berkeley Street) I had hoped to expand it if it succeeded. So Bertram Ogle of Theodore Goddard & Co and I joined the small board at the outset, he as Chairman. After some months it was discovered that the rates on the company's property had been understated by nearly £1,000 per annum; a typist's error in the vendor's schedule had not been spotted by our valuers. Bertram and I saw H.U. Willink KC who advised that Old Gate had an open and shut case against the valuers. But in May 1939 we lost this action, largely because the aggressive barrister for the defence, Gilbert Beyfus, KC convinced Mr Justice Wrottesley by his ruthless cross examination of our Managing Director that the latter had agreed to check these details because the valuers were accepting a fee below the full scale charge. This Managing Director was the man I had never felt happy about. He was a very pleasant chartered accountant named Geoffrey Procter; but unfortunately he was also incompetent.

Meantime, out of the blue, a Jewish accountant whom I knew told me that a young property man called Charles Clore might be interested in buying Cheviot's controlling interest in Old Gate. I met him briefly and he made an offer considerably in excess of anything I had expected. After a decent delay I accepted. Old Gate was highly geared and the equity capital was only £30,000 so the transaction was a small affair. I never knew why Clore did this and it must have been unprofitable to him for many years thereafter.

With these two exceptions, the hundred-odd companies I floated in the thirties after I had left Gresham are still in good shape today, although most are now part of much larger groups, to the advantage of the original shareholders.

Cheviot's second issue in October 1934 was the smallest public issue I ever made and may well have been the smallest ever. The company was Levers Optical Co Ltd, a firm of manufacturing opticians in London. I divided the capital into two classes of shares – A and B shares – which participated equally in profits until both classes had received a dividend of ten per cent, after which the A shares were entitled to a quarter and the B shareholders to three-quarters of the remaining profits. The issue consisted of 120,000 A ordinary shares of 5/- each at par, a total of only £30,000. The whole of the B ordinary shares, representing a nominal amount of £20,000, were retained by the directors. The subscription list was opened on 22 October 1934 and was closed within five minutes – heavily oversubscribed. The A shares opened at 5/9d on the London Stock Exchange.

By then Cheviot was in full flood. Business was literally pouring in and I was working six days a week, starting work again after tea on Sunday to be ready for Monday morning. I was taking on approximately one out of every four hundred proposals received, for I felt that our future entirely depended on undertaking good issues which would stand the test of time.

The first two issues having succeeded, Cheviot quickly acquired a following and, until Mussolini invaded Abyssinia in 1935, every issue was well oversubscribed, and thereafter was dealt in at a premium over the issue price.

I had a staff of one and, when I needed, I was able to draw extensively on Davie Parsons' experienced staff, for whom I paid the normal hourly rate. Since I never believed my success could last for more than a limited time, I drove myself to make the maximum amount of hay while the sun shone. I usually had a raw apple, some cheese, and a glass of milk in my room while reading office papers: my minimum working day was about fifteen hours. Never since then (except for the period 1947–52) have I been subject to such a degree of pressure. Everything else took second place to the needs of the business. On one occasion I suffered from a wooden splinter which penetrated deeply under one of my finger nails. I couldn't get it out and although it became septic I put up with the pain for several days before allowing myself the short time necessary to have it properly removed.

When I made an issue I first agreed the total purchase price and the percentage of the equity which Cheviot would purchase. Then I generally created a two-tier capitalisation for the new company or reconstructed the existing one to achieve the same result. The preference shares would always have a nominal value of £1, but the ordinary were usually 1/- shares and never more than 5/- shares. The preference were usually priced at par, the ordinary too. These two-tier issues were always sold as a package: the public had to buy both classes of shares. One was not available without the other. Although the rate of dividend on the preference shares was always fixed at a level to make them worth their issue price, they were nearly always quoted at discount for several weeks while the ordinary, which were in greater demand and represented the real plum, opened at a premium (larger than the discount on the preference). Subsequently those ordinary shares gradually went to much higher levels in a matter of weeks.

The 'package' method enabled the company to create a reasonable amount of preference capital. The creation of ordinary shares of low par value always resulted in there being far more of these than of preference shares. This in turn had the advantage of giving Cheviot a supply of ordinary shares for 'making the market' during the formative first few months after the issue.

I do not think that the total cost of launching any Cheviot issue ever exceeded ten per cent of the amount of cash we raised. It was not possible to make a reasonable profit for Cheviot from the issue charges alone, but if the issue went well we gradually met the subsequent demand for the ordinary shares, at higher prices, from those Cheviot had retained in its own account. If the shares became really popular – as some of them did – we occasionally made a very substantial profit by the time the last of our 'surplus' ordinary shares had been sold. The outcome was that everyone gained. The public who bought the original shares made a good profit over a period of a few months. The company's costs at ten per cent maximum were undoubtedly low. And Cheviot's profit was, I believe, both earned and deserved.

I doubt if the City realised quite how profitable Cheviot was. Nevertheless, competitors began to arise. This was welcome, for I could now suggest an alternative issuing house for all the issues we did not want. This in turn greatly reduced the time I had wasted in turning away persistent applicants who would not take 'no' for an answer.

The largest of these new issuing houses was London Industrial Finance Trust Ltd, which between 1935 and 1939 made thirty-one issues before it disappeared. London Industrial was the vehicle of W.J. Merifield, whom I knew quite well. The firm had branch offices in Birmingham and Manchester, and its London office, off Cheapside, had fifteen telephone lines (I had two). With a few exceptions, London Industrial's issues were of good quality, and Merifield always appeared to be a sensible chap. What the firm's own accounts showed I never knew, but I should be surprised if it ever made anything approaching the Cheviot profit. Much of its business came through a man called Arthur J. Whitehead, who, with a few high-powered salesman equipped with expensive cars and a ready flow of smooth talk, would pay unannounced visits to medium sized businesses, throughout the country. Occasionally the salesmen succeeded in reaching the Chief Executive, whose family was often the controlling shareholder. Whitehead's men would then expound the advantages of a Stock Exchange quotation, and sometimes this would result in serious interest being evoked. If so, Whitehead would bring in Merifield and if an issue resulted, Whitehead received a substantial commission.

After a while, Whitehead wanted a share of the issue profits as well. Merifield must have jibbed, because early in 1936 Whitehead came to see me. He said 'You have the leading issuing house for small and medium-sized businesses – I have the best business-gathering organisation. If you will sell me fifty per cent of Cheviot Trust – and I'm prepared to pay you a good price – we'll be unbeatable.'

Although I knew at once that I did not want to go into partnership with this man – our outlooks were poles apart – I let a few days go by and then I told him that I had decided to stay as I was. A few days after this on February 13 1936, he registered Whitehead Industrial Trust Ltd with an issued capital of £10,000 and predictably proceeded to churn out the largest number of issues of any industrial issuing house.

The quality of these issues was very mixed and in the later stages, the businesses were dressed up for flotation with over-ambitious estimates of prospects which the managements were sometimes incapable of meeting. Eventually, Whitehead gave up, leaving behind him a number of less than successful publicly floated businesses.

In the summer of 1934 I had had a fortnight's family holiday at West Wittering. For part of each day I sat on the beach with the huge *Stock Exchange Official Gazette* ('Burdett') and a bright blue threepenny school exercise book. By the end of the fortnight I had read through the whole book and had noted the salient points of over a hundred companies quoted on some UK Stock Exchange. All were then virtually unknown outside their immediate locality but all appeared to be prosperous.

Back at the office, Victor Cowdell gradually obtained the accounts of these companies and a number of them proved to be absolute winners. One of these was a firm of Kentish papermakers called C. Townsend Hook & Co Ltd. We used to buy the £10 shares at just over £12 and the well covered yield ran to double figures. G.V. and I kept many of these shares personally and when after the war *The Times* made a take-over bid for Townsend Hook, I must have made a substantial five-figure profit from this one share. That fortnight on the beach brought a rich harvest, which I reaped over a period of many years.

During 1935, I was making issue after issue for Cheviot: Capital and Country Laundries, Purnell & Sons, S. Collier & Co, Mansfields Ltd, Ismay Industries. I did not pause for breath until, as a direct result of Mussolini's invasion of Abyssinia, I hit problems for reasons totally outside my control. Some 98% of the £160,000 4½% debenture issue for Crown Flour Mills at £98% was left with the underwriters, in September 1935.

This English company was owned by Balfour Williamson & Co, but the debenture stock was secured by mortgage on the mills at Portland, Oregon. It took me several months to place the underwriters' stock in firm hands but I eventually succeeded in placing it with several Scottish insurance companies. I had regarded it as a prestige issue for Cheviot and our sole remuneration had been a fee of 750 guineas and an overriding commission of ¼%. The whole of the expenses amounted to £9,000 which was 5.7% of the amount raised and included the cost of forming a new company with a capital of £225,000. Lord Forres, the head of Balfour Williamson, was chairman and I became one of the five directors.

Purnell & Sons Ltd (now British Printing Corporation), one of the

1 A family group taken in 1906

2 My birthplace: 33 Mortonhall Road, Edinburgh, designed by my father

3 Manderston, Berwickshire, designed by my father for Sir James Miller and completed in 1905

4 & 5 Father and son both taken in 1915

6 My mother, by Henry Lintott RSA

7 My father and John Burnett, Secretary of United Wire Works, seeing me off at Waverley Station for Leicester, 6 May 1928

8 The photograph I sent out with every letter seeking a job in London, 1927

9 Edward Hill, Secretary of Gresham Trust

11 Sir Arthur Wheeler

10 G. V. Smith, Sir Arthur's partner and later mine

12 Phil Belfield of Sterling Poultry Products

13 Farming at Woodmans in 1945

14 Early days at ICFC: Lord Piercy, myself, and Julian Sorsbie

15 Lord Piercy

16 The Board of ICFC, 1960.
*Left to right:*
Lord Dudley Gordon, Dudley Robinson, Lord Blackford, W. H. Fraser, Lord Piercy, J. K. (General Manager), Colin Skinner, Lewis Whyte, and the Earl of Limerick.
*Standing:* S. V. Warren (Secretary)

17 In Charlotte Square, Edinburgh, 1964

18 Hugh Fraser and myself after winning the battle for Outrams, 1964

19 The Chairman and Deputy Chairman of ICFC in the late 1960s: Lord Sherfield (Roger Makins) and myself

other issues in 1935, provided me with many problems. Established in 1849, it had remained a small firm of general printers in Somerset until in 1924 Mr C.J. Purnell, the son of the founder, persuaded a young articled clerk, who had worked on the audit for the previous two years, to join him. This man – Wilfred Harvey – was exceptionally able and ambitious. He concentrated on the mass production of books and magazines, and in ten years the capacity of the plant had been increased more than eightfold and Purnell had handed over the management of the business to him. The rapid expansion had resulted in a high level of indebtedness and the purpose of the issue was to discharge the debts. Profits had risen satisfactorily during the previous three and a half years, yet several issuing houses had declined the business.

I met Harvey several times, and spent some time going over the factory at Paulton, near Bristol. I had no doubt as to the soundness of his trading policy, but I was less certain of his financial judgment. After many weeks of careful investigation I agreed that Cheviot should handle the £150,000 issue, and the draconian terms I laid down in order to protect the subscribers to the issue were eventually accepted in toto. A new company was formed to acquire the business from Mr Purnell who only received £1,500 in cash out of a purchase price of £95,250 – in itself a low figure. The issue consisted of 125,000 6% cumulative preference shares of £1, and a similar number of 5/- ordinary shares, both offered for sale at par. I got Monty Gedge KC our invaluable counsel to draft an article which made it impossible to change the rights of the preference shares without an Extraordinary resolution passed by the holders of not less than 75% of the preference shares then in issue, and although various attempts have been made to get round this condition, these shares still exist inviolate in The British Printing Corporation.

What finally made me agree to undertake this business was the fact that the third, and younger, partner of Davie Parsons & Co, Alan Pratley FCA, who had personally investigated the business and had established a good working relationship with Harvey, was willing to join the new board; I thought we could control Harvey in this way.

The issue was well oversubscribed and the ordinary shares opened at a satisfactory premium. It was, I think, the most profitable issue which Cheviot ever made. Four and a half years later, thanks to Harvey's foresight, Purnell's started the war with a tremendous stock of paper, a record overdraft, and a factory unaffected by German bombing. Harvey had proved to be an incurable expansionist, and eventually the more cautious Pratley resigned. Meanwhile Harvey had won the confidence of Sir Charles Lidbury, the notable Chief General Manager of

Westminster Bank, and the company made enormous profits during the war. By 1945, the 5/- shares, which I had issued at par, stood at over £5. But by now I felt so strongly that they were overvalued that, at my own expense, I wrote to every original shareholder who still retained the shares, advising him to take his profit. I had many nice letters in reply but the shareholders mostly decided to keep their shares. In the 1960s the company got into serious trouble and Harvey was eventually dismissed. Experience shows that it is impossible to exercise effective control over a dedicated expansionist for more than a limited period.

In July 1935, I had rented a cottage for a month at Sandsend, near Whitby. Mother had spent her holidays there as a child, and now she came to stay with us for what proved to be the last time. It was a marvellously happy time, and I managed to join the family for two of the three weeks she was there. We took the opportunity of driving to many places in the North Riding, and I saw Birch and the parish church at Helmsley where she had been married. Since leaving home in 1928 I had written to her once or twice every week and she knew of everything I was doing. I sent her all the prospectuses I was working on; she liked to read them even if she didn't fully understand them.

In September Mother and my sister Eveleen had their usual holiday at Callender in Perthshire, and she was to stay with us in October. But the week before the projected visit she contracted a chill, and on Friday 5 October her heart failed, and she died without warning. The degree of mental shock this caused was something I have never experienced either before or since.

In the spring of that year, Mother had agreed to sit for her portrait, which I had asked Henry Lintott to paint. He had been a friend of my Father's for many years, and so knew Mother well. Lintott was one of the best portrait painters in Scotland and the portrait, which was finished just before Mother came to Sandsend, is both a perfect likeness and a beautiful work of art. I have given it to the Mary Kinross Charitable Trust so that it may be preserved by future generations of the family. It was my most precious possession.

But back to the business. In June 1934, we had placed the shares of a very small company called Sterling Poultry Products Ltd, and this proved to be one of the major events of my life. In the 1920s, the Americans had started to hatch chicks in large incubators instead of under broody hens, and this revolutionised the poultry industry. Day-old chicks, when hatched, possess enough nourishment to require no food or water for the first twenty-four hours. So although in 1934 all Sterling's customers were in the UK, by the 1950s, Sterling Chicks were being exported by air to countries as far afield as Malaya, Kenya and India, and of course to almost anywhere in Europe.

My association with Sterling dated from 1934. Through a retired American banker, F.R.A. Shortis, I met Jack Pierce, the export manager of the Buckeye Incubator Company USA, then the largest makers of incubators in the world, A.H.J. Bull their European representative and Phil Belfield, Sterling's Chairman and Managing Director. Sterling had been established by Pierce and John Bull in 1929 with a capital of £2,000 and in 1934 86% was owned by Pierce and another Buckeye director personally, with the two British directors holding the balance of 14%. The two Americans wanted to sell a substantial part of their holding. While Belfield, who was an Essex farmer, could not afford to buy them out, he wished to invest all the cash he could raise in the business. Sterling's net profits before tax had risen to £4,626 in the year to July 31 1933, and net assets amounted to £14,929: all derived from the original £2,000 capital. At that first meeting I realised that in Phil Belfield I had met a most exceptional man. As well as being a highly skilled farmer he was also a first rate business man with high standards. To crown it all he was a born leader of men.

We decided to float Sterling. I agreed a value of £28,750 for the existing business, which the original owners were to receive partly in cash and partly in shares of the new company formed for the public issue.

The issue, which was fully subscribed, consisted of 15,000 7% cumulative participating preference shares of £1 (entitled to a maximum dividend of 10%) and 15,000 ordinary shares of 2/-. Both were issued at par, thus producing £16,500. I subscribed for a substantial part of the issue; also, Phil and I bought some of the ordinary shares which the Americans had received as their share of the purchase price. With Phil and John Bull, a first rate man, the three of us possessed de facto control of the new company. Although I never joined the board, I became the unpaid financial adviser to the company for the next twenty-seven years.

After the war, Sterling had its one and only rights issue. Jack Pierce of the US Buckeye company had become a bit of a nuisance and we wanted to ease him out. When I was in New York in 1947 I bought his shareholding for about £50,000. Jack was one of the ablest negotiators I ever encountered so it was far from easy. Before leaving London, I had to get permission from the Bank of England for the transaction and they gave their written consent to my buying these 2/- shares at a price not exceeding 16/-.

New York was so full that Jack and I had to share a double room at the Barclay Hotel. We talked until about 3 a.m. without getting anywhere and, after putting out the light, I did not dare to go to sleep in case Jack might find the Bank of England letter. I soon noticed that he was not sleeping either, so by 5 a.m. we had started to talk again. He received all the detailed monthly figures for Sterling which were devastatingly good, so I concentrated my argument on the pound sterling, suggesting that it was a dangerous currency to hold. He then told me that, while he agreed with this up to a point, he had read the Bretton Woods Agreement in anticipation of our meeting. He pointed out that sterling could not be devalued by more than 10% without the consent of the other parties which, he affirmed, would certainly not be forthcoming.

At that point, I nearly gave up! However, as we were finishing a late breakfast, still in our beds, he agreed to deal at 10/6, provided this could be converted to dollars at the current rate of exchange. So we went together to J.W. Seligman, the banking firm which we both knew, and when they had seen my Bank of England permit (it was a bit tricky making quite sure that Jack did not see the terms of the document) it took Seligman two days to sell approximately £50,000 sterling for US dollars, after which I parted from Jack with possession of the shares and his letter of resignation from the Sterling board. The sad sequel to this was that Jack, who had seemed in normal health to me, had a fatal heart attack three weeks later. We were all genuinely sorry, for he had many endearing qualities and had played a useful role in the pre-war years.

Apart from the cash injection of £45,000 from the rights issue I have mentioned, Sterling grew entirely from its original capital of £2,000. In 1951 Phil produced the first hybrid chicks in the UK – a very considerable genetic achievement which he had worked on personally for the previous five years. In 1961, Carl Ross, then Chairman of Ross Foods, who had badly wanted to acquire Sterling for some time, seduced one of the newer working directors and made a bid without warning which, frankly, was so high that it could not be rejected. By then Sterling were quoted on the London Stock Exchange, with Rowe and Pitman as brokers. Phil and I had both sold some shares in order to obtain the quotation and the three of us no longer controlled the company.

Freddy Proctor, a partner of Peat Marwick Mitchell whom I knew well, was advising Carl Ross (though Ross had made the bid without consulting Freddy), and a few days later, Phil and I went to see them both at Ross's suite at the Savoy where the discussion went on for fully twelve hours. Ross had recently twice failed in take-over bids and I felt certain that he could not risk a third failure. Phil left most of the talking to me, and as the hours went by, I stuck like glue to the fact that, with the degree of shareholder loyalty we possessed, he would never succeed unless his terms were recommended by us.

The original bid had been a little over £3 million (four Ross 5/- shares for five Sterling 2/- shares). By the time we left the bid had been increased to nine Ross shares for ten Sterling shares which raised the value of the bid by £376,460 to £3,405,183, at the current price of both shares. On our part, we had agreed to recommend the bid. Phil added that as soon as everything had been completed he would resign. I doubt if Ross believed he would do so but Phil, of course, did exactly this, just as soon as the deal was completed and we had sold every one of our Ross shares (this had been arranged beforehand). Deprived of Phil's guiding hand, the business subsequently went downhill and the very high price paid by Ross became absurd. But for the outstanding ability of Alex Alexander, then Ross's No 2, the outcome would have been disastrous. Eventually, Ross and his son were eased out, the Imperial Group bought the business, and Sir Alex Alexander is now in charge of the whole of their food division. I have the warmest regard for him.

The take-over was a tragedy, however, and several lives were upset as a result. Phil Belfield, on ICFC's behalf, became part-time Chairman of a large farming company near Evesham but otherwise he shunned the business world. He died from a sudden heart attack on 15 October 1971 when he was seventy-four. I deeply regretted the passing of a true friend and one of the outstanding people I have known in my lifetime.

About the time we floated Sterling Poultry Products in 1934 the Standard Life Assurance made a take-over bid for the shares of a small and old-established business called Heritable Securities and Mortgage Investment Association Ltd. This had a successful record over many years in advancing mortgages secured on local property. The shares were quoted on the Edinburgh Stock Exchange and, as there was a large uncalled liability, the price was low. The manager, George Sturrock, had been a friend of my Father's whom I knew well, and the company was sound in every way.

I had gradually bought quite a number of Heritable Securities shares for Mother at a large discount on their asset value, to yield over 20%.

This bid was, of course, above the market price, but in my view quite inadequate. It was obviously impossible to reinvest the proceeds in anything of comparable quality without a drastic loss of income. I wrote to the Board of Heritable Securities urging them to hold out for a more equitable price, but Mr Sturrock, as I had feared, was upset by this letter. He was then not far from reaching retirement age and the prospect of handing over his excellent little company to a strong concern such as Standard Life had perhaps influenced him unduly. When Standard Life succeeded in acquiring over 90% of the shares I decided to fight it in court rather than give in to something which I believed to be less than fair. Theodore Goddard & Co instructed their Edinburgh agents, who in turn briefed a young barrister, Mr Jock Cameron (now Lord Cameron). Although I stated my case fully on paper, I was then so busy that I was unable to go to Edinburgh to meet Mr Cameron.

We lost the case, largely because the judge felt that, as nearly all holders had accepted the offer, and as Standard Life was a most respectable company, there could not be much doubt as to the merits of their case. The costs were considerable, but I paid without regret, feeling that at least I had done everything possible. My one sorrow was the hurt to Mr Sturrock's feelings. There was an amusing sequel, for as a result of this action I got to know the partner of Gordon Falconer and Fairweather WS the solicitors who acted for us and who was then Chairman of Morrison & Gibb, the Edinburgh book printers. Through him, I met Mr Haines, the recently appointed Managing Director of Morrison & Gibb, whom I could see was rapidly converting this run-down company into a first rate business. Over a period I bought shares in this concern very cheaply, and during the next few years I realised a substantial capital profit which many times exceeded the cost of the abortive action, for which I still feel totally unrepentant.

By then I had become used to people asking for my advice on their personal financial problems and, occasionally I took the initiative. In my first year in London for instance, I met Gwen Ffrangcon-Davies, the actress, at a party given by some mutual friends. I thought her a delightful person, and after a while I asked her how she invested her savings! I remember her laughing heartily over this and telling me she did not save anything. Whereupon I produced pencil and paper and took her through her (financial) life to the age of sixty, working out the effect of her saving 5% of her current earnings over that period. All this was done sitting on our host's staircase. At her request I gave her the calculations.

On another occasion, in my Cheviot period, the Chairman of St James's Advertising – Colonel Percy Izod – asked me to go with him to see Marie Stopes, who wanted his advice on some financial matters. After dinner at his home, he and I visited her somewhere near Dorking. It quickly became apparent that she wanted us to tell her how to finance the establishment of birth control clinics throughout the country. Of course neither of us could help, and we returned to our wives who had been highly amused by the whole affair and plied us with embarrassing questions. Marie Stopes I remember as a plain, middle-aged woman, very intense, and absolutely single-minded on the subject of birth control.

On a lighter note, I remember going to a dinner party in Kensington in 1928. I did not know my hosts, who were friends of Edinburgh people I knew well. Their children were a little younger than I, and they and their friends were very much in the social swim. I found myself at dinner between a gushing debutante on either side, who wanted to know what I had been doing that summer. Wimbledon? No, I had never been. Henley? No – and so on. Finally one of them said 'Well, what have you been doing?' By that time I felt a trifle aggressive. So instead of saying 'working', I replied – 'Africa – I sort of walked across from east to west – big game and all that.'

That restored me to favour. Until we all went off to some night club they listened to the rubbish I invented, and swallowed the lot. My geography had always been tolerable, and I had read enough Rider Haggard to do the rest. I assured them that the old cliché of holding one's fire until one really could see the whites of the tiger's eyes was true. But I said the crocodiles were the most frightening of all, and in Northern Kenya one nearly always had to wade across the rivers. Later in a letter inviting me to something else, my hostess told me that my African experiences had 'made the evening'.

I never repeated this caper. But the importance of being able to assess varied types of people was something that I took seriously. I thought of trying to find a course of lectures on psychology but I never got round to it. Later on I came to feel that one can only learn how to deal with people by experience. The original Rockefeller is reputed to have said that he would pay various salaries for degrees of skill, but 'the man who has mastered the art of negotiation can write his own ticket, for there is no limit to what I will pay him'. I entirely agree with this philosophy.

So I developed my own rules for the game. My first principle in every negotiation was to make it as easy as possible for the other side to agree with me. Ideally, I sought to end up by the other side proposing as their idea what I was trying to achieve. I always tried to open with the least controversial issues. Get these sorted out and a growing atmosphere of agreement builds up.

Next lesson: one of the most effective tools of negotiation is flattery and, if you can accurately judge the doseage your patient is capable of swallowing, the outcome can be truly incredible. Alcohol, which is more commonly used, is not in the same league. Very few people are totally immune to flattery – the art is to spot just what they are starved of and then to supply it in a form that is designed to win their confidence – for once the 'confidence layer' is penetrated you will accomplish things that previously would have been utterly impossible.

In nearly every negotiation during my life I have worked on these lines and have sought to keep the atmosphere relaxed, friendly and informal. I doubt if I have ever thumped the table and if my opposite number did so I used to reckon that I had passed the half-way mark to succeeding.

In his wartime broadcasts, the Radio Doctor (later Lord Hill) used to emphasise the importance of seizing what he called 'the magic moment' to go to the loo. Likewise, in nearly every negotiation there is a 'magic moment' and if time runs out before it comes the discussion will probably end in failure. On the other hand, I have not infrequently seen a successfully concluded negotiation thrown away because one of the two parties continued to talk about it quite unnecessarily after agreement had been reached. In the process he said something which reopened the matter with fatal consequences.

Lastly I would emphasise the value of silence in the right place. Few people can cope with this, especially if it is set against the background of a tense situation at a peak of the negotiation. At such a time two or three minutes is an eternity, and if you possess a sufficient reservoir of self control you should say absolutely nothing, and just keep looking at your friend across the table. If he can't stand it any longer and is the first to break the silence he will usually make a move that you can turn to your advantage.

It could be that the extent of the equity participation is being discussed and you are seeking to obtain 12–15%. If silence finally gets on the other man's nerves and he breaks it by saying 'I must tell you that nothing over 20% will be acceptable to us: repeat nothing' this silence has indeed been golden.

Another way of putting this fundamental point is – always try to get the other side to make the first move on any crucial point. It may prove to be a more advantageous starting point than expected.

On another level, I could be thoroughly aggressive if I felt the occasion demanded. One undoubtedly mellows with age. But certainly until I was over sixty, if I felt anyone had behaved really badly or unfairly I usually returned the compliment with a high rate of interest added! Most of us have had the occasional really bad case where the normal procedure would probably be to telephone the man in his office, tell him bluntly what you felt about what he had done, or tried to do, and then having made it crystal clear that all future contact was ended, put down the telephone.

In one very extreme case, I went so far as to telephone the offending person at his home just before midnight. To do this successfully one has to be word perfect and very brief, otherwise one is liable to be upstaged by his hanging up first. This may sound crude but I believe W.S. Gilbert gave us a wealth of fundamental wisdom when he wrote 'let the Punishment fit the Crime'.

An example of the sort of trouble one occasionally faces occurred during the winter of 1935–1936, when I had an experience in Cardiff which I will assuredly never forget. In the late autumn of 1935, William Ogden, then the senior partner of Ogden, Hibberd, Bull & Langton, a London firm of chartered accountants, told me that three leading firms of retail bakers and grocers in South Wales, all household names, had asked him to fix the terms for the merging of their businesses. The executive directors had all wanted the merger for some time, but it had been bitterly opposed by the elderly proprietor of one of the companies, who had recently died. He had, however, instructed his trustees to sell his shares only for cash and so a small preference share issue was necessary in order to provide this money.

I went with Ogden to Cardiff where we met the three principals and their professional advisers and it was agreed that Cheviot would make the issue. Nothing of note happened until, in March 1936, about a fortnight before the prospectus was due to be advertised, a woman telephoned me at home in Ealing one weekday evening at about half-past eight.

She told me that one of the three firms, which she named, had falsified its accounts for several years, and had lost money in increasing amounts during that period. Both its auditors and solicitors, she said, almost certainly had no suspicion. She had now decided that she ought to tell me this. Then she rang off. She had an educated, Welsh voice. I imagined that she might have been the discarded mistress of the proprietor. This particular business was being acquired on much more favourable terms than the other two: perhaps this woman had now explained why this was so.

I rang Bertram Ogle of Theodore Goddard & Co at his home and the maid gave me a telephone number where he could be reached that evening. I dialled the number and, to my astonishment, I cut into a conversation between Monty Gedge KC and Bertram! For the next half an hour I had a consultation with both of them. They agreed that I should go to Cardiff the next day and invite the man in question to explain this telephone call. I was advised about the possible slander implications of what I was about to do. So, as a result of that crossed line, I left Paddington very early the next morning well briefed.

What I had been told proved to be true in essence. For a long time the man concerned denied it. He became very angry and at one point he seized me by the throat. Eventually he suddenly burst into tears, and asked me what he should do. I asked him for the original contract we had signed, tore it up, and told him he could be thankful to be treated thus. He was, as it happened, a non-conformist lay preacher, well known in the locality.

I then went to the Cardiff office of Colonel Gerald Bruce, the senior partner of the solicitors acting for Hopkin Morgan Ltd the largest of the two remaining vendors. I saw him together with the principals of the other two businesses, Cyril Morgan and Bill Harris respectively of Hopkin Morgan Ltd and William Harris (Merthyr Tydfil) Ltd. When I had told them all what had happened, their relief was very evident and Bill Harris thanked me for saving them from what would have been an appalling situation.

By that time, and contrary to normal practice, Cheviot had signed the contracts because of the terms of the will. When we had all relaxed a little, I told them that I would have to study the new figures before I could say to what extent we would have to change the detailed terms of these contracts. There was a long silence. Then Gerald Bruce told me that they were extremely grateful and so they would give me time. But they were not prepared to do anything else. They had me well and truly over a barrel.

Next day Ogden arrived and we all conferred. The withdrawal of this 'cheap' business made a substantial difference to the issue. The amount to be raised was unchanged, but the capital and income cover for the preference shares which Cheviot had contracted to buy was now much less.

At the end of the day, we broke up with no solution in sight. Ogden had to go back to London, and that night, at the Angel Hotel in Cardiff, I sat in my bedroom trying out numerous alternatives in order at least to avoid any loss to Cheviot. As matters stood, I foresaw a loss of rather more than £6,000. When I went to bed about 2.30 a.m. I had used up all the hotel notepaper in the bedroom, after which I had used lavatory paper.

The next morning I woke up with a new idea. There were two Cardiff brokers at that time, who were jealous of one another, and who had both wanted to act for the issue. So I put on paper the terms of a conventional preference issue, the only difference being that it was very highly priced. This gave Cheviot a profit of nearly £4,000. That morning I called on both these brokers and told them that these were the terms. If they wanted the business, the first one who said snap and placed the whole of the sub-underwriting would be the broker to the issue. By the next day this plan had worked and Henry J. Thomas & Co of Cardiff became the new company's brokers, placing the whole of the sub-underwriting and so relieving Cheviot of all risk.

To my astonishment the offer for sale of 75,000 6½% cumulative preference shares of £1 each at 21/- in Morgan Harris & Co Ltd was about twice oversubscribed on March 19 1936. I had undoubtedly underestimated the glamour of the two local names, and Henry Box's hard selling had done the rest. No one lost in the end.

But the manner in which I had been treated left a deep scar. I did not bother to find out what eventually happened to the lay preacher who was the origin of the trouble. I wrote off South Wales and never again did I do any business there.

1936 and 1937 were years of continuous issues under various labels. They also marked the zenith of my co-operation with F.S. Lewis the broker with whom I had done so many issues. All these issues were successful, of good quality, and profitable. During this period I had no conventional holidays but I used any spare time I had to plan a new house which my financial position would now justify. Sheila Margaret, our second daughter, was born on 11 June 1936 and 'Orchard Way' was now too small for us. We had also decided to live further away from London and had chosen Haslemere, where I was fortunate in being able to buy several acres of the over-large garden of a Victorian house in Three Gates Lane. Over a period of some months, I bought adjoining plots and acquired twelve acres of beautifully situated land in total. The site was near to the centre of Haslemere, with a view to the south east extending to fifty miles. I asked Mr W.S. Grice FRIBA, from whom I had bought 'Orchard Way' to act as my architect though I think it would be fair to say that we designed the house together. I wanted a beautiful house which would match my Father's high standards.

One Friday afternoon I received from the architect the eleventh edition of the detailed plans, which he told me embodied all the points agreed between us. On the Saturday, I sat down with the plans and spent the entire day tracing the likely movements within the house of every person who would be living there. I did this for each season of the year, I considered illnesses, parties, guests who stayed in the house, business meetings and so on. By Sunday evening I had finished – and I had 115 queries! Fortunately, Grice was a remarkable man; he would need to have been. A week later we spent a good part of the Friday night together and he only left after lunch on the Saturday when we had sorted everything out. If I ask myself whether it was worth all this meticulous trouble, I am convinced that it was. When the building was finished there was only one small detail at the top of the main staircase which I would have changed had we been starting again.

The house took nearly two years to build and cost rather more than £28,000, including the land. We moved from Ealing to Haslemere in the summer of 1937 and were fortunate in finding as staff three sisters, all in domestic service, who wanted to work together. A young gardener, Jim Stent, who lived about half a mile away, also came to us. He was a tremendous worker and a highly intelligent man, who stayed with me until he died from chronic bronchitis in 1976. His widow and their three children are all family friends.

'Springfold', as we named the new house contained nine people. In due course, we had a housewarming party. The number of people who came terrified me (I think there were quite a few gate-crashers) and I realised that I had less than nothing in common with the majority of them. I felt that Tim Grice and I had created an artistic gem, yet already it was involving us in some of the least attractive aspects of human society.

In my business life I had come to know various people who, like myself, had made a large amount of money over a relatively short period. All of them now possessed Rolls Royce cars, some had yachts, and nearly all had country mansions. Most were overweight, and drank a massive amount of hard liquor. All this made me the more determined not to change my relatively spartan way of life which, I am sure, is one of the reasons for my still being fit and active at the age of seventy-seven. Hard work is undoubtedly healthy; the killers are over-indulgence and worry. A successful business, which one enjoys, is a prescription for good health.

By 1937, although I did not know exactly what I ought to do with my surplus capital, I certainly did not want it for myself. At that time the sensible thing seemed to be to give it to my family for their protection. So this was what I did. By 1938 I had decided that I didn't wish to continue acting as an intensive money-making machine. I had enough to be financially independent even if I never earned another penny. I was thirty-four and possessed a degree of experience in dealing with the finance of small and medium sized businesses which was possibly unrivalled in the UK at that time.

After much thought, I decided to find out whether a second career in politics was a possibility. I realised that I knew practically nothing about the political world but I hoped that my experience could perhaps be useful, and addressing a public meeting held no terrors for me.

Which of the three Parties was I to approach? Whilst I had respected Stanley Baldwin, and particularly his handling of the General Strike and his moderation in the period which followed, I had no regard for Neville Chamberlain, and the whole philosophy of the Tory Party at that time was too right-wing for my liking. While I worked happily with most people in the City, when politics were discussed I felt out of sympathy with most of what was said.

My natural home could have been with the Liberals but I still distrusted Lloyd George whom I saw as the *Eminence Grise*. So I wrote to Arthur Greenwood, the Secretary of the Parliamentary Labour Party. I was largely in sympathy with what I felt the Party then stood for, and was prepared to join it if I could make an effective contribution.

In due course, I had a pleasant reply from Mr Greenwood who suggested that I should lunch with him at the House of Commons. In the event this proved a total disaster. Greenwood soon became somewhat the worse for the drinks he was having before lunch and much of his conversation consisted of telling me dirty stories at which he laughed heartily. This sort of talk has always embarrassed me from the time I was a schoolboy and I remember that lunch as one of the most boring I have endured. The outcome was that I wrote off politics and never again considered it seriously. On the whole, though I may have been over-hasty to judge on the basis of one meeting, I now think this may have been fortunate. I do not believe that I was cut out for political life.

Almost by chance, another way of severing my links with my existing business interests presented itself. G.V. Smith (by then equipped with a Rolls and a country 'cottage' at Findon in Sussex) had three sons, and Jim – the eldest – was working at Cheviot on an informal basis. He came with me to meetings and took notes. He was without doubt, a 'sharp' boy. But I did not fully trust him. At that time, however, he was the apple of his father's eye and in due course, as I had feared, G.V. told me that Jim was very interested in Cheviot's business and he asked me if I would take him into the firm.

I knew at once that I did not want him. But when this approach came in the early summer of 1938, it was at the time I was trying to get myself off my own hook. Furthermore, I was mentally very tired and in need of a complete change. So, on an impulse, I told G.V. that if he gave me a realistic price for the Cheviot goodwill, I would sell him the business. At the same time, if he wished, I would sell him my minority stake in the 'outside' broking firm, Brodie.

I was careful to add that, after a good holiday, I would form another Trust and carry on in much the same way except that I would in future only do a limited number of first class issues each year.

For some time G.V. argued that the existing set-up had worked so well that we would be foolish to break it up. This was, of course, perfectly true. But as we talked, I realised that Jim was going to become a major factor in Brodies even if I kept him out of Cheviot, as I should have done. This was unfair to Victor Cowdell, who was a much abler man than Jim and contributed so much to the smooth running of Brodies, but it was a classic case of nepotism. The truth was that G.V. and I had drifted apart. I felt that success had spoilt him and my approach to Arthur Greenwood had shocked him. In the end we agreed a deal, and I got a sensible price for my Brodie and Cheviot shares. Thus I deliberately brought to a conclusion the remarkable money-making machine of which I had been the principal architect. I still believe that I was right to have done so.

Within a few days of selling Cheviot, I had registered a new company, The Montrose Trust Ltd (another Scottish name). I owned all of its issued capital of £5,000. This was all the permanent capital I needed, for by then it was no longer necessary for me to buy 'prestige' by having a substantial capital. I wrote personal letters to all my business associates, and the replies made it crystal clear that virtually all of them would continue to do their business with me.

G.V. Smith had secured the services of a man called T.A.W. Allen who had worked with Merifield in London Industrial Finance Trust, and he and Jim Smith were now the two executive directors of Cheviot. They never succeeded in getting it off the ground. Increasing losses resulted, and after the outbreak of war, it was liquidated.

Of G.V.'s two other sons, Philip, the next in age, came into Brodies and eventually took it over from his father. He was quite a clever and reliable boy and he made a success of Brodies after the war. But the underlying conditions for the type of business changed considerably as the years went by, and eventually he had to close down.

# CHAPTER NINE

## *1938 to 1942*

In October 1938, after the sale of Cheviot I was mentally and physically very tired, and so I decided to go to America. I sailed in the S.S. *Montrose* and after a day in Quebec where she called, I went on to Montreal. *Montrose* was the vessel on which Crippen had been arrested, so by then it was an old ship and the continuous noise of creaking plates once we got out into the North Atlantic was a bit wearing. Jules Thorn's brother, a delightful and brilliant Viennese doctor, was on board with his wife and we had many interesting talks. As an Austrian Jew he was emigrating to North America. I also had some talk with Mackenzie King, then Prime Minister of Canada. I didn't take to him. Quebec I thought very romantic on my brief visit and it brought back a lot of schoolboy history. I also greatly liked Montreal and, instead of the intended few days, I stayed for nearly three weeks at the Windsor Hotel there. I had introductions to the heads of the Bank of Montreal and of brokers, Wood Gundy and these opened many other doors. I was taken to some of the modern pulp and paper mills and to one of the big hydro-electric plants.

The snow lay everywhere before I left, and I spent my last weekend in the beautiful Laurentian Mountains, seeing them in ideal conditions although the cold was extreme. I then went on to Toronto, where there was no snow and everything was much more British. I met a number of interesting financial people, but I was not entirely obsessed by business. On my first Sunday I went to the evening service at the Scottish Church for Dr Sclater, the Minister, had been a well known figure in Edinburgh. When I came out into the mild winter night I stood for a few moments listening to groups of people talking to one another on the steps of the church. All had Scottish voices and I might have been back in Edinburgh!

I was taken by Wood Gundy to Niagara where the Falls were even more impressive than I had expected. Then from Toronto, I went by overnight train to New York. The city was a revelation to me, and I fell in love with it from the first hour. In 1938, the efficiency and energy of New York penetrated one's whole being. I had very few introductions and none to any of the top people. Lord Forres of Balfour Williamson & Co had written to Balfour Guthrie, their American company, but I did not take to the Scot then in charge of the New York office.

The man I met whom I really liked was a tough but kindly American broker of about my own age called Josh Davis. He was then a partner in Reynolds & Co, and, at the end of my stay, he and his senior partners entertained me to lunch and made it clear that if I was prepared to emigrate to America, there would be a partnership for me at Reynolds. I thanked them warmly and promised that I would think it over carefully.

The hospitality I received in New York had been on a scale which I had never before experienced. I was taken to several theatres and at one of these, where the current hit review *Hellzapoppin'* was running, I found myself sitting beside Gary Cooper, He had his wife – a very plain little woman – and a much older woman with him, and was a quiet relaxed type who looked exactly as he did in his films. In a stay of about a week, I was never back at my hotel until well after midnight, and the next morning I was usually on my way to Wall Street at about 9 a.m. Then I boarded the *Queen Mary* (travelling cabin class, rather than first) and had a thoroughly enjoyable homeward trip on this beautiful ship, getting back just in time for Christmas 1938. For the first part of the voyage I slept most of the time as I recovered from the hectic New York life. But, though I was physically tired, the complete break had been mentally refreshing and I now felt ready for anything. With what lay ahead, I needed to be.

The Munich crisis had occurred before I left for Montreal. During the days when the outcome was in the balance we had had three guests at Springfold for the weekend. We listened to every news bulletin and on Sunday afternoon I drafted a letter to Neville Chamberlain which the five of us discussed and signed. We said that we were prepared to go to war to support Czechoslovakia. We suggested that the well-equipped Czech army, with their powerful frontier fortifications would prove a tough nut for the German army to crack. We also reminded the Prime Minister that it was always fatal to give in to a bully.

Next day, I had taken a bus from the Bank to Whitehall – all business was at a standstill – and walked into Downing Street. There was a large crowd of people standing silently opposite No. 10, with only a small number of police. I walked up to the door of No. 10 and rang the bell. No policeman enquired into my business. The door was quickly opened by a uniformed porter to whom I said 'Will you please see that Mr Chamberlain gets this letter as quickly as possible?' He took it, glanced at the envelope, and said: 'Most certainly, Sir', in a voice which would have charmed a bear.

Back at the office, I rang up the Czechoslovakian Embassy and told a man who sounded very tense, what I had done, saying that I thought many people in Britain would be feeling much the same as the five of us. He asked me to hold on – he would like the Minister to hear what I had just said. After a little while, a tired, soft, continental voice said: 'Masaryk speaking'. After I had said my piece, he said he was very grateful and naturally he hoped I was right. I could not have been more wrong, in that most of our people supported appeasement, and that is something which still makes me feel ashamed.

During the summer of 1938, the Officers' Emergency Reserve had been created and the Government asked for volunteers. I had applied, and in due course I was formally accepted. Asked if I had any preference I said 'Counter Intelligence'. I knew, of course, that with nothing beyond schoolboy French, I would have been useless working on the Continent, but I thought I might do a reasonable job if I were infiltrated into some doubtful group at home. I was observant, possessed a photographic memory, and had cultivated the art of asking seemingly innocent questions. I felt I could apply much the same technique if I were posing, say, as a British Fascist. Probably the biggest factor behind my choice was that I really wanted to do this.

After a while, I received a personal letter from the War Office asking me to call. When I presented myself on the appointed day, a messenger took me up three floors in a lift, along several corridors, and then across a covered bridge into another building. In the room to which I was taken were two pleasant, middle-aged men, both in mufti, whose names I never knew. After enquiring about my background, starting with my parents, and my business experience, the senior man asked me why I had expressed this preference. At the conclusion of the interview, the senior man said: 'You mentioned you were observant. I must now take you to the main entrance to comply with the regulations. Would you like to lead the way?' I walked slowly and at least once I turned round to view the scene as I had seen it on the way up. Finally, we reached a particular lift, which I recognised and sure enough, at the ground floor, we were beside the main entrance.

After my return from North America, I had a further letter asking me to come again. This time I was taken to a different floor and saw an older man with an assistant, both again in mufti. We had a short talk, and then he said, 'Now I am going to disappoint you. I must tell you that unfortunately we can't accept you. If you'll give me your word to treat this in absolute confidence, I will tell you why this is.'

I gave him my assurance, and then he said, 'The answer is your complete lack of languages. We have more than two hundred suitable volunteers, none of whom we can use at the present time, though all speak at least two languages perfectly. I hope that this is of some comfort to you.' I cannot imagine that after forty years of silence there can be any harm in recounting this. This certainly was a disappointment to me and for some time after that nothing happened. Then one day I received by registered post another letter from the War Office. It appointed me, in the event of hostilities, to the post of 'controller of the decontamination of clothing' in a large area embracing nearly the whole of the East and South East of London. At that time it was expected that the Germans would use poison gas, and the provision of large scale decontamination facilities was probably sensible.

But why had I been chosen, without even being asked beforehand? At the time, I assumed the letter was intended for someone else, so I rang up the War Office, quoted the reference number, and spoke to a polite civil servant. He rang me back after he had got out the file, and told me that there was no mistake. I said 'But I wouldn't know how to decontaminate a pocket handkerchief – I'm a merchant banker, and what I imagine you need is a sort of laundryman'. 'Exactly so,' he said, 'Are you not a director of Capital and County Laundries Ltd?'

This, of course, was true. Cheviot had floated the company in February 1935 and I had later joined the board as a non-executive finance director. But I knew nothing about the trade and had only once looked over Rogers & Cook, their London laundry in South Lambeth Road. I said this over the telephone, but it appeared to make little impression. In the event of war, Rogers & Cook was to be taken over as the operative centre for 'my' area and the man at the other end of the line kept saying 'But you are a *director*!' The whole thing was ridiculous. Nevertheless, for some weeks I spent occasional days at Rogers & Cook, where the technical processes were explained to me, and I made copious notes. By now it was June 1939.

I was then on the board of several industrial companies, one of them being The Newall Engineering Co Ltd which Cheviot had floated in July 1936 for a remarkable man called Sydney Player, its Chairman and Managing Director. I was a non-executive finance director of Newall and in June when I was in Peterborough for our usual board meeting, I told my fellow directors this story over lunch by way of light relief. But on the way to the station, Sydney told me that if war came, Newall would at once become a key firm because the jig borers they made were essential to the manufacture of aircraft or any high precision armament. The European alternatives came from Switzerland and Czechoslovakia, so Newall would become the only supplier. 'And if that happens', said Sydney, 'we shall need you.' On the station platform he asked me to allow him to speak to two senior people in the War Office with whom he was in touch. The outcome was the cancellation of the ridiculous 'decontamination' appointment and I later received a less formal letter instructing me, in the event of hostilities, to place myself at the disposal of Newall Engineering. I saw that Sydney genuinely wanted me and I was confident, as we walked up and down the platform waiting for the London train, that I could tackle the job he had outlined.

Meantime, I had plenty of business to occupy me. From about mid-1938 the pace had slackened, but I was still fully occupied five days a week. Montrose made two further issues for companies which Cheviot had originally floated. Cheviot, meantime, was doing no business.

Early in 1939, the Clydesdale Bank had introduced me to James Howden Hume, then Managing Director of James Howden & Co Ltd, established in 1862 as 'Boiler Auxiliary and General Engineers'. The generation of the family which had created the business had obviously been first rate but the generation which followed let the business get into low water and in the early 1930s, the bank had a preliminary meeting with a Glasgow accountant to discuss a possible receivership. The accountant in question advised the bank to talk to 'young Jimmy' before taking any action. The outcome was that the Bank supported Jimmy Hume with enough credit and authority to give him a reasonable chance. From then onwards, the business never looked back and the prospectus which I published on 19 June 1939 showed that profits had risen continuously from £23,871 for the year to 30 June 1936 to £105,452 for the ten months to 30 April 1939. The net tangible assets were £220,710.

I wanted this prospectus – Montrose's first major issue – to strike an entirely new note in a number of ways. I left everything in Howden as it was – warts and all. I did not revalue any of the fixed assets, which were all stated at cost less depreciation, and were greatly undervalued. I did not even say this, and contented myself with stating the bare facts and letting them speak for themselves.

The issue was the most difficult one I ever made because of the background conditions. But I had absolute confidence in Jimmy and his team and was determined not to give up, although at the time it seemed we were attempting the impossible. The offer was of 150,000 ordinary shares of 10/- each at 16/6 per share, so that Montrose had to underwrite £123,750. The team was my old Cheviot one – Theodore Goddard acting for the issue, Davie Parsons acting as the registrars on this occasion, and F.S. Lewis' now larger firm of Snell and Swaffield, Sidney J. Lovell & Co acting as the London brokers. I had entrusted the accounting investigation to Mellors Basden & Co, for by then I had formed a close friendship with Ted Basden, the senior partner – an outstanding accountant with unusually good business judgment. Of the 150,000 shares offered, 100,000 were purchased from the family, and we had to pay the full purchase price three days before the lists opened. The remaining 50,000 shares were newly issued, the proceeds going to the company.

I knew it was going to be difficult to underwrite the issue (the underwriting terms were 3% with an overriding commission of 1% – the normal rates for the smaller pre-war issues). But in the event it proved to be impossible, so virtually the whole of the sub-underwriting was taken by myself and my family trusts, by Ted Basden of Mellors, Basden & Co and by F.S. Lewis of the brokers.

I went to see Nicholson, the relevant General Manager of the Midland Bank, who telephoned me the next morning to say that the bank would agree to my request to lend Montrose £100,000 for a fortnight to enable them to pay for the family shares. I cannot now be sure whether or not the Midland asked for my personal guarantee – I do not think they did. It was a very acceptable gesture of confidence, and I have always felt grateful to the Midland for this.

The list of applications opened on Thursday 22 June 1939, and attracted genuine applications (all quite small) for slightly over 200,000 shares: the issue was thus oversubscribed. In its way, this was a triumph. It was, I think, the last equity issue before war was declared on 3 September. The shares, after allowing for total expenses of £13,132, had cost Montrose 15/10 ½d so our profit of 7½d per share was £4,687, plus the 1% overriding commission and a small margin in hand after paying brokerage – in all, a profit to Montrose of about £6,000. All modest figures, as I had intended they should be.

Brodies had sent the prospectus to their clients only. There were no stags, buying the shares simply with a view to selling immediately at a profit, so the price opened at a small premium and gradually moved up. The company prospered and is now known as The Howden Group. Jimmy Hume retired some years ago but I don't think either of us will ever forget those days in June 1939 and I well remember the relief I experienced when the Midland give me the figures for the applications received; and I knew that we were home and dry.

In the event, war came only ten weeks after the Howden issue. Towards the end of that period the *Daily Express* declared in banner headlines – 'There will be no War'. But, although the mood in Britain was far from warlike, all that I did during this period was on the assumption that the war would come fairly soon. I put Montrose on a caretaking basis with Davie Parsons & Co and sold everything which I felt was especially vulnerable, such as property shares. I left most of the proceeds on deposit with Barclays, except for buying a few West Country brewery shares. I expected their beer business to benefit from the influx of people from the large cities.

On Thursday 31 August I had a telephone call from Sydney Player asking me to come to Peterborough as quickly as possible; I went that night. The train left on time, but all the lamps in the carriages had been removed and the only light was a blue lamp in the guard's van. One saw few lights anywhere during the journey, which took a long time. Initially, I stayed in Peterborough at the Campbell Hotel but then I moved to Archdeaconry House beside the Cathedral where I was the only paying guest of Canon and Mrs Blakeney. Before going to Peterborough, Canon Blakeney had been Vicar of Melton Mowbray Parish Church. The young Malcolm Sargent had been his organist there and he stayed at Archdeaconry House on two occasions when he was conducting concerts in Peterborough Cathedral.

My job at Newall was to organise all the purchasing so that the flow of incoming material kept pace with the four-fold increase of output asked for by the Ministry of Defence. For this we were given the highest priority rating. I had taken over a small department which had no proper stock records, and these had to be introduced post-haste. The output target was reached within the required time and then left well behind. I dealt with every serious bottleneck personally and this took me to many parts of the Midlands to talk face-to-face with our suppliers.

On one occasion in 1940, we were on the edge of a major crisis because Firth Brown were very late with the main forgings for some of our jig borers and we were within hours of production being halted. Eventually, Sheffield telephoned me to say that our batch would be dealt with by the night shift and so, taking a three ton truck, I set off on my own a little before midnight. I had never driven a truck before and, with the headlights reduced to a slit in the blackout lamp shields, and with all the direction signs removed because of the threatened invasion, the journey took a long time.

I have always had a 'good bump of locality' but I made several bad mistakes that night and at one point, when I was quite wrongly in the fen country, the road suddenly made an acute right angle turn and although I braked hard I broke through a fence. I got out and there, within inches of the front wheels, was a deep drainage ditch full of water. Finally I got to Sheffield about 6 a.m. and the forgings, which were still very hot, made more than a full load. With the extra weight I found the truck considerably easier to drive than when empty. The return journey was uneventful.

But this is shooting ahead of events. Back on Friday 1 September 1939, when I arrived at the works, Sydney had told me that they had received instructions from Whitehall to protect the most vital parts of the factory from blast, and the Army had just delivered a large number of empty sandbags. No one had time to supervise their installation, so would I do it? It took about a week to complete and gave me time to decide what changes were necessary in my own department.

On Sunday 3 September, I had brought a portable radio to the works as the BBC had said that there would be an important announcement. At 11.15 a.m. we listened to Neville Chamberlain's broadcast which told us that we were now at war. I recall the bitterness in his voice. Very shortly after this, the first air raid warning was given by the local sirens. This proved to be a false alarm but, at the time, it was very much in keeping with what many of us had expected. At Newall, we put on our tin hats and filled our sandbags at about double the normal rate until the 'all clear' sounded. During the next twenty-four hours there were two more abortive warnings but, after that, nothing more for a long time.

Later, however, I was in Coventry on the second morning after the terrible raid which virtually destroyed the centre of the city. At that time I was a 'fire watcher' at Peterborough Cathedral and had been on duty for part of that night. Up in the vast spaces beneath the roof, my co-watcher and I heard the swarms of German planes going over, and, a little later on, were told the target had been Coventry. I had an appointment with Alfred Herbert, the Engineers, and drove through the city en route. The fires were out by then but smoke was everywhere, as was the stench of burning. It was an unbelievable and truly awful sight. Many streets were closed, being either deep in rubble or with some partly demolished buildings which were liable to fall down. Police and Air-raid wardens were everywhere, many of them digging amongst the rubble searching for bodies.

The only other sight I witnessed comparable to this was on Sunday 15 September 1940 when I left Haslemere by train at about 9.00 a.m. to return to Peterborough after one of the brief visits to my family. This was a day of almost continuous raids on London which marked the climax of the Battle of Britain and after many stops we were turned out at Wimbledon where we were told that the line ahead had been badly damaged.

There were a few buses running, but, rather than queue for them, I set off on foot. It took a long time because of blocked roads and some 'unexploded bomb' notices. These meant making as yet unmarked detours and it was easy to get lost. Several raids occurred during this period and twice I saw tight packs of German planes flying quite low south of the Thames. For a moment, they were directly overhead and one saw the swastika markings clearly. I saw no British planes during that day. I spoke with many people and eventually I got to a tube station where the trains were running fairly normally. I got out at Oxford Circus to see what central London was like; it was beginning to get dark then, probably around 7.30 p.m., and the whole of Oxford Street west of the Circus was closed. Fire engines and fires were everywhere and, as I stood at the barrier looking along Oxford Street, the whole of the front of the John Lewis store collapsed and slid across Oxford Street until the burning rubble started to invade the shops on the south side of the street. Alas, many firemen must have been ungulfed.

I went back to the underground and thence to King's Cross where the lifts had been stopped because of an air-raid in progress. At every underground station, the platforms were packed with people settling down for the night with their blankets and perhaps an inflatable mattress. They lay at right angles to the platform, leaving a narrow strip which passengers used to get on and off the trains.

People talked freely and a new arrival would be asked what it was like 'on top'. Inhabitants of the East End of London were naturally much in evidence and so was the traditional Cockney wit. All different sorts of British people showed themselves at their best that day. What a pity it takes a major war to bring out these characteristics.

Once at King's Cross I found that my train was in, but it left about two hours late, in complete darkness, and at little more than walking pace until clear of north London. Here and there, men were repairing bomb damage and we were switched to another line. It was about 2.30 a.m. when I let myself into Archdeaconry House in Peterborough.

By May 1941 I had been working virtually without a break for twenty-one months at Peterborough and I was conscious of being very tired. One afternoon, crossing a yard in the works, I had a sudden blackout. I was taken back to Archdeaconry House, and put to bed. The Blakeney's doctor came to see me, told me my blood pressure was very high, and prescribed sedatives and complete rest. But during the next few days I got much worse, and my own doctor came from London to see me. He was Dr George Genge-Andrews OBE, a wise and dedicated G.P. with a particular interest in psychiatry. He told Sydney Player that in his opinion this was the early stage of a nervous breakdown. He had come by car and I went back with him to the London Clinic in Devonshire Place. Genge, who had been my doctor for ten years, came to see me twice each day, seven days a week, during the eleven weeks I was there. The cause of my breakdown was not, however, the degree of overwork to which I had subjected myself for many years, or even the extreme pressure of the last twenty-one months. The reasons were more personal.

I had become deeply attached to Mary Connon, the Edinburgh arts graduate who had worked with me as my personal secretary and helped in the build-up of Cheviot. When Dolly, Mary and I realised in 1938 what was happening, we had each tried to do the right thing. Mary had left to work, first, elsewhere in London and then in New York, coming back to England just before the outbreak of war. The future of the children had dominated all our actions and none of us had the emotional toughness to come unscathed through the situation which confronted us.

This, then, was the real cause of my breakdown, and Genge had known of it for some time. His professional view was that a divorce could not be avoided and this was eventually accepted by all of us: first, with great generosity, by Dolly, and later by Mary and myself.

One of the few people who knew about this was my friend, Phil Belfield, Chairman of Sterling Poultry Products Ltd. He came to see me in the Clinic and then having talked to Genge, he asked me to go to his farm in Devonshire as soon as I was able to travel. By August 1941 I was able to go to Phil. I spent the first ten days sleeping a great deal, and, at that time, after a walk of a few hundred yards I had not sufficient strength to lift up my feet and wash them in the basin in my bedroom. Very gradually my daily walk increased until later I began to do a little light farm work. By early November that year, I was able to go to London where Genge examined me. Though reasonably satisfied, he wanted me to go back to Devonshire.

At that time, however, I hoped to return to industry and Andrew Craig an electrical engineer, whom I had come to know well during my Newall period, had asked me to stay with him at Walsall. Andrew and his wife were an extremely kind west of Scotland couple and I had a happy stay in their house on the outskirts of Walsall. Occasionally I went with Andrew to visit a factory, but I could see that Genge was right and that I could not have coped with any pressure. When I saw George Genge-Andrews again and he told me that a period of quiet country life was essential, farming seemed the obvious answer. Through an advertisement in the *Farmer and Stockbreeder* I met Frank Streatfeild-Moore on 7 January 1942. We liked each other and it was agreed that I should come to work for him at his farm at Shefford Woodlands, about eight miles west of Newbury. Frank had inherited this 1000-acre farm and was living in part of the large house, looked after by an old family retainer. After a public school education, he had done the full course at the Cirencester Agricultural College and farming was his whole life. I had no experience to offer, and I did not know exactly how much work I would be capable of doing. So I suggested I should come without any payment other than my keep.

This worked admirably; Frank soon taught me to plough and we staggered our hours so that, when he came in for his mid-day meal, I took over and, together, we kept going with a five-furrow plough from first to last light. After some weeks, Frank asked me to look after the sheep. There were several hundred of these and, every day, a new area of the kale had to be staked out and the sheep moved to it. The area had to be accurately staked because, if the sheep had too much to eat, some of them would become 'blown' and one would find them on their backs with enormously distended stomachs. If not promptly dealt with, this could prove fatal.

Each morning I was out at first light. The farm was pretty high up on the Berkshire Downs and it was often very cold indeed but I felt well, and my energy began to return. I came to London periodically to see George Genge-Andrews for a check-up. I felt very different in the noise and bustle of London, and Genge told me that I would deteriorate if I indulged in any short cuts to full recovery. I remember his hearty laughter when I said I wanted to have another attempt at getting into Intelligence. Years later, after his death, I discovered that he himself had been connected with MI5.

I did not relish the prospect of going back to the City just to make more money whenever the war might end. I did not need more money; I had, of course, settled capital on Dolly and the children, but even then, there was enough for all of us. As the weeks passed, I began to realise how interesting farming could be and I began to think of making it my future life.

# CHAPTER TEN

## *Woodmans Farm*

On 23 March 1942, I had had a telegram from Lord Forres, suggesting that I should come over to Chipperfield, in Hertfordshire, the next day to see a 200-acre farm known as 'Woodmans' which was for sale with possession of the land only, not the farm house. Balfour Williamson, the merchant bankers of whom Lord Forres was Chairman, and with whom I had the Crown Flour Mills connection, had moved from the City to a large house about a mile from Chipperfield and I drove over in my 8 h.p. Morris. The lovely Georgian farmhouse at Woodmans was let on a ten-year lease to a London physician named Graham-Howe and the lease still had five years to run. Forres would have bought the farm himself if he could have lived in the house but, although he had offered the Doctor a considerable sum for early possession, this had been refused.

The absence of a house was solved for me by Balfour Williamson making available a prefabricated (and movable) wooden laboratory at a chemical works they owned near Erith. Looking at a sketch of it, I decided this would make a home until the house became available. The sale of the farm on behalf of a retired Watford coal merchant was being handled by Humbert & Flint. The asking price was £12,000 and the property had been on the market for some time because of the house being unavailable.

I went back to Frank the next morning having offered £10,000, and a few days later this was accepted. I had bought 205 acres of land, three cottages, a lodge and a beautiful five-bedroom, two-bathroom Georgian house, three hundred yards up a tree-lined drive from the main road. Even at that time, it was not an expensive purchase. Forres and his brother Gerald Williamson kindly suggested that I should stay at Balfour Williamson's while the 'laboratory' was being erected on the farm. I had paid £100 for the building as it stood at Erith and, when it was erected in a corner of a pleasant field to the rear of the main house, it gave us a large sitting room, two good bedrooms, a kitchen, larder and bathroom. Although it was not beautiful we were warm and comfortable.

I took over the farm on 15 April 1942. It was in a pretty run down condition but I thought it wiser to make no changes until I had become thoroughly acquainted with it.

Mary Connon and I were married on Saturday, 30 January 1943, at Clapham Registrar's Office, near where Mary was then living. She had been working at the Admiralty until a few days before, and the little 'laboratory' house was only just finished.

During the next two and a half years, we were absorbed in making a success of the farm. We started to build up a herd of attested Ayrshires and concentrated on milk production. But I knew how profitable the sale of day-old chicks could be, so I engaged a good poultryman, made one of the barns into an incubator house, and installed a large 'Buckeye' incubator. We had about 3,000 pure bred birds of our own and supplemented these by buying hatching eggs from good local breeders. I began advertising 'Woodmans Farm Chicks' in 1943; the business grew rapidly, and I bought more incubators until two large barns were entirely devoted to chick production. By 1944 we were milking 110 Ayrshires at the peak of the season in a modern Alfa-Laval plant. That summer the British Council sponsored a film to give audiences throughout the Commonwealth a representative picture of British farming. The producer decided that Woodmans was the most suitable of any of the farms he had visited. For three days, technicians and electric cables were everywhere and the land girls enjoyed the 'close-ups' taken of them milking. We were told that the result was very good but the film was never shown in this country.

The farm was by now a hive of activity. Each week, on hatching day, we despatched chicks to upwards of a hundred customers. I would take these to Kings Langley station from where they would travel all over England. For several years, we had a stall at St Albans for the Saturday general market in the main street, selling chicks, table birds and eggs. I looked after this myself for the first two years, from 9 a.m. until about 5.30 p.m. usually taking in well over £100. The stall was attractively decorated (shades of the Players Hiring Company!) and a band round the top carried the name 'Woodmans Farm Chicks' in letters which could be seen from a distance. On a fine summer day the job was a pleasure but on a cold winter's day or a wet one, working under a tarpaulin cover, the occupation had its drawbacks.

Although dealing with the public has its difficulties many of the contacts it brings are very rewarding. I aimed to make each section of the farm large enough to employ a first rate specialist, and both milk production and poultry had achieved that. Now, I added a third section:

market gardening. My excellent gardener at 'Springfold' in Haslemere, Jim Stent, was now married and he moved to Woodmans in 1943. We built a large glasshouse and had 16 acres of vegetables and soft fruit which Jim tended with the help of a sixteen year old boy. Most of it was bought by local greengrocers but in the autumn of 1943 we had three surplus acres of beautiful Brussel sprouts which we could not sell locally so I asked a Covent Garden merchant to make an offer for the crop as it stood. He came out the next Sunday, left his expensive car at the farm, and walked over with me to see the sprouts. 'Very nice,' he remarked 'but there is a glut of sprouts. The best I can do is to offer you so much a hundredweight at the farm.' I realised that the price he was offering would not pay for the picking and told him so.

As a result of this incident, I determined to establish a retail outlet of our own. I had always believed that food grown without artificial fertilisers was more positively healthy and I had become a founder member of The Soil Association founded about that time by Lady Eve Balfour. With our dairy herd and poultry, we produced a lot of manure and, although I had to use chemical fertilisers for the corn and the grass leys, only natural manure and compost were used for the market garden.

I found a small shop on the north side of George Street, two doors from Baker Street in London, and took a seven year lease at a moderate rent, calling it simply Woodmans Farm Shop. A licence to open this was required, but after I appeared before a Committee my application was granted. It was considered that by selling compost grown food we would be doing something different. This attracted the spontaneous attention of the local Hertfordshire press and also some of the national press. One day a female reporter from the *News Chronicle* came to the farm by appointment. Just as I was expounding the merits of our compost-grown food a man opened the office door and said 'I've got five tons of super-phosphate for you, Guv. Where do you want it put?' When I had told him, the reporter and I had a good laugh. Happily, she believed me, but nevertheless I took her over to the market garden section so that she could see for herself the great mounds of manure which were added to each day. The article appeared in a prominent position soon after the shop was opened at the beginning of July 1944. The widowed mother of one of our young farm workers, Mrs Rose Marshall, not only took on the management of the shop, but drove the van each morning from the farm with all the produce picked on the previous afternoon.

We started with peas, broad beans, carrots, spinach, new potatoes, chickens, eggs and honey. Each day, virtually everything was sold by noon. We soon found it necessary to stock all the basic things a woman bought in a greengrocer's shop, so we started to buy fruit and some vegetables at Covent Garden. We kept our compost-grown produce separately and sold our Covent Garden vegetables at cheaper prices. There was a market for both. Mrs Marshall had a friend in London who went to Covent Garden daily and they shared the work in the shop.

From the first, the shop made a reasonable profit after paying the farm a full price for its produce. Durrants Hotel in George Street bought our home produce and later we developed a considerable trade with various good restaurants. Some of our customers came considerable distances in order to buy our produce. They included a number of well-known artistic and theatrical personalities which made working in the shop all the more interesting. The flying bomb period gave us some problems but Mrs Marshall never once missed a day. The V.1. flying bombs made a distinctive noise and when one heard the motor cut out, one knew the explosion would follow within a minute or so. If it was near, it was necessary to take cover and, on several occasions, Mrs Marshall had to stop the van hurriedly and do this. Later, we had the V2 rockets which were unpleasant. The nearest we got to one was when I was in the shop one day and a V2 fell at the back of Selfridges, two blocks from us. Quite a lot of glass around us was shattered but our windows held, perhaps because our door was always open. The blast briefly affected our hearing and, for some time afterwards, we were sweeping up the dust in the shop.

By the end of 1944, I had bought the next farm – Cottingham and also Tenements Farm to the north of the Chipperfield-Bovingdon road, which had no buildings but represented good land at a cheap price. I was then farming 510 acres and had built two more bungalows near to ours for our head poultryman and farm manager respectively. The latter had overall charge of all farming operations with an experienced man in charge of the dairy herd responsible to him.

With the shop and its two employees, I now had a total staff of twenty-two people including three German prisoners of war. The farm was operating at a satisfactory overall profit. I was keeping detailed accounts, and from these I knew the contribution made by each department, and day old chicks were the largest profit earner. At the beginning of 1945 Arthur Wells, who had been an unqualified managing clerk with Davie Parsons & Co for many years, accepted my invitation to help with the management and to take charge of the bookkeeping and costing.

I had obtained a licence to build one more bungalow for his occupation near the main house, and Mr E.J. Waterhouse, our excellent local builder, produced a good three-bedroomed house on what was a lovely site. It was called Little Hyde which was the name of the field in which it was built. Arthur put a little capital into the farm – about £2,500, I think – and became entitled to a generous share of any future capital profit.

George Genge-Andrews's prognosis had proved to be remarkably accurate, and my general health steadily improved. I had been examined by a Medical Board in St Albans in July 1942 to decide whether or not I was eligible for military service. In due course, I got an official piece of paper which told me that I had been classified as Grade Four (pretty low in the scale, I think) and that I should not be wanted. A year later, had I applied for regrading, I am sure the result would have been different, but by that time the farm was producing so much food that I felt the best thing I could do was to carry on and produce still more – which is what happened.

By 1945, I had become very interested in Lady Eve Balfour's work. It was clear that properly controlled research was necessary to determine the real value of organically grown food. This had been attempted on a limited scale in New Zealand and it seemed to show that a group of children fed largely on such a diet grew more quickly, and had a reduced incidence of dental decay, than those on a 'normal' diet. On the daily route to the shop, we passed John Groom's Orphanage at Edgware and I had a preliminary talk with them about this. What I had in mind was the possibility of feeding a reasonable number of the children on a diet nearly all produced organically, and then having independent medical checks undertaken to compare their progress with that of the other children. I began to prepare for this project in 1945, isolating some land to keep enough of the dairy herd to supply about ten children. We could not have produced a complete diet but milk, chicken, eggs, a wide variety of vegetables and a good deal of soft fruit, apples and honey would have been possible. I intended by deep freezing to keep the full supply going in the off seasons, giving the children strawberries at Christmas for instance.

George Genge-Andrews, while sceptical, was ready to organise the necessary medical committee. By that time the farm as a whole was of absorbing interest to me and if over the next five years, we could have carried out a dietary experiment on reasonably scientific lines, I felt that I would have an interesting alternative to financial life in the City.

As to the City, I had had little opportunity to keep in touch with the Stock Exchange during my Peterborough period. Early in October

1940, having decided that Hitler had probably missed the bus and there would be no successful invasion, I bought a number of blue chip equities, investing most of the money I had put on deposit fourteen months earlier. Prices had then risen appreciably since the low point of June 26 1940. But to have bought anything in June 1940 would have been an outright gamble and, in any case, I was too busy at that time to give it a thought. By October of the same year, it was possible to believe that Germany would fail to win the war and, if America eventually came in, that she would lose it. When we settled down at Woodmans I took the *Financial Times* regularly and occasionally I would do some Stock Exchange business. Sterling Poultry Products, which was then my largest holding, was growing each year under Phil Belfield's guiding hand. I looked after the trusts for Dolly and the children in exactly the same way as I looked after my own funds and, by about 1943, the value of all these funds had more than regained their pre-war worth.

One other event of financial interest occurred during these war years. During 1944 I did all that I could to enable the board of The Texas Land & Mortgage Co Ltd to prevent their excellent company from falling into the hands of Mr D.C.F. Lowson, later Sir Denys Lowson.

I had been a Texas shareholder for a long time and had come to know its chief executive, Mr G.A. Mitchell, and also his son George, who was about my own age. Both were splendid people and the company was successfully and conservatively managed. As with all these mortgage companies there was a substantial uncalled liability on the £10 shares; only £2.10.0d per share was called up at that time. There was no reason to suppose this would be changed in the future.

On 15 September 1943, however, an 'outside broker' with the grandiose name of National Securities Corporation circularised the Texas Land shareholders, warning them of the dangers of the uncalled liability and bidding 75/- each for their shares. This, the brokers claimed, compared with the last quoted price of 43/9d though one of Lowson's companies had in fact bought 1,500 shares at 74/- the previous month. (The asset value was £9.10.0d. per share.) The circular frightened many shareholders into selling and, as a result, Lowson obtained control by a small margin. He nominated himself and four others for election to the Board at the annual general meeting in December 1944. At this meeting, I attacked Lowson pointing out that once he had eliminated the uncalled liability he could re-sell his Texas Land shares at a considerable personal profit to the unit trusts which he managed and that these voteless unit trust holders would be mere pawns enabling him to control Texas Land. (He had recently used this technique with Eugene Ltd and later on he repeated it with Texas Land, as I had foreshadowed.)

I said at the meeting 'I make no comment on the ethics of such transactions – the facts speak for themselves. But I hope that a full report of this meeting will be studied by the Council of the Stock Exchange, the Board of Trade, and the Association of Unit Trusts.' After the meeting which inevitably resulted in the election of the Lowson clique, an angry Lowson told me that if I did not withdraw my remarks he would sue me. I didn't withdraw and never heard from him again in this connection.

In November 1946 a High Court libel action by Lowson against Mr J.G. Archibald, the Chairman of Texas Land, and the Mitchells lasted for five days before Mr Justice Stable. Lowson denied any prior contact with National Securities Corporation and defence counsel then produced this company's original letter to Lowson submitting their draft of the vital circular, and Lowson's reply returning this draft amended in his own handwriting.

At that point Lowson's case collapsed. The record was allowed to be withdrawn, and the settlement provided for Lowson to pay £11,000, which amply covered the defence costs. Only a limited number of copies of the full transcript were to be preserved and the Mitchells were debarred from broadcasting this transcript, though they could lend it to anyone who asked for it. I did so, and the facts disclosed were shocking. It is sad that such a man as Lowson was able to become Lord Mayor of the City of London in 1953. Publicity attending his subsequent business transactions, exposed by the *Investors' Chronicle* in the 1970s, merely confirmed my earlier impressions. George Mitchell was so deeply shocked by the whole dirty business that he withdrew from the City, and devoted himself to local government and charitable work thereafter, being given a CBE in 1966.

# CHAPTER ELEVEN

## ICFC – The First Phase

The groundwork for the next stage in my career was laid on 23 January 1945 when Sir John Anderson, then Churchill's Chancellor of the Exchequer, announced the forthcoming formation of two new finance companies to be set up within the private sector. The smaller company was to be called Industrial and Commercial Finance Corporation (ICFC). The concept of ICFC was born with the publication of the Macmillan Report in 1931 which pinpointed a gap in the supply of medium and long term capital up to £200,000 for smaller businesses (the 'Macmillan gap'). Lord Macmillan was a Scottish law lord and his committee was a distinguished one.

No effective action was taken for the next twelve years, but in 1943 three committees (Treasury, Board of Trade, and Bank of England) were set up to report on the problems of post war finance. Although the reports of these committees had all been finalised by the end of 1943, there were still large areas of disagreement between the findings, and the clearing banks were reluctant to finance any institution. Early in 1944, Montagu Norman whose views were very much in line with those of the clearing bankers, became seriously ill and was succeeded as Governor of the Bank of England by Lord Catto of Cairncross.

Catto realised that if the bankers did not set up an effective new Corporation the Government would do so. At a critical meeting of the Committee of London Clearing Bankers (CLCB) on 11 May 1944, Catto's statesmanship prevailed. However, while the Bank Chairmen had been won round, the powerful Chief Executive Officers' committee had not. The Chairman of this committee, Sir Charles Lidbury, then the Chief Executive of Westminster Bank, was an able and formidable figure widely respected throughout the banking world. His view was that banks 'could eat up what little problem there may be'. He and Mr William Piercy, who was to be the first Chairman of ICFC, knew each other and Piercy later told me that Lidbury had said to him in 1944 'the damn thing isn't wanted'.

However, as a result of the CLCB meeting on 11 May, Lidbury's committee was instructed to draft detailed proposals for setting up

ICFC. Lidbury dominated this drafting committee and there followed five months of tortuous negotiations, essentially between Sir Charles Lidbury, Sir Otto Niemeyer (Bank of England) and Sir Wilfrid Eady (Treasury). Niemeyer's contribution was outstanding and his clear vision and rugged commonsense proved decisive. The Scottish banks had wanted to set up their own company but in the end were persuaded by Catto to participate in the formation of ICFC.

On 6 October 1944 Catto was able to write to the Chancellor of the Exchequer, Sir John Anderson, with precise proposals for the establishment of two companies to finance industry. The outcome was the Chancellor's statement in the House of Commons on 23 January 1945. The issued share capital of ICFC was to be £15 million with, in addition, loan capital of £30 million, so that its total resources were to be £45 million. Both its share and loan capital were to be held by the English and Scottish Banks except for a token 3% to be held by the Bank of England, in those days still a quoted public company in which the Government then held no shares.

The other new company – Finance Corporation for Industry Ltd – was to deal with loans over £200,000 and its capital, with a large uncalled liability, was to be held mainly by insurance and investment trust companies, except for 15% held by the Bank of England. The joint stock banks were to provide extensive loan facilities to the Finance Corporation for Industry, protected by the uncalled liability of the institutional shareholders.

I was naturally much interested in ICFC for it appeared to be going to follow much the same course as I had advocated in a twenty-nine page memorandum I had written in 1938, advocating the establishment of a Scottish company to finance small businesses. Sir William Whyte, then General Manager of The Royal Bank of Scotland was genuinely interested in this idea. I had given a copy of this memorandum to Sir Henry Clay of the Bank of England and in 1942 I had followed this with a four-page note on 'The Post-War capital issue market' which I had also sent to the Bank. My 1938 Memorandum had set out in detail the methods I proposed to employ and one of my central points was that a minority share of the equity of every business undertaken should be secured in order to provide a counter to the inevitable losses. Provided the majority of the investments were profitable this would be effective. However, by 1945 when I joined ICFC I had come to feel that equity participation should be confined largely to high risk business where instead of matching risk with higher interest rates one did so by a minority equity interest, the extent of which would be geared to the degree of the risk. Based on my extensive experience of small businesses in the thirties I was convinced that a minority stake in a well managed small business, in spite of certain obvious risks, could be very profitable. In 1938 this view was contrary to accepted opinion. Even in 1945 it was still in advance of most City opinion which felt that a minority stake in a private company left one powerless when a crisis arose, and so was to be avoided. But from 1948 the ICFC Board did largely accept the value of minority equity holdings which have proved a fundamental, perhaps the fundamental, reason for our success.

It is possible that my 1938 Memorandum might have resulted in the formation of a small Scottish company to try out these ideas for filling the 'Macmillan gap'. But Munich and then the outbreak of war in 1939 effectively prevented this.

In 1945, after talking it over with Mary who had always believed that I would eventually return to the City, I wrote on 17 February 1945 to the Bank of England offering my part-time services to ICFC as a consultant. Apart from the possible John Groom Orphanage experiment with organically grown produce, nothing would have to be changed now that Arthur Wells was established at the farm. The acknowledgement of my letter stressed that the Bank would not be responsible for making any of the appointments, but it undertook to pass on my letter to the Chairman as soon as he was appointed. I heard nothing more until July 1945 when Mr William Piercy, the recently appointed Chairman of ICFC, wrote asking me to meet him. On 27 July, we met in a room at the office of the accountants Deloittes, overlooking Finsbury Circus, and talked for about half an hour.

Years later, Bill Piercy told me that this talk had been something of a turning point for him. Certainly it was for me, and I realised at the time that I had met someone with whom I instinctively felt on the same wave-length. This had happened earlier with Arthur Wheeler and with Phil Belfield. Piercy told me that he was committed to having a banker as General Manager but I assured him that I had absolutely no wish to be Chief Executive and, furthermore, I could not accept a whole-time appointment. While this was clearly not what he wanted, he said he would work out something on the basis of three or four days a week.

In July, after much thought, I had voted for Labour under Attlee and I felt that his surprisingly large majority was in the best interest of the country at this critical period. (Mary who had a university vote, in addition to her ordinary one, gave them both to Churchill.) In August 1945 Mary and I had our first holiday. Our faithful little Morris took us to just beyond Penzance, where we spent a happy fortnight with our baby daughter Elizabeth, who had been born on 2 June 1944.

On our return, I had a call from Piercy, and we met on Wednesday 29 August at the offices of the National Bank of New Zealand. I also briefly met James Lawrie, the newly appointed General Manager of ICFC who was then secretary and London manager of the National Bank of New Zealand and was not due to take up his new appointment for another fortnight. My impression of him was that of a pleasant person endowed with intelligence and wit. Piercy asked me to join ICFC as a part-time consultant (on a three-four day per week basis) and, when I agreed, enquired how soon I could come. I said next Monday would be possible and we shook hands on that. The salary was an afterthought to both of us; he suggested £1,000 a year and although, at the time, I would have preferred nothing except out-of-pocket expenses, he obviously saw difficulties in such an arrangement and I let it go at that. During all the years I spent at ICFC, I never raised the question of my own remuneration for, compared with other matters, it was of no importance.

Piercy's appointment as first Chairman of ICFC had not been announced until 7 June, while ICFC itself was registered in July 1945. This appointment was unexpected and the decision was largely a personal one of Lord Catto's, who had known Piercy during the First World War when Piercy was a temporary Civil Servant working in the Ministry of Munitions under Catto. Later in that war, Piercy went to the United States as a representative of the British Ministry of Food. In 1919, he had been appointed a CBE.

After the First World War, with many offers to choose from, he had joined Harrisons & Crosfield Ltd as Marketing Director and later became joint Managing Director of Pharaoh Gane. In the Thirties, Piercy went to the City to organise the first unit trust, and did important creative work in evolving methods by which the small savings of the general public could be safely channelled into quoted Stock Exchange securities. He was a member of the London Stock Exchange from 1934 to 1942. At the outbreak of the Second World War, Piercy was fifty-three, a successful and mature business man whose fertile brain had already made its mark in the City and whose counsel was valued in academic, political, and business circles. Again, he was absorbed into the Government machine. He headed the British Petroleum mission in Washington where he was principally responsible for the successful introduction of pooled distribution of petrol. He was successively a principal Assistant Secretary in the Ministry of Supply and the Ministry of Production, and then served as Personal Assistant to the deputy Prime Minister (Attlee).

Piercy, who had been a life-long Liberal, joined the Labour Party during that period, though he remained dedicated to a mixed economy. His outstanding ability and experience in a wide variety of fields won him a place in the inner circle of the intellectuals in the Party. Yet the other side of his complex character ensured his success in the business world. He made a considerable personal fortune in his eight years on the Stock Exchange. He sent his son to Eton and afterwards to King's College, Cambridge. He pioneered the Unit Trust movement, primarily for social motives, although at the same time securing for himself a substantial share of the equity of the management company.

Without doubt he was capable of being devious and although later on many of the staff of ICFC thought they knew where they stood with him, this was far from being so, as some of his conversations with me disclosed. He was a widely read man and in conversation would often quote from one of his favourite authors. These quotations or some throw-away line often contained the real pith of his thoughts, rather than the rest of the talk which could sometimes suggest the very opposite. Catto must have recognised in this complex mixture most of the qualities which were needed for this difficult assignment and future events were to justify his choice.

The board, of which Piercy was Chairman, was as follows:

| | *Age in 1945* | *Appointed by* |
|---|---|---|
| Lord Piercy of Burford | 59 | Bank of England |
| Mr W.H. Fraser WS | 69 | The Scottish Banks |
| Lt Col Lord Dudley Gordon | 63 | Barclays Bank |
| The Earl of Limerick | 59 | National Provincial Bank |
| Col The Hon G.K.M. Mason (Lord Blackford from 1947) | 58 | Midland Bank |
| Mr R. Hugh Roberts | 62 | Lloyds Bank |
| Mr Colin M. Skinner FCA | 63 | Martins, District and Williams Deacons Banks |
| Mr Edward de Stein | 58 | Westminster Bank |

The individual directors were nominated by the various banks without any collaboration between them so that at the outset many of the directors did not know one another. But, with the exception of de Stein, who resigned in November 1946, the Board formed a cohesive whole and the Corporation was fortunate to have such a wise and conscientious body of men to guide it during its difficult formative years. Edward de Stein, a successful and experienced merchant banker had only accepted the appointment 'as a matter of public service'. Writing in April 1945 to Rupert Beckett, then Chairman of the Westminster Bank, he says 'I also want to make it quite clear that I do not believe that the Company will be a success. . . . However, I understand from Lidbury that the Banks are prepared to face the real risk of loss, and on this understanding I am prepared to serve on the Board, though it does not sound a very cheerful job!' To this Beckett replied 'I am in agreement with your estimate of the prospects of the Finance Company. I fear that many projects of this nature which have a political origin will prove that such an emanation does not produce successful financial or commercial results.'

Happily, the rest of the Board believed in the aims of the new institution. All were men of character and their collective experience covered a wide field: Willie Fraser, an Edinburgh lawyer; Dudley Gordon, an Engineer; Mark Limerick, with a career both in the City and Industry; Hugh Roberts, a Midland industrialist with a wealth of first hand experience of small businesses; and Colin Skinner, one of the leading Chartered Accountants in Manchester were he was universally respected. Keith Mason emerged as the most important of the Board appointments and in effect became the unofficial non-executive Deputy Chairman of ICFC. He had been a professional – and gallant – soldier during the First World War and when promoted to colonel when he was serving under Allenby in the Middle East, he was then the youngest serving officer in the British army to hold that rank. Had he remained in the army he would undoubtedly have been one of the senior commanders in the Second World War and well able to stand up to Churchill. But, sadly for this country, he left the army for politics and was Conservative member for North Croydon without a break from 1922 to 1940. He was a deputy Chairman of the Midland Bank and a director of a number of leading companies.

Although they were entirely different characters, he and Piercy hit it off from the start. Keith was a man of great character and wisdom, and possessed immense moral courage. Without his stabilising influence during the period when Piercy's relations with the Clearing Banks were at their most difficult, the history of ICFC might have been very different.

At 10 a.m. on Monday 3 September 1945 I arrived at the National Bank of New Zealand's office at 8 Moorgate, EC2. I was met by Piercy, again saw Lawrie briefly, and was introduced to the staff, which consisted of Ted Cole (who had been there for a week) and several competent looking girls. It was then hoped that we would move to our office at 7 Drapers Gardens early in October. Ted, who had come from the Abbey Road Building Society, was fully occupied with this move and though we had permits and all the help the Treasury could give us, it was only Ted's dogged perseverance which enabled us to move early in January 1946.

Meanwhile, except for Piercy, we were housed in two rooms on the attic floor of the National Bank of New Zealand, where there was one telephone. Piercy gave me a schedule of about twenty-five applications which had been prepared by Deloittes, and also a file containing rather more than fifty applications not yet acknowledged. These letters were very similar to those I had dealt with in the Thirties and by the end of the first day I had reduced everything to about forty applications which seemed to me to justify detailed examination. I saw a lot of Piercy throughout the day and it was interesting to find how easily we agreed upon the dividing line between acceptable and unacceptable business. Our backgrounds had been very different but our experience had been largely complementary. He was eighteen years older, but this never cut any ice in all the years we worked together. We both left well after 6 p.m. and I soon realised that I would have to forget about my three or four day week. In fact I worked all that first week (when the staff effectively consisted of Piercy and myself), including a large part of Saturday, and I was to work full-time for the next sixteen years. Had anyone then told me that this would happen I would, however, have dismissed it as nonsense. For the moment, although I was well aware that I had been taken for a ride by Piercy (the part-time aspect we had agreed had obviously been nonsense) I was already fascinated by the challenge of the tremendous problems which clearly lay ahead. The only honest answer is that I found the situation distinctly amusing, and, in spite of the genuine interest I had then developed in farming, it was exciting to be back in my native habitat: the City.

In the Thirties, my first priority had been to build up a profitable issuing house business which would endure, and in order to ensure this, I took on less than 1% of the issues we were offered. But ICFC had been specifically created to *help* the small and medium sized business. To carry out this mandate we had to accept a considerable degree of risk. We had not been set up just to engage in safe business. Yet unless we were able to do this at a reasonable overall profit, ICFC itself would not endure. During that first week for much of the available time Piercy and I discussed this vital point and found that so far as the major points were concerned, we talked the same language.

On Monday 10 September, I was joined by Maurice O'Connell, a chartered accountant with several years of invaluable experience with SARA (Special Areas Reconstruction Association). 'MO'C', a delightful Irishman, was an experienced investigating accountant and he arrived just as the flow of accounts, for which I had asked, was starting to roll in. Then two days later, Lt Col Colin Kirkpatrick arrived. He had been a stockbroker before the war and he started to deal with the daily flow of new applications. Until 27 September, when the three of us were joined by 'Rocky' Stone, a brilliant young chartered accountant newly demobilised from the RAF, it was impossible to keep pace with the applications then pouring in. During October, four more people joined us, and in December a further three. One of these was a young engineer, Scammell by name, and although he himself was not a success with us, this appointment led to the formation of ICFC's Industrial Department. At the beginning of November, I had bowed to the inevitable and had agreed to accept a full-time appointment. Lawrie's task in handing over to his successor at the National Bank of New Zealand took much longer than had been anticipated and it was not until December that he was able to devote most of his time to ICFC. Thus, in the vital first three months, I had to discuss anything needing confirmation with Piercy, which in practice worked admirably. Lawrie, who was a good administrator and also had a flair for spotting talent, spent most of his limited time in recruiting staff. Although Piercy had the last word, ICFC is largely indebted to Lawrie for the high quality of its initial staff.

The Controllers and Accountants (five persons) still occupied the attic room with its one telephone. Working conditions were appalling, but in spite of this (really, because of it) a bond was forged between us which created what became known as the 'ICFC spirit'. I think that every one of us who joined the Corporation during those first months did so because he believed in its aims, and wanted to take some part in establishing it as a new force in the City. This created a corporate enthusiasm and as more people joined they too became infected. On 14 November, Piercy was raised to the Peerage – one of a number of peers then created by Attlee.

The ICFC board took its responsibilities seriously and every director did his homework meticulously. We presented a detailed submission for every case on the agenda and for some time the Controller in charge of each case came to the Board to introduce it and answer questions, which were always numerous and searching. As I was doing the bulk of the vetting of these company applications for finance during the autumn of 1945, I was present at these early Board meetings from October onwards. By the end of 1945 I had a good relationship with the Board, without as yet really knowing any of them, but during the thirteen years in which I was General Manager, I got to know Fraser, Limerick, Skinner and Keith Blackford well and continued to see all of them until the end of their lives.

The pace of that first week continued unabated through the autumn and many fundamental procedures were decided. For instance, we opted for fixed rates of interest. Even when the loan under discussion was for twenty years, we felt it was important that our type of customer should be able to calculate accurately his yearly commitment during the whole of that period. We were conscious that much of industry had just left the sheltered life of cost-plus wartime contracts for the task of developing peace-time products in a competitive climate, such as had not been experienced during the preceeding six years. One typical case was some small manufacturing business occupying leased premises which required long-term finance to purchase plant for its new products. It also needed massive additional working capital to finance the raw material which had previously been a 'free issue' from some Government department. With little in the way of fixed assets and with the floating assets probably charged to its bankers, we were exposed to the high risk which had been envisaged for us.

For secured loans our rates varied between 4% and 4½% while for unsecured loans and preference share capital the rate was usually 5%. Where the risk was greater, we sought to balance the excess risk by a modest equity participation, which was something I was particularly anxious to establish. We tried to produce an individual scheme tailored to fit the requirements of each business. Often at the end of a day the Controllers would gather together and we would sometimes break new ground in designing a financial structure to fit a specialised need.

Towards the end of November, an extraordinary incident occurred. We had agreed a £50,000 secured loan to Novello & Co Ltd, the music publishers. The security was impeccable; in complete contrast to the high risk cases which were then flooding in. Novello banked with the Westminster and, in accordance with our normal custom at that time, we automatically advised the Bank of the terms of the loan we had agreed with their customer. This quickly reached Lidbury's desk and, unknown to us, he thereupon asked the managing director of Novello's to come to see him. Lidbury told him that there was no need for him to go to ICFC for the £50,000; the bank would give them the money. The managing director – who came straight round to see us afterwards – said he had reminded Lidbury that they required this loan for ten years.

To his astonishment Lidbury waved this objection aside and in his presence dictated a letter confirming this, which the managing director showed me. Later that day, Lidbury telephoned Lawrie and told him that, as Novello's were old customers, the bank would look after their requirements. After consulting Piercy and talking to Novello's managing director, Lawrie went over to see Lidbury who was his usual bluff and hearty self. His line was 'of course, we are going to do the business for these old customers'. Later during that memorable day, Lidbury telephoned Piercy and said to him 'I'm afraid I've upset your General Manager. Tell him to propose himself for lunch at the Bank.'

Though most of the other senior bankers were more subtle than Sir Charles Lidbury, it gradually became all too clear that we were an unwanted child. Barclays and the Commercial Bank of Scotland were the exceptions to this general view and years later, A.W. Tuke of Barclays told me that once the decision to set up ICFC had been taken, Barclays felt that it was both sensible and fair to support us. But this attitude was exceptional. Of the first 430 applications which we received up to 20 February 1946, three were introduced by the Westminster Bank. In all, only 89 of the 430 came from our shareholders, and of this number, Barclays accounted for 47. During 1944, Lidbury had sought to write into our constitution a proviso that would have made it obligatory for every application to us to be sent in the first instance to the applicant's bank, who would then have decided whether or not it was suitable for us. Niemeyer, in a sardonic letter to Lidbury, succeeded in killing this. Had he not done so, we should have had only a brief life; for the pattern set by these first 430 cases did not change substantially during the next decade.

Little more than a month after the Novello incident another first class application which we had all but lost ended up in our hands. This was £100,000 4% fifteen year loan to Monckton Coke and Chemical Co Ltd, to build a new coking plant and I was the controller in charge of the case. The company had placed a firm order for the plant and as a first payment was due early in January 1946 I had done a rush job and completed the legal work by the end of December. This was before we could hope to have the consent of the Capital Issues Committee which vetted all but the very small new capital issues and whose consent, in this case, we regarded as a formality. At that time, nationalisation of the coal mines was being implemented and about 65% of all coke ovens, particularly those directly associated with collieries, were being included. On 31 December, when we were ready to complete, the company was advised by the CIC that the loan from us would not be necessary as the Ministry of Fuel & Power was prepared to supply the funds. I discussed the matter with Piercy and on 2 January 1946 I went to see Mr A.E. Watson CB CBE, a principal assistant secretary at the Ministry of Fuel and Power, armed with a memorandum which recorded the tremendous amount of work we had devoted to this case in the previous six weeks.

I judged Watson to be an exceptional man, and so I put all my cards on the table face upwards. I told him that we were having a real struggle to get ICFC off the ground and that Monckton was at this moment a key factor in this. After perhaps a quarter of an hour he said that if it was not too late, he would try to get the CIC to reverse its decision, and in parting we agreed that neither of us would make a written record of this unusual meeting. The CIC reconsidered the case on 9 January and its consent, dated 16 January, still exists. The company was not nationalised, and it subsequently fulfilled all our expectations. I have never forgotten Mr Watson, any more than I have Mr Jones of Turners Asbestos, who opened his file for me in 1925.

Shortly after this was reported to our Board, de Stein called on Piercy and made it clear, now that Monckton was not to be nationalised, that he regarded this excellent case as one which should be turned over to one of the existing City institutions. We had no intention of doing this (here we were already taking an entirely different line at ICFC to FCI) but in those very early days we could not be absolutely sure how resolute the rest of the Board would be on this issue. Piercy succeeded in avoiding a confrontation and we completed the case. As 1946 progressed, it became evident that the Board as a whole did not share de Stein's extreme view, and on 5 November 1946 he resigned on this principle. In fact, none of our cases was turned over to the City establishment. In contrast, FCI kept religiously to its appointed role as a lender of last resort, and this was the real cause of its financial crisis in 1958.

Our Moorgate period ended when, at last, we moved to 7 Drapers Gardens on 7 January 1947 where we occupied the ground and first floors at a rental of 7/6d per foot on a three year lease from the Drapers Co. Unknown to any of us at that time, Ted Cole and Alan Coventry (then Assistant Secretary) had spent the previous day (Sunday) scrubbing the floors. Charwomen were unobtainable, and these two were determined that we should find a clean office next day. The rooms were austere and pretty cold but we had ample space and quite soon all the senior staff had a telephone. Lawrie now started to devote the whole of his time to us, and morale was high.

With the move, we had adopted a five day week. The male staff, including Lawrie, numbered twelve and twenty cases, totalling applications for £979,800 had been approved by the Board by the end of December 1945. In February 1946 each of the three Controllers was given an assistant. Peter Wreford, who had just joined us from the RAF came to me. He was twenty-nine and had been trained in Coutts Bank before the war. We hit it off from the start and our partnership was a particularly happy and fruitful period for both of us. When he left ICFC at the end of 1958 to set up in business on his own account, he was Manager of 'EDITH' (Estates Duties Investment Trust Ltd), an offshoot of ICFC. He has since had a meteoric career as executive Chairman of Gresham Trust.

Thanks to having Peter, I was able to deal with a greatly increased volume of business. I dealt with all the Scottish cases, and at Piercy's request I established personal contact with the heads of the Scottish banks in Edinburgh, seeing J.B. Crawford (Bank of Scotland), Sir William Whyte (Royal Bank), J.M. Erskine (Commercial Bank) and J.T. Leggat (National Bank of Scotland). All were courteous but reserved. It was clear to me that the Scottish Banks had a more intimate relationship with their customers than their English counterparts, and if they had a customer whom they trusted it was likely that they would do his (good) business even if it was not textbook banking, and that ICFC would never hear of it. To cap this, the Scottish bankers complained that we were taking their money out of Scotland. They had provided 10.86% of our capital resources and in these early years barely 5% of our portfolio was Scottish. It was not until 1966 that our Scottish portfolio equalled the capital which the Scottish bankers had subscribed, and this in spite of the fact that during these twenty-one years our overall terms were marginally more favourable to our Scottish applicants than to their English equivalents. The truth was that many of the applications which were being introduced by the Scottish banks – and also by some of the English ones – were for business where they felt the risks were too great for themselves. For our part, we were not prepared to pick up the left-overs and this also led to some friction.

When the Scottish banks agreed to give up their conception of a separate institution for Scotland, they had insisted on a Scottish Advisory Committee being formed and in March 1946 the eight Scottish banks each nominated one member for the Committee, each of whom was paid the princely sum of 100 guineas a year. The Committee lasted for twenty-one years and although it was never able to make any overall contribution, we did benefit by being able to consult the members individually about particular cases. But we were not infrequently told by a Scottish applicant that because a member of the Committee was interested in a competitor, they could not talk to us unless we undertook to divulge absolutely nothing to our Scottish Committee!

Towards the end of 1947, John Erskine, the forceful manager of the Commercial Bank and in some ways a good friend of ours, pressed Piercy to agree to some measure of delegation to the Scottish Committee. Piercy reluctantly agreed that cases up to £10,000 should be decided by this Committee presided over by Willie Fraser whose judgment we all respected. This procedure started in January 1948 and lasted for about two years. During the first eighteen months, only two cases were sanctioned, for £7,500 and £6,000 respectively. Both proved disastrous. The outcome was that the minute of delegation was withdrawn by mutual consent and the Scottish Committee reverted to being a purely advisory body. To pick the wheat from the chaff had appeared to them to be a fairly easy matter, all the more so because of their wealth of local knowledge. In fact, as we knew to our cost, it was a difficult business which we were gradually learning the hard way.

During the rest of 1946, pressure continued high. Each day was crammed with meetings and I spent many evenings reading office papers. But at weekends, two days of physical exercise on the farm worked wonders. Fiona Margaret, our second daughter, was born on 24 June 1946 and Robin David, our son, on 19 February 1949.

By March 1946 we were preparing at ICFC to draw on the borrowing facilities from our shareholders for the first time and the rate of interest had to be fixed. The Chairman of the CLCB (Committee of London Clearing Bankers) at that time was Edwin Fisher of Barclays. Three months earlier, Niemeyer had said to Piercy that if our lending rates ranged from 3½% to 4% rather than 4% to 4½%, at any rate one shareholder (meaning the Bank of England) would not be displeased. Piercy related this to Fisher and the rate at which we borrowed was fixed at 2% where it remained until it was raised to 3% on the 1 February 1952. One outcome of this was that we lent a total of £985,000 in 1946–47 at rates varying between 3⅜% and 3¾%!

In June 1946 we made an investment of £20,000 in Sir George Godfrey & Partners Ltd, which was the start of a series of applications from this quickly growing business of aircraft cabin pressurisation specialists and, when we floated the company in 1955, I largely wrote the prospectus. By then, we had a profit of £1,250,000 on our Godfrey position and for many years this held the record for a single case. Due to the premature death of one of the three original executive directors, and our being asked to buy most of his shares, we had over 40% of the equity. Denis Theed and Dick Knight, the two controlling shareholders recognised that the company could not have succeeded as it did without frequent injections of capital at a time when the risk was considerable. I dealt with them throughout these nine years and we have remained personal friends ever since.

In June, I was appointed Chief Controller and in November 1946, when several of our early cases were in trouble, Piercy set up a Cases Committee consisting of himself, Lawrie and myself. After an intermittent start, this Committee settled every case from February 1947 onwards and in time it became the most important instrument within ICFC. It was intended to act as a filter for applications for finance and it also fixed the precise terms for the business which we wished to do.

As 1946 had progressed it gradually became apparent to many of us that there were fundamental differences between Piercy as chairman and Lawrie as general manager. The latter saw our role in terms which sometimes contained a substantial element of idealism. From July 1946, Lawrie, on his own initiative, only attended Cases Committee if I was away. Although the sad truth was that this saved a lot of time and argument without changing the outcome, this state of affairs clearly could not continue indefinitely. Meantime, Piercy and I continued to read the whole file of each case as well as the individual Controller's submission. We seldom differed as to whether or not to do the business but there would sometimes be a marginal difference between us as to the rate of interest to be charged – Piercy's rate always being lower – and on equity participations we could differ quite widely. I felt strongly that unless we matched every excess risk with adequate equity we should never be able to offset our bad debts and leave a reasonable profit after doing so, but it took me a long time to convince Piercy of this. At that time both he and our Board had serious reservations about the value of a minority stake in a private company.

Our business continued to grow in 1947 in spite of very little publicity and no press advertising. Without doubt, we had proved the existence of the 'Macmillan gap'. At the January board meeting, fifteen cases totalling £1,339,036 were approved. The negotiation of all this business had been handled by four Controllers (Guy Drummond, Denys Oppé, Julian Sorsbie and myself): only one more than in the previous year. During the first three months of 1947 working conditions for all of us were again difficult. We had the fuel crisis and the temperature was below freezing point for most of that time. Our offices were electrically heated and for about three weeks we were without any heating or light during most of each day. We sat wrapped in overcoats, wearing gloves, and it was a great relief when, towards the end of March, the thaw came at last.

Early in April 1947 we carried out our first public issue for The Viscose Development Co Ltd, which I dealt with personally. This was a one-for-one rights issue to shareholders to raise £129,000 and in addition the company wished to obtain £100,000 by a debenture on its fixed assets. In the preceding year, Piercy and I had agreed that we should carry out our own issues in due course. This small public company had no City connections and so was the perfect case for us to start with.

Because of the volume of current business with which I was dealing by the end of 1946, I had acquired another assistant in Roy Jenkins, and he worked with me throughout the Viscose issue and thereafter, until he left in May 1948 to enter Parliament. He joined us as an 'Assistant Economist' in January 1946 on being demobilised, it being understood that we should lose him when he found a suitable Parliamentary seat. He did first-rate work and when he left I took a couple of days off to canvas for him in Central Southwark, which he won. He knew the seat would disappear at the end of that Parliament so it was a courageous thing to do at the time. I got to know him well and also his able and delightful wife, Jennifer, and I certainly saw him at that time as a future Chancellor.

I wanted to use the Viscose issue to start to reduce what I regarded as the excessive profits made by issuing houses in the pre-war years (a poacher turned gamekeeper situation!). The going rate for underwriting commission was about 2½% and I suggested to Piercy that we should underwrite Viscose for a commission of 1½% without any fee and that the company should pay only our actual out-of-pocket expenses, which was an entirely new departure. Piercy was so enthusiastic that we eventually fixed the commission at 1%, and our Board agreed to allow me up to £5,000 'for the purchase of shares in the market should this appear desirable'. I did not allow applications for excess shares, and apart from giving a very small amount of underwriting to the three jobbers concerned, I kept the rest for ourselves.

344,000 5/- shares were issued at 7/6d and 29,168 shares were allotted to underwriters, of which we got 26,624. We made a realised net profit of £9,773.18.5d, mostly by dealing in the shares. This was a satisfactory result for us, yet the cost to the company had been very moderate.

As we had expected, there was a considerable reaction from the City establishment. Both *The Times* and *Financial Times* ran special articles with banner headlines. Piercy had two visits from Lionel Fraser of merchant bankers Helbert Wagg and Rufus Smith (later Lord Bicester) of Morgan Grenfell, representing the Issuing Houses Association. They endeavoured to obtain an assurance that we would not again underwrite any issue. Of course, Piercy did not give any such undertaking, though he assured them that underwriting was never likely to be other than a very minor part of our business, and this they wisely accepted on the 12 May 1947. As the result of the Viscose issue, the rates of underwriting commission began to fall. Soon 1¼% became normal.

Sir Horace Wilson came to the April board meeting in 1947, having been nominated by the Westminster Bank to replace Sir Edward de Stein. It will be remembered that at the height of the Munich crisis in 1938, Neville Chamberlain had sent Wilson to see Hitler and he was Head of the Civil Service from 1939 to 1942. Although at the time of his appointment he was out of favour in Whitehall, he remained a useful member of the Board for five and a half years.

In May 1947, I paid a brief visit to Montreal and New York with Denis Theed to help him set up a Canadian subsidiary for Godfreys, engage a managing director, and buy land on which to build a factory. Whilst in Montreal, I spent a day with our counterpart, the Industrial Development Bank, set up by an Act of the Canadian Parliament in 1944. They lent on security and had no equity investments. They had a staff of seventy, expected soon to reach 100, and during the previous two and a half years had authorised 380 cases. We had gone over on the maiden post-war voyage of the *Mauritania*, sailing from Liverpool on 26 April, and we came back on the *Queen Elizabeth*, getting to Southampton on 16 May. Travelling first class on these magnificent ships was a unique experience. The ship was akin to a large five-star international hotel and the food, in contrast to our still rationed supplies at home, was extraordinary. I have a diary note which reads 'Fourteen items on lunch menu – ate two'. Sir Simon Marks and Israel Sieff of Marks & Spencer were travelling together on the *Mauritania* and as ICFC had already financed some of the Marks & Spencer suppliers, I knew Sir Simon. He and I met every morning and walked around the boat deck for about twenty minutes. Once he talked for the whole time about how to ensure that girls working in M & S washed their hands after using the lavatory. He saw this as essential, even if they were not dealing with food, and he told me of the various methods of mass communication which had been employed to encourage them to form this habit. None had been particularly successful!

As 1947 wore on the number of sick cases among companies we had financed increased. At a Board meeting on 14 October, £140,000 was provided for bad debts. Our sick list and doubtful cases then totalled £654,800, so the provision was only 21% of this, which was not enough. Even so our loss for the year to 30 September 1947 was £116,035. For the rest of the year, the position worsened and receivers were appointed to several of our companies. Piercy and I both knew from experience how important it is to find the right type of man for this difficult job of receivership. We recognised we had the ideal man in Ronnie Leach FCA of Peat Marwick Mitchell & Co (later Sir Ronald Leach CBE, senior partner of this firm). My friend Ted Basden (Mellors Basden & Co) also acted for us in several difficult receiverships where he did a superb job.

By the beginning of 1948 the rift between Piercy and Lawrie had, most unfortunately, become very wide and their relationship had deteriorated to a point where neither could talk frankly to the other. On 16 January, I was appointed Assistant General Manager, and Julian Sorsbie succeeded me as Chief Controller. My new appointment made little practical difference. I continued to negotiate many cases, though I also spent a lot of time with the Controllers and even more with our 'after care' people where I concentrated on the most troublesome cases. I played absolutely no part in administration, which Lawrie continued to control with his accustomed competence. My relations with him were reasonably good and I most certainly did not wish him to leave for I had absolutely no desire to become responsible for a great deal of administration for which I felt I had no natural capacity, or even adequate experience.

What I wanted was to be free to build up a sound business for ICFC while at the same time fulfilling our appointed role, and this I thought I could do. What I was to be called mattered nothing to me. There was also a personal reason why I wanted Lawrie to stay. The farm had continued on an even keel, but if I could not have two clear days a week (Saturday and Sunday) to devote to it, I knew it would have to be sold, and that I most certainly did not want. It was, therefore, a black day for me when on 5 April 1948 Lawrie wrote his letter of resignation. At that time, he had no alternative post and it was not until mid-July that he accepted an appointment as Chief Executive of the newly created National Film Finance Corporation (NFFC) and left us at the end of that month. This proved to be a successful appointment for him and his undoubted ability left its mark in a field which suited him.

The solution that I then sought was the appointment of joint General Managers, and George Davies, our excellent Secretary, would have been the right man for this. Unfortunately, owing to the premature death of an uncle, George had to take charge of his family's hundred-year old business in Honolulu (now part of Jardine Matheson). I believed that Rocky Stone had the necessary ability and character but I failed to persuade Piercy, who felt that he was rather too young. Lawrie invited him to go to NFFC but Rocky did not wish to leave ICFC and on 6 July, he succeeded Davies as Secretary. In the years which followed he made an outstanding success of whatever he undertook and during the next eleven years he, Piercy and I worked together extraordinarily well.

At the end of July, after several disappointments, Piercy was introduced to Mr L.G. Pinnell who had just retired after a good career in the Indian Civil Service. Sir John Anderson, for whom Pinnell had worked when Sir John was Governor of Bengal, thought highly of him. Piercy and I saw him early in August and Sir Horace Wilson had a talk with him. He was a first class Civil Servant but he was in no way suitable as a joint General Manager. Piercy, however, felt that with Pinnell as Chief Administrative Officer and Rocky as Secretary, I would be free to concentrate on what I wanted to do. We settled it one evening sitting by the lake in St James's Park after dining at the Reform Club; there seemed to be no viable alternative. He had said 'This will be a partnership between the two of us, and ICFC will eventually emerge as a great institution.' I knew that I could work easily with Piercy and I felt sure that together we could overcome ICFC's problems. On 7 September 1948 I was formally appointed General Manager and Pinnell joined as Chief Administrative Officer.

# CHAPTER TWELVE

## *ICFC – General Manager: The First Stage*

In September 1948 the staff of ICFC numbered fifty-five in total. In the previous twelve months we had lost seven senior men, all of whom had been replaced from within the Corporation. Peter Wreford, whom I regarded as exceedingly able in every way, had been promoted after Roy Jenkins joined me, but since Roy had left at the end of May, I had been without any 'permanent' personal assistant. Now the need for a first-rate and experienced person was paramount. Most unselfishly, Peter Wreford came back to help me and once more we worked together most effectively. A strong bond, which exists to this day, grew up between us and my relationship with Peter, now covering a period of thirty-four years is, I believe unique for both of us. Mrs Joy Slaughter, who had worked for George Davies, became my personal secretary. Joy stayed with me for the next five years when she left us in order to devote herself to her baby son. She was a wonderful person, liked and trusted by everyone. I owe an immense debt to her as well as to Peter.

There were only three Controllers now, and Sorsbie, although Chief Controller and a most able technician and negotiator, was the one on whom I could least depend. Both Drummond and Oppé were outstanding and I completely trusted their judgment. O'Connell, as Chief Accountant, was sound but lacked decisiveness. He had a staff of six, which included Geoffrey Scarlett, a very able chartered accountant who later became General Manager of ICFC. Michael Maurice, a brilliant and able man but by nature an extremist on whom one could not always rely, was in charge of the vitally important Technical Department which then contained seven men with a wide variety of practical experience of industry, most of whom were very good. The small Legal Department was in good hands and Nicholas Momtchiloff in Economic Intelligence had a staff of three. He himself was greatly respected by everyone in the office – not least by me.

The core of the problem which had to be urgently resolved was: (a) to reduce to manageable proportions the number of new cases which got into trouble in their early years and (b) to minimise our losses on existing cases which were then growing at an alarming rate.

The cope with (a) we had a Cases Committee meeting twice a week, now enlarged to include Sorsbie and Maurice whenever the latter was able to attend. Piercy and I continued to read the entire file of every case and kept this up for the next twenty-three months, by which time we felt the crisis was behind us.

Controllers always came to this Committee, which was completely informal. 'Take a pew', was Bill Piercy's usual greeting to whoever was joining us. (He had asked me to call him by his christian name on that evening in St James's Park so from now onwards I will do so here.) The discussion was often enlivened by his mischievous wit, which at its sharpest could be extremely funny. We had no secretary, for Bill continued to write the minutes himself and quite blatantly slanted these on occasions so as to emphasise his own viewpoint.

The second problem (b) was much more difficult. During the summer of 1948, Maurice and I had recruited what was officially called a Management Team though in office slang this became a 'breakdown gang' or 'the fire brigade'. It was a mixed team of seasoned people with experience of industry, consultancy and cost accounting. They were intended to move into a business when trouble was brewing, diagnose the cause and propose the remedy. Over the succeeding years, our experience was that, when headed by an outstanding man, and provided it got to work before the rot had gone too far, such a team could succeed. But we were always short of first class 'business doctors'. Henry Drysdale, the dour and brilliant Scottish Chartered accountant, was our star performer. (Earlier in this narrative I have referred to the part he played in investigating the scandal of Combined Pulp & Paper Mills Ltd.) I had first met him in the mid-Thirties through Bertram Ogle after Henry, over a period of several years as Executive Chairman, had restored the ailing company which owned Pullars of Perth and Eastman's and asked me to help him negotiate its sale to Johnsons of Liverpool, which in due course we succeeded in doing. When an ICFC business was in trouble, he would go to the company for several days with one of his trusted technicians, after which he would outline the salient points of the problem to Piercy and myself. Sometimes he would simply say 'The whole thing is too far gone – in my opinion it's for the knacker'. But during a period of nearly ten years he never failed with any case which he agreed to undertake; a remarkable record.

At this time, I was very conscious of the fact that we only had limited time in which to change course before we would find ourselves in financial deep water. The accounts for the year to 30 September 1948 confirmed this. The number of bad and doubtful cases had grown from seven in the previous year to eighteen and by 2 November when the Board met, another two names had been added. We provided a further £135,000 but once again, this was minimal. On the other hand, Cases Committee was beginning to prove effective and we believed that the process of selecting our new business was now under proper control. The year's outcome was a small profit which lowered the accumulated debit balance of £145,210 to £113,249.

After my appointment as Assistant General Manager in January 1948, at Bill's suggestion I had made personal contact with some of the merchant banks in the City. Denys Oppé in particular also followed this practice most successfully. Sir Nutcombe Hume of Charterhouse (as he became) invited us to participate in a number of its cases but in the event, we undertook none of these. I never fully trusted 'Nut' and certainly some of these approaches were just attempts to off-load second-rate speculative business. On the other hand, I developed a close rapport with Jack Hambro, then Olaf's deputy, and this led to some profitable business with Hambros Bank.

Whenever a quoted share was involved, A.F. Graham-Watson – known as 'Fitz' and then senior partner of Rowe & Pitman – was usually involved, for he was very close to Hambros. Like me, he came from Edinburgh, and was one of the wisest stockbrokers of that period. We did one business jointly with M. Samuel & Co and there I found both Lord Bearsted and Charles Leatham most friendly. Tommy Brand of Lazards, one of the most brilliant of all the merchant bankers at that period, was another person I saw quite a bit of. Siegmund Warburg (whom I regarded as fully the equal of Brand) went out of his way to be friendly to ICFC and to me personally and our business relationship with his firm started in 1948 in this way. I got to know Lionel Fraser of Helbert Wagg, though at that time we did no business. He had great charm but while I liked him, I never quite felt that I trusted him completely. He and Nut Hume both possessed a veneer which, when penetrated, usually proved to be pretty insincere.

When one remembers that only three years before this, we had been a largely unwanted newcomer to the City, tribute must be paid to many people in the square mile who were open-minded and friendly. By the close of 1948, therefore, we had been able to break the ice. There was just one important exception: namely our own shareholders. Our relationship with them varied widely. Barclays remained uniformly helpful, and a good relationship had developed with Martins and the District Bank. In the autumn of 1948 I had gone to Scotland with Bill on a series of official visits to all the Scottish banks. With the exception of J.B. Crawford of the Bank of Scotland, who made it plain that he felt ICFC's General Manager should be a banker, all were friendly and John Erskine of the Commercial Bank went out of his way to be especially so. The ICFC Board was concerned about our poor relationship with some of the senior bank executives and in December 1948 they invited the senior executives of the London bankers to a 'tea and sherry party' at Drapers Gardens to meet me. Cecil Ellerton of Barclays and Arthur Ensor of Lloyds radiated warmth and encouragement but, on the whole, I doubt if this and other similar parties achieved anything.

On Thursday 23 December 1948 we had our first Christmas staff party in the large basement room which later became the staff canteen. We invited the children to come with their parents and we all played games which at times became hilarious. I dressed up as Father Christmas and gave them their presents. This was a most successful party and perhaps it is a pity that we never repeated it. At Christmas I sent a personal message to the staff in which I referred to the contribution which each individual department was making and underlining its importance to the whole effort. I made special mention of the telephone operator and the reception staff, reminding them that every new customer got his first impression of the Corporation from them. Although we were then in the midst of a great deal of serious trouble, I firmly believed that we should overcome this and so I wrote confidently. 1948 had been a most difficult year but happily it was to be the low ebb of our fortunes.

1949 marked a turning point for ICFC. There was no magic about this. It was a product of unremitting work on the part of Bill, Rocky and myself, and the dedicated effort of all the senior staff. I had moved to a room on the first floor adjoining Bill's corner room. There was a communicating door between these two rooms which was probably the most used door in the whole of the office. We were continually swapping ideas and discussing each new turn of events. There wasn't a dull moment. During the first part of 1949 the number of sick cases continued to increase, as more of our early cases (many of which we should never have undertaken) went sour. The amount of time which about half a dozen of us spent on these was appalling, and this only gradually eased as receivers were appointed and the pressure was transferred to them. By 30 September 1949 the number of sick cases had risen to 25 and we provided an additional £340,000 for these, compared with £135,000 for the previous year. Eleven of these 25 cases were now in receivership. After this provision, the year's profit before tax was £149,394 which, compared with £84,834 for the previous year, was still much too small.

We had now completed £3,969,000 of new business with an expenditure of publicity (including the production of a new brochure) of only £704. Publicity had cost a mere £92 during the previous year. People with good business were coming directly to us in increasing numbers.

At the start of 1949, we had made a new departure by buying a business from its receiver. This was Richard Crittall & Co Ltd, a well known firm of heating and ventilating contractors established in 1911. The receiver was Ronnie Leach of Peat, Marwick Mitchell & Co. During the latter part of 1948, Ronnie and I had had various discussions about Crittall. He convinced me that the firm, which then had 800 employees, could be saved. There was an order book of over £1,600,000 and a tax loss of some £500,000.

£300,000 of new equity capital was required and we needed a partner. Bill suggested Harley Drayton, at that time one of the boldest of the leading financial figures in the City. So, taking a single sheet of paper containing all the relevant facts, I went over to 117 Old Broad Street to see him. As recorded in my diary, the two of us were together for nine minutes and when I left Harley had agreed to participate 50/50 with us. He and I talked the same language.

This rescue operation, which had been carried out in the face of the disapproval of at least one of our shareholders, was justified by future events, and the company is now part of the Crown House group. Many years later at a lunch party, Ronnie Leach related how he and I had dealt. He said that at what was intended to be our final meeting he and I had reached an impasse. There was a very long silence and then I apparently said 'I wish that I could speak French, for I believe that what I want to say can only be properly expressed in that language. In crude Anglo-Saxon, it is simply "Take it or leave it".' Ronnie took it and we have had an unbroken friendship from that day to this.

In complete contrast to this, was Ronnie's appointment as receiver of Minneapolis-Moline (England) Ltd by the company's bankers in January 1949. We had an investment of £172,500, all of which we lost. The company had been promoted by Sale, Tilney & Co Ltd in May 1946. Sale, Tilney had held the sole UK selling agency for this well-known American company's farm products since 1938 but, in August 1945 with the expiry of 'lend-lease', they began to explore the possibility of manufacturing the products in England. When the British company examined the detailed specification of the American-made combine harvester, which was to be their first product, they found it impossible to purchase in the UK some of the raw materials with identical specifications. Instead of buying these in the US they re-designed the parts to compensate for the differences in the British materials. This inevitably led to other alterations and eventually it was decided to 'make a job of it' in order to adapt the combine to the heavier grain yields in the UK.

The outcome was that the re-designed British-made combine was full of teething troubles. It continually broke down in the harvest field, and within a few months the business was ruined. Apart from a tax loss of about £500,000, the assets mainly consisted of unassembled parts of combines which had proved to be faulty and the American company refused to grant another manufacturing licence in the UK following this experience.

We were not entirely free of political pressures. In April 1949 Piercy had a personal letter from Sir Stafford Cripps (then Chancellor of the Exchequer) expressing his hope that ICFC would be able to help Lady Reading who was then promoting export sales of the work of British craftsmen to North America. Stella, Dowager Marchioness of Reading, was the widow of Rufus Isaacs, the first Marquess and a most remarkable woman. She told the two of us with great clarity why she needed £100,000, and not a penny less. We had expected a request for £10,000 so when we were presented with an unconditional demand for ten times that amount at a nominal rate of interest, there was a noticeable pause in the proceedings. Bill then explained that we were not a charity, but she brushed that aside. She paid us a second visit, bringing a personal message from the Chancellor. We held out the possibility of a £10,000 loan on generous terms. She realised that she was not going to deal with us on her terms and so, with great dignity, she departed and that was the end of it.

By 1949 we had financed a number of businesses operating in the development areas. DATAC (Development Areas Treasury Advisory Committee) had made secured loans to many of these firms. We had usually subscribed for share capital and in any event nearly always ranked behind DATAC in our role as risk takers. Inevitably, the casualty rate among these cases was high. The Treasury officials who dealt with DATAC's affairs were naturally reluctant to increase the already high level of unemployment in these areas, while we could not afford to throw good money after bad. We had frequent meetings at the Treasury when these situations arose – Shillito and Grant are names I remember in this connection – and I usually represented ICFC. Nearly all of these meetings were difficult and sometimes there were really angry passages because, after my own fashion, I also could be tough, and by 1949 our judgment of the prospects of success in overcoming industrial crisis situations was reasonably good.

I would say that we came nearer to being interfered with by the Treasury over DATAC cases than by anyone else during our early years. Had Bill not supported me when Sir Wilfred Eady, the Second Secretary of the Treasury, later spoke to him to 'suggest' that I had been too tough on some particular occasion, the Treasury officials would have got their way and ICFC would, in due course, have lost many hundreds of thousands of pounds. I had the utmost respect for the intellect of these civil servants but all of them were to some extent living in an ivory tower, far removed from industrial reality. At top level in the Treasury, relations were good. Sir Wilfrid Eady came to lunch twice during 1949 will Bill and myself. He would have liked us to accept a slightly higher degree of risk in the average case but in the majority that we discussed the difference was only marginal. Eady was a realist.

During that period, Alec Barrie was Chairman of DATAC and I got to know him well. He was a Scottish Chartered Accountant brought up in Dundee and was then a partner of McClelland Ker & Co. His wife had been a student at Edinburgh University at the same time as Mary. Alec was an exceedingly able man but he was also much more than that. His wisdom and humanity were profound. He died in his office of a sudden heart attack when only fifty-one – he had been grossly overworking for a long period for he had never spared himself when something difficult had to be done. On one occasion, when we were in Whitehaven together, we took a day off and with a borrowed car, supplemented by quite a lot of walking, I showed him the Lake District which he had never seen. It was a unique day and even the summer weather was perfect. At Carlisle, waiting for the night train to Euston, Alec said to me 'I'm afraid I thought your life almost entirely consisted of employing your natural aptitude for negotiation. So today has been a bit of a revelation to me. Do give yourself a chance to do some of the other things in life, as you've done today.' We were both shy people so we said no more, but I have never forgotten this episode. Alec's premature death robbed the country of an outstanding man who would shortly have become a public figure.

Catto, the Governor of the Bank of England, came to lunch from time to time. I always felt that his viewpoint and ours were very similar. He was one of the few people outside ICFC who really understood our business and the fact that he absolutely believed in ICFC was, of course, of enormous importance.

Throughout the Fifties, Bill used to invite prominent members of the Labour party whom he knew to lunch in the office and sometimes he would ask me to join them to make a party of three. In this way, I met Nye Bevan, Ernest Bevin, James Callaghan, Stafford Cripps, Hugh Dalton, Hugh Gaitskell and Harold Wilson. Later on, I met Attlee in the same way. These were always relaxed occasions where one had the opportunity to see our guests' real characters. Nye Bevan, whom I had been prepared to dislike, was an utterly different person in these surroundings to his public image. On one of his visits he and Bill were having a discussion about some philosophical matter and Bill had just stated his viewpoint. Nye sat back, considered this, and then he said 'You put that well, but I believe Shelley summed it up best of all – do you remember?' – and Nye proceeded to quote quite an extensive part of one of Shelley's poems. I have no doubt it was accurate, and he could not possibly have known that the conversation would touch on this subject.

Dalton I never cared for, but the austere Cripps was patently sincere. I also greatly respected Ernie Bevin who was clearly possessed of tremendous strength of character and seemed to me to be a patriot of much the same type that produced our nineteenth-century Empire builders. When, at the height of the cold war, he made a major speech as Foreign Secretary standing up to Stalin, I was in the House with Bill. Ernie caught sight of Bill as he emerged from the Chamber after the speech, and had a drink and a sandwich with us. Lord Macpherson of Dromochter was with us but it is Ernie's shining eyes that I remember, for he was uplifted by what had just happened. He had taken a considerable risk in speaking out as he had done, and his superb moral courage was very evident as he talked that evening.

Hugh Gaitskell and James Callaghan each came only once when I was there, though I met Gaitskell on a number of occasions and liked him very much. Callaghan came to lunch on 20 November 1952 but my recollection of him only extends to his being a pleasant and courteous guest. I was present on two occasions when Harold Wilson came. At the time, he was President of the Board of Trade and the pattern of both visits was the same. He arrived twenty minutes late, but made absolutely no reference to this. (Bill at that time was probably just as busy as he was.) He then plunged into the discussion of a number of subjects which interested him and on which he wanted to hear Bill's views. Sometimes after Bill had replied, Harold would say 'Ah – that's good' and diving into one of his jacket pockets he would bring out perhaps twenty bits of paper and, selecting the one he wanted, he noted what had been said. I never remember him smoking a pipe, only cigars. Attlee I only met after he had retired and was in the Lords. He came over as an outstanding man of complete integrity who conveyed a great deal in few words. I liked him greatly.

During 1949 we tried to make use of the spare time which some of the recently retired Generals then possessed, especially if they had technical skills which could be applied to industry. General Sir Charles King, for instance, who as a young man had been in charge of the re-building of Quetta after the terrible earthquake, was invaluable as Chairman of two firms of building contractors. General Sir Frederick Pile, a man of great character and boundless energy, made an excellent Chairman of Fothergill & Harvey and also of Cementation. Lieut-General Sir Wilfred Lindsell and Major General Roger Reynolds also did excellent work for us. On the other hand, we never succeeded in fitting in a man who possessed no specialised experience even though he had had a distinguished career in one of the three services. Such a man is usually out of his depth in the commercial world.

In May, 1949 we agreed to lend £250,000, which was £50,000 over our top limit, to Marchon Products Ltd of Whitehaven in the West Cumberland Development Area. Marchon was the creation of two brilliant men, Frederick Marzillier and Frank Schon (now Lord Schon of Whitehaven) then respectively forty-three and thirty-eight years old. Both came to this country in 1939 as refugees from Austria and in 1940, when the blitz destroyed their small firelighter factory in London, they moved to Whitehaven. After the war, although neither of them was a chemist, they acquired German chemical know-how and started to manufacture a range of synthetic chemicals for the new and fast expanding detergent industry.

Starting from rather less than nothing on their arrival in Whitehaven, they had built up net assets of £121,185 by the end of 1948, while for that year the net profit before tax was £98,746. They employed 350 people and Colgate Palmolive Ltd, which had recently paid £60,000 for 10% of the equity, was about to place orders to the value of over £1½ million per annum. Julian Sorsbie was the Controller in this case, though (as the six voluminous files bear witness) the real Controller during the next six and a half years was Bill himself. Schon had caught his eye at the outset. Although the risk was considerable, I, too, was anxious to do the business. I had been on holiday while the details were being settled, and when I saw these on my return (the day before our Board meeting) I was completely taken aback, and for the first time Bill and I faced an absolutely fundamental difference of opinion. This concerned the equity option which I had discussed with Sorsbie before leaving, and which had now been dropped. Next day, Bill readily agreed that I should put my point of view to the Board and in fact I only had to say a few words to convince them. But, although opposed by Keith Blackford, Bill was adamant and his minute read 'If possible, a four year option being obtained for £60,000 on 10% of the equity. . . .' Naturally, Schon did not accept this and contracts were exchanged on 4 August which gave Marchon three months to decide whether to grant the option and redeem the loan at 102½% in ten years' time, or without any option, to redeem at 107½%. In due course, Marchon naturally opted for redemption at 107½%.

At the time I was determined to attempt to put this right and secure us an equity stake, if and when the opportunity arose. I had to wait for nearly three years but in April 1952 the chance came, and we bought 10% of the equity for exactly £60,000. By then the earnings yield was considerable and honour was satisfied. Bill had been so keen to secure this business for ICFC (which was absolutely correct) that he had allowed Schon to out-manoeuvre him on the question of conceding equity to us, which is remarkable when one remembers what a wealth of shrewdness Bill possessed.

Schon was the executive chairman of the company and under his leadership the business went from strength to strength. In 1951 he was concerned about the reliability of the supply of sulphuric acid, a major raw material for Marchon. In that year, with Bill and Alec Barrie's active help, DATAC agreed to lend £1,700,000 for a sulphuric acid plant with a capacity of 75,000 tons per annum, and costing £2 million. By a most fortunate coincidence, a large and shallow deposit of anhydrite had been discovered beside the factory and this supplied the raw material. Once again, Schon built this complex plant without employing outside specialist contractors. It was successfully commissioned early in 1955, a great tribute to Schon and the Marchon team who designed and erected it. All this had been carried out by a new associate company, Solway Chemicals Ltd, and by the end of 1952 we had a total investment of £404,666 in the group – £254,666 in Marchon and £150,000 in Solway. So much for our £200,000 limit.

In the autumn of 1955, out of the blue, Albright and Wilson Ltd made a substantial cash offer for Marchon and Solway, and we all had a difficult decision to make. On the one hand, a period of rapid growth clearly lay ahead and we had no doubt that the team of executive directors was fully capable of handling this. But additional large funds were going to be required and between us – DATAC, ICFC and stockbrokers Cazenoves (who had successfully placed a £600,000 debenture issue a year earlier) – we had really pulled out all the stops. In the end, the offer was accepted with some regret, and when it was completed in December 1955, ICFC had realised a capital profit of £269,646. Had the £250,000 Marchon loan remained in its original form our profit would have been £18,700. I believe the extent of our profit was absolutely justified for we had accepted a high risk initially and the help which Bill himself gave them over a period of six and a half years had been very considerable. Marchon had become his pet lamb!

On one of my visits to Whitehaven I had noticed a number of horizontal tanks, and as these were new to me I enquired their purpose. Marchon by then was supplying all the liquid hair shampoo sold by various firms under a variety of trade names. I was told that each tank contained the product sold to one of these competitive firms and I innocently asked what the difference was. The reply was 'Each has a distinctive scent, otherwise there is no difference'. Thereafter, every time I read the luscious advertisements telling women of the special qualities of a particular shampoo, I thought of that row of tanks.

One of the Solway directors appointed by DATAC was Sir Henry Tizard. I saw him from time to time, both in Whitehaven and London and got to know him reasonably well. I believe he probably had the most original mind of any man I ever knew, and although I am sure he could be both obstinate and difficult, as Churchill had found on some occasions, to my mind he was fascinating, extremely stimulating and great fun into the bargain.

During the summer of 1949, Noel Hall who was then the Principal of the Administrative Staff College at Henley-on-Thames, asked me to talk to a group of his students about ICFC. The evening went well and for a good many years thereafter I used to do this once in each term, spending the night at the College. The groups of 12-15 students were men earmarked for promotion in some of the large banking and commercial firms and the Civil Service, while there were always a few from overseas. The discussion which followed these talks was always stimulating.

When he was Professor of Economics at LSE, before becoming Chairman of the Electricity Council in 1962, Ronald Edwards organised a weekly seminar at the LSE at which a paper was presented by a wide variety of people chosen by Ronnie as leading exponents of the subject then under discussion. There were industrialists and bankers, trade unionists, scientists, senior Civil Servants and the Chief Executives of some of the nationalised industries, including the BBC. Anyone who had delivered a paper had an open invitation to come to future seminars. On 15 May 1951 I read a paper on ICFC (the questions I then had to answer were undoubtedly the toughest I ever encountered) and thereafter I went to many of these seminars. By this time, they had become a forum for the inter-change of economic and industrial ideas and the packed room probably contained rather more outsiders than students. Ronnie was a marvellous person who enriched everything he touched. How fortunate Beechams were to secure his services as their Chairman towards what proved to be the end of his life.

Catto resigned as Governor of the Bank of England in 1949 at the age of seventy and Stafford Cripps appointed Cobbold, the Deputy Governor to succeed him. In 1947 Hugh Dalton, prior to his sudden resignation on 13 November 1947, had sounded Bill out about his willingness to succeed Catto as Governor, and early in 1948 Bill had told me in strict confidence that this was a possibility. He and Dalton had been friends ever since they met at the LSE in 1910, Bill being the elder by a year and a half. In February 1946 Dalton had appointed him to the Court of the Bank of England with George Gibson and Robin Brook. (The Bank was nationalised on 1 March 1946.) In 1950 and again in 1954 Bill was reappointed and only retired from the Court in 1956 on reaching the age of seventy.

In 1948 Bill wished to talk over with me the various alternatives which he was considering were he to be appointed Governor in the following year. Had this happened, Lord Blackford (undoubtedly the outstanding member of the board of ICFC) would have been invited to succeed him and I believe that he would have accepted. Keith would have made an admirable Chairman and the relationship with our shareholders during the difficult Fifties would certainly have been different. In Dalton's *Memoirs 1945–1960* on pages 287–8 he records that after he resigned he sent a note to Stafford Cripps headed 'Bank of England – next Governor' in which he said 'Of the present Court of the Bank, only Lord Piercy, in my opinion, is worthy of serious consideration'. Perhaps in the event, this note proved counter-productive.

In January 1950, we had a lunch party at Drapers Gardens to meet the two men who were soon to take over the direction of Philip Hill & Partners from Meredith, the ex-financial editor of the *Daily Mail*. They were Kenneth Keith and Harry Moore, two young Chartered Accountants. Bill knew Meredith and we were a party of six with Julian Sorsbie and myself. We all liked Moore but none of us took to Keith. It was clear that the possibility of any meaningful business relationship was remote and so it proved to be.

On 10 March 1950 Bill and I had a visit from Isaac Wolfson of Great Universal Stores and his Finance Director. Isaac obviously felt that ICFC was by now sufficiently well established to justify a direct contact. He did nearly all the talking and the hour he spent with us was always interesting, and sometimes hilarious. He enquired at the outset whether we would like to discuss a loan of £150,000 to Tyne Plywood or one of £10 million to 'Gussies'. We indicated the former and after a little discussion he must have sensed that there were no bargains to be obtained. He therefore switched the conversation to a rapid exposition of his philosophy for Gussies, blended with some of the most skilful sales talk I ever remember hearing. He showed us a copy of the enormous coloured catalogue issued on 3 September 1939 and the current one about one-fifth of its size with the furniture prices up by about 450% and one identical carpet up by 650%. Then out of his bag came Gussies' internal monthly accounts – about a hundred large pages. In was his custom, he told us, to put his 'personal tick' against every item as he read, and we noticed his tick appeared many hundreds of times. To end this tour de force, he turned to us, beaming all over (and, of course, not intending to be taken seriously), and said 'Lord Piercy, Mr Kinross, will you let me enroll you as spare-time agents? The commission will be 8¾%.' His parting shot was that he had spent more than £300 of his time with us and that it had been a great pleasure.

I believe that went for all three of us (I omit the Finance Director who had not uttered a single word throughout) and over succeeding years we lunched together on a number of occasions. We both liked and respected Isaac and though we only very occasionally did the odd piece of business, these meetings were invariably enjoyable. On one occasion he told us that he was looking for an executive Chairman of the Anglo Portuguese Bank, which he had bought, and in Bill's presence he announced that he would like me to consider this seriously. I immediately made it clear that I was not interested. The whole thing was done so adroitly and charmingly that no one was embarrassed.

In the summer of 1950 I got to know Jules Thorn and in September of that year Henry Drysdale and I sold him an engineering business in Spennymoor named Smart & Brown which was one of our very sick cases. Jules paid very little for it – it was not worth much – but he agreed a very fair profit-sharing formula and over a number of years he made such a success of the business that we got back the whole of our original investment. Now this factory has become an enormous complex and is one of the major production units in the Thorn empire. This negotiation laid the foundation for further deals and for a personal friendship which we both cherished to the end of his life.

In September 1950 following a long period of friendly negotiation, Sterling Poultry Products took over all my farming activities and after a successful farm sale I had no further financial interest in Woodman's Farm except as a landlord. It was sad to see our lovely attested Ayrshire herd broken up but I was fortunate to have been able to keep the farm for as long as this.

Antony Hornby of Cazenoves was another visitor, and the excellent relationship we always enjoyed with Cazenoves began with Antony and has continued unabated with Luke Meinertzhagen. Pope, the business manager of *The Times*, came from time to time. He used to tell us of some of the difficulties they encountered over would-be advertisers in their Personal Column. 'Ex Bank Manager just released from prison badly wants job' resulted in fourteen serious replies and he was engaged by a good firm at £500 a year. On the day that Pope told us this, they were considering whether to insert an advertisement from a man offering to have an eye removed for £2,000 plus all surgical costs.

Our ICFC branch system dates from June 1950. There was ample evidence to show that we were getting a relatively smaller amount of new business from the Midlands and the North of England because many people in these areas did not wish to come to London to see us. We asked Ernest Ralph to visit Manchester and Birmingham and his report convinced us both that Birmingham, with its great diversity of small businesses, was the better choice. The estimated additional cost of the office was only £2,020 per annum. In April 1950 Lord Balfour of Burleigh (B of B hereafter) had succeeded the Marquess of Linlithgow as Chairman of the Committee of London Clearing Bankers (CLCB) and although the Chief General Managers and some of the Chairmen did not like our incursion into the provinces, Bill's close relationship with B of B proved decisive. Ernest Ralph was chosen as the Manager of this first branch which was officially opened on 17 October 1950.

It was not until 28 March 1952 that we were able to open our second branch office in Manchester. Our shareholders did not like this at all and it was largely due to Colin Skinner, who won the support of the three northern banks, that we succeeded. Bill and I had difficulty in persuading Guy Drummond to accept the managership of this branch. However, seven years later when we wanted him to return to London, Guy was so entrenched in Manchester that he refused this offer of substantial promotion. The quality of life in a provincial city is in some ways better than in London.

In August 1950 with the cold war worsening, one could not exclude the possibility of a third world war breaking out. I had suggested to Bill that it might be wise to have a potential evacuation office in the country where in the meantime we might keep some of our essential records. Through Edmund Thompson I found a suitable house near Pateley Bridge in West Yorkshire, which had a secondary use as a staff holiday and convalescent home. The Board sanctioned a total expenditure of £10,000 for the purchase and repair of 'Grassfield' and for a number of years it served us well.

That same month the Board discussed a note from the Chairman concerning the need for increased facilities to deal with the effect of estate duty on medium-sized and smaller businesses. By then we had completed one or two 'death duty cases': that is, purchasing a substantial minority interest in some family business from a deceased estate, where the working directors were anxious to prevent it from falling into the hands of a competitor. Our relationship with our customers was such that when some unexpected death occurred and shares had to be sold it was natural that they should turn to us. It was, therefore, agreed that we should continue to take on the best and most needy of these cases. But our shareholders who still provided the whole of our funds (and this continued for a further nine years) expected these to be used solely to finance businesses, which, because of the geographical limitation imposed by our articles were bound to be their customers. They did not wish their money to end up in the pocket of an individual, or his executors.

When we investigated the potential demand for this specialised form of finance, we discovered it was much greater than we had thought. It took two and a half years to overcome the considerable opposition from our shareholders but this investigation eventually led to the formation in March 1953 of Estate Duties Investment Trust Ltd, designed purely to take up stakes in small companies which came on the market through family circumstances. Sir Oscar Hobson reviewing its formation in the *News Chronicle* used the headline 'Introducing EDITH' and that is how it has been known ever since.

In December 1950 our Board approved an investment of up to £250,000 in another new company which was registered on the 27 March 1951 with the name of Ship Mortgage Finance Co Ltd. Once again, because of opposition from our shareholders, our subscription was reduced to £200,000 or 20% of the issued capital of £1 million. The Shipbuilding Conference subscribed £250,000, Hambros Bank £100,000 and a number of leading insurance companies took nearly the whole of the balance.

By then it was clear that the demand for mortgages on ships to be built in British yards was far in excess of the limited amount which our shareholders wished us to undertake. Sir Charles Hambro and Bill who met weekly at the Bank of England had talked about such a company and Hambros who had a long experience of ship mortgage business, were natural partners for us. I in turn talked to Edmund Thompson, then one of the leading shipping solicitors in the UK who found the ideal manager for the proposed company – Cornelis Ary Lensen, who possessed the specialised experience which was essential. Sir James Milne, the first chairman, had retired as general manager of the Great Western Railway Company when it was nationalised and the board over which he presided at Ship Mortgage Finance was comprised of Sir Philip d'Ambrumenil, Sir Amos Ayre, J. Ramsay Gebbie, and Lord Piercy. I was appointed as Bill's alternate director and was intimately concerned with Ship Mortgage affairs until I finally retired from its board in August 1974.

Peter Wreford was the first Secretary in 1950 and Lensen, who remained Manager for sixteen years, proved excellent at the job. Only once during that period did we come near to incurring a bad debt and even then Lensen eventually recovered the whole of our loan.

To return to ICFC: by the time our fifth annual general meeting was held on 6 June 1950 (the accounting year had by then been changed to 31 March) Bill and I were satisfied that the worst was behind us. We provided £190,000 compared to £340,000 for doubtful advances (there were twenty-seven of these) but we were confident they had now reached their peak. For the first time we had made a maximum, rather than a minimum provision. The resultant profit before taxation was £360,630 against £149,393. Repayments and realisations during the year amounted to over £1 million. Shortly after this, Bill and I stopped reading the entire file of every case coming to Cases Committee.

At Christmas 1949 I had sent another message to the staff from which the following extract is probably the kernel: 'Ours is a task of high importance for we can do much to help to create great businesses of the future and if, as a team, we continue to work together with the enthusiasm and harmony which are such a notable feature of ICFC, we shall deserve to succeed. Let us never forget that according to how we do our work, we shall influence for good or ill the lives of the many thousands of people who work in the businesses which we finance . . .'

A year later, in 1950, with our affairs in good order, I no longer felt that a message was necessary. Also, our staff was still of a size where I knew everyone personally.

At the beginning of 1951 – on 23 January – a bizarre but not insignificant incident occurred when W.G. Edington, then Chief General Manager of the Midland Bank, asked me to lunch with him privately at Head Office. His purpose was to enquire if I would be prepared to take over the chairmanship of ICFC from Bill, who he said, was neither liked nor trusted by himself and his fellow chief executives. My response can be imagined – as can that of Bill to whom I reported this unexpected invitation. We decided it was best to treat this as if it had never happened, and neither of us, I believe, subsequently spoke of it to anyone.

Almost exactly nine months later, on 22 October 1951 I was due to lunch at the National Provincial Bank Head Office with my friend L.J. Williams whom I had known for about twenty years and who was then general manager of the Bank. I was a little surprised on my arrival when he told me that we were to be joined by Lord Selborne, then chairman of the Bank, and that they wanted to have a confidential talk with me about ICFC. Selborne was a courteous and sincere man who explained that, as he did not know Bill, he was taking advantage of my lunching with L.J. He then enumerated a number of matters which he said caused concern to him, and, he believed, to some of his fellow chairmen. He felt that we were doing business which was outside the 'Macmillan Gap' and he instanced two National Provincial customers with whom we had dealt as examples. He quoted several instances of 'large sub-underwriting commitments' which he felt were not our legitimate business. He touched on our advertising, then only just beginning, and said that as we had not been created to supersede existing financial institutions he did not feel we were justified in 'touting for business'. He ended by saying that he greatly hoped we would not assume that ICFC necessarily had access to £45 million. That, he said, would be a great mistake.

In the ensuing conversation I said that if we were to confine ourselves to accepting business which practically no one else wanted, it would not be very long before our shareholders lost their money. However, I failed to convince him, and while I believe he recognised that I also was sincere, the talk resulted in stalemate. He had said that he naturally expected I would wish to tell my chairman of this conversation, which of course I did. There was, alas, nothing new in it, and Bill, wisely I believe, decided not to approach Selborne. I, therefore, wrote an ordinary bread and butter letter to L.J. and we heard no more.

The relationship with our shareholders was often extremely difficult, particularly in the Fifties. I believe the only way for us to have avoided friction with them would have been to have literally accepted the role designed for us in 1945. FCI did this, and so followed a very different course until the merger with us in 1974. In 1958 the Bank of England had to inject £5 million interest-free for five years by an advance of moneys uncalled on part of their FCI shareholding, and they also agreed to lend a further £10 million in certain circumstances – 'the £15 million umbrella'. This remarkable rescue operation proved effective, though it probably resulted in a very cautious lending policy by FCI in order to avoid any repetition of the crisis of 1958, the outcome of having acted as a lender of last resort for the previous thirteen years.

In ICFC's case, it was apparent from the outset that the 'Macmillan Gap' existed and this resulted in a flood of applications. Had we not been free to deal with these on their merits alone, we should unquestionably have had a life of only a few years, which is what men such as Lidbury had expected would happen.

Our accounts for the year to 31 March 1951 left us in no doubt that the changes we had made over the previous three years were now bearing fruit. After providing £150,000 (£190,000) for doubtful items (an over-provision) the profit before taxation was £580,665 (£360,630). We had now advanced £20,252,402 and had 325 customers. The number of sick cases had fallen to twenty-one. For many years thereafter our profits rose each year and for the year to 31 March 1953 we paid a maiden dividend of 4% on our share capital, increased to 5% in 1954.

In several respects these 1951 accounts marked the turning point. The opening sentence of *The Times* which was typical of press comment, read – 'The Industrial and Commercial Finance Corporation has good and solid progress to report'. The next day Harold Wincott, editor of the *Investors' Chronicle* who by then occupied a unique place in British financial journalism, telephoned to say that he would like to devote his next middle page weekly article in the *Financial Times* to ICFC. As a result of this, we had the pleasure of having Harold with us at Drapers Gardens for the best part of a day. The article appeared on 15 May 1951. The concluding sentence reads: 'All in all, ICFC would seem to have come to stay and to fill a most useful niche in our economy'.

In November 1951 Bank rate, which had remained at 2% for twelve years was raised to 2½% and by March 1952 was 4%. This marked an end to the policy of cheap money. From the late summer of 1951 a mild trade recession had deepened and on 19 November the Chancellor sent a restrictive directive to the Capital Issues Committee. We had a more severe credit squeeze in 1955–57, prolonged by the Suez crisis of 1956. Compared with subsequent squeezes these were both mild, though Bank rate rose to 7% in 1957 – then regarded as an extraordinarily high level.

ICFC's situation during that summer and autumn of 1955 was unprecedented. For much of this period we could only undertake the most pressing cases for small amounts and nearly all with existing customers whose need for further finance was both urgent and well founded. In order to do this, we had to withdraw from a number of cases where our offer of finance had not yet been accepted so that no firm contract existed. It was a heart-rending task, and all one could do was try by every means to minimise the harm to ICFC. The staff were magnificent; there is no other word for it. The worst period lasted for about four months (July to October 1955) during which I spent a wholly disproportionate amount of time seeing customers who were understandably very upset.

During October 1955 Bill wrote to the Governor of the Bank of England and to Sir Edmund Compton at the Treasury, telling them that we had only accepted £50,000 of new business since July, and without additional resources we could not do any new lending before July 1956. The result of this was that at the quarterly meeting of the CLCB on 3 November 1955 the Governor directly intervened and we were given a further £1 million for the period to 30 June 1956. Writing on 26 October, just before this vital meeting, Aldenham had said that the CLCB 'may be persuaded to abstain from pressing for an early reduction in the £22½ million limit but I do not think that they will be persuaded to agree to any increase even though you would not expect to use that increase for several months'. The £1 million we were given was therefore directly due to Catto's intervention and it came in the nick of time.

During the fourteen years from 1945 to 1959 the state of our relationship with the CLCB depended to a great extent on who was its Chairman. The initial honeymoon period lasted for just over two and a half years. On 7 April 1948 the Marquess of Linlithgow (Midland Bank) who was chairman of the CLCB from April 1948 to April 1950, asked Bill for fuller information. In July this became a suggestion that 'ICFC's auditors should supply the Banks with a comprehensive report on the Corporation's administration and operations and an estimate for the present and potential risks carried by the Corporation at the end of their financial year on 30 September 1948.' Catto killed this with a douche of commonsense at the Bankers' quarterly meeting on 5 August 1948. It had originated with the General Managers, as so often was the case. In November 1949 the CLCB requested quarterly details of individual loans of over £50,000 and of bad or doubtful debts over £2,000. While Bill made it clear that there was no reluctance on our part to supply information more frequently, provided we were not asked about the names or cases, Linlithgow was told that if these two points were pressed it was likely that 'two or three' of the ICFC directors would resign. They were not pressed, due I think to Catto's influence.

In April 1950 Linlithgow was succeeded as Chairman of the CLCB by Balfour of Burleigh (Lloyds Bank) and he in turn by A.W. Tuke (Barclays Bank) in April 1952. Both were highly intelligent men who understood the banking business and Bill's relationship with them was good. It was not until Aldenham (Westminster Bank) took over the chairmanship from Tuke in April 1954 that our four years of good chairman-to-chairman relationship ended and the worst period of all started. There were times in 1955–56 when Aldenham and Piercy were barely on speaking terms. One issue which kept recurring during the whole of the fourteen years was our shareholders' commitment to an eventual total of £45 million. In November 1950 for instance, Linlithgow argued that 'it is difficult to believe that the £45 million can have been anything more substantial than a notional figure', and he maintained that it was open to shareholders to call in their loans to ICFC at any time.

In January 1952 the CLCB gave us notice that from 1 February the rate of interest on our borrowings would be ½% over Bank rate with a minimum of 3%. This marked the end of a fixed rate of 2% which we had enjoyed for over six years. Bill pointed out to B of B, then Chairman of the CLCB, that we had used all of the money drawn down in making long-term loans at fixed rates of interest which could not be revised. He took the point and the outcome was a two-tier level of interest rates under which we accepted the ½% above bank rate formula for all 'new' borrowing from 1 February 1952 but all the 'old' money drawn prior to that date, was to be charged at 3% until repaid.

Clearly the degree of risk in continuing to do all our business at fixed rates of interest when our borrowings were now at a fluctuating rate was considerable. But the experience of more than six years of lending at fixed rates had confirmed our original belief that this was necessary for our type of customer. We therefore decided to continue this policy, even though it cost us dearly between 1952 and 1959. From 1959 when we achieved freedom to borrow in the market, it became possible to match our loan commitments with equivalent borrowings at reasonable intervals and so contain the degree of risk.

David Robarts (National Provincial Bank) succeeded Aldenham in April 1956 and remained in the Chair of the CLCB for four years, being succeeded by Sir Oliver Franks in April 1960. From the outset of the Robarts period, Bill established a good relationship with him. During 1956 this resulted in several difficult matters being settled to everyone's satisfaction. Then on 6 February 1957 Bill met Robarts and Franks for talks about ICFC's future capital requirements, in an atmosphere which was friendly and constructive. The two bankers agreed to try to obtain their Committee's consent to a further £1 million to 30 September 1957. At their meeting on the following day they succeeded, and for once the amount for which we had asked was not reduced. However, the credit squeeze itself increased in severity and despite strenuous efforts on Robart's part we were only able to obtain about 50% of the new funds we needed. This became more and more irksome to everyone concerned and in July 1958, at Robarts' instigation, discussions in earnest began about the future long-term financing of ICFC.

After a useful preparatory meeting in the summer there was an interval until Robarts returned from holiday towards the end of October. But then events moved quickly and, writing to me on Saturday 8 November 1958, Bill says 'The other great event this week is the bankers' move. What has thawed them I cannot imagine, except that two decent men like Robarts and Franks feel as bad as we do about this cat-and-mouse business which really – without any touch of animus – one can impute above all to Aldenham's peculiar character. However, if we can get this done right, it may mean open water for us.'

On the 19 November, when he was nearly seventy-three, Bill went into the Woolavington Wing of the Middlesex Hospital where Sir Eric Riches performed a successful prostate operation. But by then the basis of the 'new deal' had been agreed with Robarts and Franks. During December, Rocky and I had a series of meetings with Neville Henle of Coward Chance who was drafting the new articles of association and I also saw Chesterfield, then Chairman of the General Managers Committee of the CLCB, and R.G. Thornton of Barclays the previous Chairman: both good friends with whom I had no difficulty in ironing out the detailed points. By early December, Bill was well enough for me to discuss the various draft documents with him in the Middlesex. He went to convalesce with friends in Dorset, but by the end of December he was back in London and I spent a morning when together we went through all the papers line by line.

By the middle of January 1959 Bill was back at the office. I went with him to one of the meetings with Robarts and Franks at that time and it was clear that both were determined to reach a lasting agreement with us. By 29 January this had been achieved and early in February both the CLCB and the ICFC Board had approved our new charter, and we celebrated this by recommending a 6% dividend for the year to 31 March 1959, an increase of 1%. It was a triumph for Bill and also for David Robarts who had conducted the whole negotiation with statesmanship. Time has amply confirmed the wisdom of what was then agreed.

The principal outcome was that the restrictive articles of association, which made us completely dependent on the shareholding banks, were replaced by a normal constitution. We could now borrow money from any source provided our directors, no longer to be nominated by the shareholding banks, agreed. Our potential resources were increased from £45 million to £57 million and in July 1959 we raised £10 million by public issue of twenty-three year loan stock at 5½%. For the first time, our borrowings were put on a long-term basis at fixed rates of interest. £4 million of this issue was used to reduce our bank loans to £15 million. They were eventually to be eliminated by future public issues.

But to return to 1952: in October, to the regret of us all, Sir Horace Wilson resigned from the Board, having reached his seventieth year. I had this typical letter from him dated 4 October 1952:

> My dear Kinross,
>
> I should not like Tuesday to come and go without a word of farewell to you, and through you to your excellent band of colleagues. I am very sorry to have to leave you.
>
> I have watched with admiration the progress that has been made and congratulate you on a very outstanding achievement.
>
> Many thanks to you personally for all your kindness.
>
> Yours very truly,
> Horace Wilson

By 1951/52 I began to be able to find time to speak at various functions. In November 1951 I read a paper at Nottingham University for Brian Tew who had been in charge of our Economic Intelligence Department in our early days, and was now Professor of Economics at Nottingham. The title was 'New Issues for Small Scale Businesses'. A few weeks later I made the principal speech at a luncheon of the Institute of Cost and Works Accountants. On this occasion with Mary's invaluable help, I wrote a speech of which I am not ashamed now.

On Friday 14 November 1952 I read a paper in Edinburgh to the Chartered Accountants Students Society at a meeting presided over by my old friend Francis Gamley CA which had a surprising outcome. The title was 'Financing the Small Business' but after dealing with that in the main part of the paper I decided to float some ideas which went back to my Cheviot Trust days. I suggested the creation of a specialised company – x – which would sell through the branches of joint stock banks units of 1d nominal value of selected ordinary shares held by x. I said 'It must be the aim of x to make these penny units available to the public just as easily as a postage stamp or a packet of cigarettes. Each customer would be given a share book which would constitute his evidence of title. At stated intervals the book would be sent to x who would then pay over accrued dividends above a minimum figure. A minimum investment of say £10 would be required at the outset.' I instanced Woolworths then quoted at about 40/- for the 5/- shares. The 1d units in a new specialised company could, therefore, be sold at about 8d to give the holder a stake in Woolworths. I dealt with possible solutions to a number of points and though I emphasised that the cost of servicing such an operation would be substantial, I suggested that the 'spread' between the buying and selling price would cover this. Woolworths for example might be quoted by x at 8d to 8½d and £1 million of turnover would therefore provide x with a revenue of £62,500.

Next morning, to my astonishment, when I got to Kings Cross I found my paper headlined in the national press. The *Financial Times* had a leading article headed '1d Equity Units' in which they said 'Obviously there is a great deal for thought in this idea'. The *Scotsman* and the *Glasgow Herald* in addition to two column reports also carried leading articles which gave a cautious welcome. The *Daily Herald*'s caption was '1d shares for the little man is his idea'. On Monday when I got to the office there were already a number of letters from people totally unknown to me. My first inward telephone call was from the *Daily Mirror* asking for an immediate interview.

On Tuesday 18 November Harold Wincott devoted the whole of his weekly middle page article in the *Financial Times* to my paper under the caption 'A Pennyworth of Woolworths'. Then towards the end of the week the weeklies, including *The Economist*, devoted a good deal of space under headlines such as 'Penny Shares for the Small Man', while at the same time the provincial papers began to take it up. By now I was genuinely alarmed, for the situation was getting out of hand. The Institute of Scottish Chartered Accountants had given the Scottish press and the Edinburgh representative of the FT, copies of my paper in accordance with their normal custom, but nothing else had been done. Putting an end to it, however, was very much like fighting a forest fire. Eventually it died down, though not before the *Wall Street Journal* had entered the fray and I had received well over two hundred letters from unknown correspondents, some from Europe and North America.

Looking back, I believe there was the germ of a good idea which might have caught on, but I would have had to convince a number of senior people in the Civil Service and in banking of its feasibility. At best it would have taken a lot of time, which I did not possess at that period. This totally unsought publicity cast a short-lived shadow over my warm relationship with Bill Piercy, on whom publicity in connection with ICFC had hitherto concentrated. Thereafter I was always careful to keep well out of the limelight (which in any case I never wanted) and nothing like this ever happened again.

Between July 1952 and March 1953 ICFC had a long drawn out struggle to obtain the institutional support we needed to form EDITH. Tuke, who believed in this concept, personally overcame the opposition within the CLCB and on 31 July 1952 he won consent to our investing an initial £200,000 (20% of the proposed capital). But by late November we had only succeeded in obtaining one firm promise (from the Commercial Union Assurance for £200,000). The Prudential had given us a negative answer, and this decision stopped everything for the time being. At that time most of the institutions felt that buying minority equity holdings in private companies was fundamentally unsound. The shares would be unsaleable and, if trouble erupted, the Trust as a minority holder would be powerless. They foresaw the whole thing grinding to a halt once the initial capital had been invested. Julian Sorsbie, Denys Oppé and I discussed this individually with many of the institutions but the most we accomplished was to convince some of them that there was a genuine need for such a Trust to enable many excellent family businesses to continue as independent entities. Early in January 1953, Keith Blackford, probably the most far-seeing of the ICFC directors apart from Bill Piercy, and who had always recognised both the possibilities and the need for EDITH, went entirely on his own initiative to see Sir Alan Barstow, then Chairman of the Prudential. The outcome was that the Prudential board reversed their previous decision and agreed to subscribe £200,000. Following on this, five of the leading insurance companies agreed to participate. Thus Keith's action effectively broke the impasse.

On 23 March 1953 the initial share capital of £1 million was subscribed by seven insurance companies, nineteen investment trusts and ourselves. The original board of six consisted of Piercy (Chairman), Blackford (Guardian Assurance) R.K. Lochhead (Commercial Union), H. Ockford (Industrial & General Trust), C.W.A. Ray (Prudential) and H.R. Thiemann (Legal & General). We decided to second a senior member of the staff to devote the whole of his time to EDITH and in 1953 Julian Sorsbie was the natural choice. I suggested to Bill that EDITH should have entirely different professional advisers from ICFC. The outcome was that Peat, Marwick, Mitchell & Co became the auditors and Theodore Goddard & Co EDITH's solicitors.

From the outset EDITH was a success. ICFC's investigating machinery, which by then was working most effectively, examined each case which then went to Cases Committee before being submitted to the EDITH board. Thanks to the care which has always been taken over the initial selection, very few sick cases have developed over the years. The fears about the lack of an adequate return flow of funds – which to some extent also bothered us – have proved to be illusory. In fact a return flow started spontaneously around the third year and has gone on ever since.

I myself believe this is mainly due to the restless age in which we live. Many people now seem to get bored without fairly frequent changes. This leads them to 'do something' and so they amalgamate with some friend who possesses a suitable business and then perhaps the two together will offer some of their shares to the public. But in some way or other, nothing seems to stand still for very long and in the process EDITH is usually forced to turn at least part of its holding into cash (usually at quite a substantial profit).

At about the same time that EDITH commenced business, Private Enterprises Investment Company and Safeguard Industrial Investments were formed to do the same thing. They were managed by Warburgs and London & Yorkshire Trust respectively – but the former gave up after some years, while the latter gradually switched to investing mainly in quoted securities, which as its chairman Sir John Keeling once said to me, was a much easier type of business. The fact was – and is – that without a comprehensive investigating organisation such as ICFC possesses, buying minority holdings in private businesses can be a hazardous undertaking. I feel that some of today's spate of newcomers to the field may learn this to their cost.

In March 1952, Geoffrey Lloyd, the Minister of Fuel and Power, announced in the House of Commons that a sum of about £1 million would be available for loans to business for the installation of fuel-saving equipment and insulation, and shortly after this the Treasury asked ICFC to administer the scheme. We were to vet the creditworthiness of the applicants and thereafter the making and administration of the loans as agents for the Ministry. Peter Wreford was chosen to take charge of the operation when it started in May 1952, and when Peter succeeded Julian Sorsbie as Manager of EDITH in 1955, Christopher Attlee took his place. Both Peter and Chris administered the scheme with great competence. By September 1957, 948 loans had been approved for a total amount of just over £4½ million. The last loan was made in 1960. Over the whole period the bad debts amounted to rather less than £100,000.

Shortly before Christmas 1952 Bill and I met the General Managers of the Scottish banks in Edinburgh to discuss the opening of a Scottish branch. With John Erskine's support we obtained unanimous agreement and in May 1953 our first Scottish office was opened in two rooms at 33 Charlotte Square with Andrew Allan as its Manager. A branch in Glasgow followed in May 1961.

These visits to my native Scotland were always enjoyable and usually I managed to spend a little time with some of the Edinburgh investment trust managers whom I knew. Bill and I nearly always had a meeting with Carlyle Gifford, senior partner of Baillie Gifford & Co. He was an outstandingly wise man who so often got his timing of investment decisions spot on.

In March 1953 the Treasury asked Bill if ICFC would find two experienced members for Advisory Committees which were to administer about £1 million of US funds – a 'left-over' from Lend-Lease. The industrial fund amounting to £700,000 was to be administered by the Board of Trade, while the agricultural fund of £300,000 was under the care of the Ministry of Agriculture. They were known as the Revolving Loan Funds for Industry and Agriculture. Although I was then considerably overworked, Bill felt I was the obvious person for the Agricultural Committee, while he joined the Industrial Committee. Sir Stanford Cooper FCA, a former Chief Executive of the Ford Motor Company in the UK, was Chairman of the Agricultural Committee and from April 1953 we had many meetings. Over the period of five years a total of about £460,000 was lent, by which time £190,000 had been repaid. The average was about £980 for grain drying and storage equipment, and about £450 for agricultural machinery. Every person receiving a loan undertook to make the plant available for his neighbours' use at an appropriate charge. In all of this I had first-hand experience of the generosity of the US at that period. No strings were attached and there was a complete absence of red tape. The Committee completed its work in January 1959 when the Minister Mr John Hare came to our final meeting to thank us.

During the 1950s and the very early 1960s I had approaches which would have meant my leaving ICFC for executive directorships in two leading merchant banks. These and other offers were all from the private sector of the City with one exception. This came without warning on 28 March 1956 when the Minister of Fuel and Power, the Rt. Hon. Aubrey Jones PC, asked me to go to see him. After briefly referring to the success of the fuel saving scheme he told me that he was looking for a successor to Joseph Latham as Director-General of Finance in the National Coal Board. Latham was to become Deputy Chairman of the NCB (he was knighted in 1960) and after some preliminary talk Aubrey Jones offered me the post.

At that time we were within sight of securing for ICFC the permanent niche in the financial structure it now occupies, and until this was safely accomplished, I had no intention of being diverted. I said this to Aubrey Jones, adding that in any case I was not the right man for the job. This clearly annoyed him and he told me in his clipped slightly academic voice that he was offering me one of the plum jobs in the nationalised industries and he hoped I did not think he was doing this without a great deal of careful enquiry. He talked for a little about what was involved in the job and then he asked me to think it over and give him an answer by some date which he named. Although I had already made up my mind, I thought it best to fall in with this. Within the week I wrote a polite note to the Minister that ended the affair. I told Bill what had happened but no one else knew.

I had been somewhat tempted by one of the merchant bank offers, but I realised that I was too spiritually bound up with ICFC when it came to the crunch. When in 1961 I retired as General Manager and for the first time was free to accept a number of non-executive directorships I had more invitations than I could accept. All of these, of course, had Bill's blessing and I believe the process of cross fertilisation they produced resulted in some spin-off which indirectly benefited ICFC. What I now realise is that throughout these twelve years or so I never really came near to leaving my first love! It all went back to that evening with Bill in 1948 beside the lake in St James's Park. What he had then said had abundantly proved itself, and one just doesn't break up a true partnership.

## CHAPTER THIRTEEN

# *'The Successful Investor' and Backing the Right Man*

During 1951 Harold Wincott, editor of the *Investors' Chronicle*, and I got to know each other well. While in many ways we were very different people, we also had much in common; we were both shy and so the deep mutual friendship which eventually developed did so only gradually. In 1952 he suggested that he should write occasional articles in the *Investor's Chronicle* describing my investment philosophy. He said 'Will you tell us how you feel about markets, and, in so far as is possible, what you are actually doing?' The first article appeared in March 1952 and was written by Harold under the pseudonym of 'Candidus'. Just before publication, he telephoned me to say that he would have to invent some title for me and he had decided on 'The Successful Investor', which became my nom de plume. A month later, a second article appeared, but this resulted in a lot of correspondence from readers and I had to say that I could not cope with such frequent articles. In April 1956, 'Candidus' made a fresh start and in July of that year Harold persuaded me to write the articles myself and thereafter I wrote two or three each year. I made changes in the portfolio in each article, giving my reason for each change. In June 1958 the portfolio consisted of twenty-five shares, only five of which were blue chips.

In 1960, I discussed the pros and cons of buying assets at a discount; I suggested ways of spotting shares due for re-rating, and the attraction of many high-yielding shares. In several articles, I stressed the importance of buying good management and outlined ways in which I thought this could be judged. In February 1960, I wrote of the merits of investment trusts but emphasised that these could only perform in line with the quality of their management. Nothing daunted, I then picked out seven investment trust management groups as representing, in my opinion, the best at that time. The article, published on 26 February 1960, which incorporated a true story of a recent happening to me, 'caught on' and people at cocktail parties in the City used to tell it to me and enquire if I knew who the 'Successful Investor' was. None of them was ever near to guessing the truth! Once again, I felt that if only I had succeeded with the War Office in 1938, I could have become a reasonably successful intelligence agent.

At about that period, I added Great Portland Estates and Rank Organisation to my *Investors' Chronicle* list to help fill the gap left by take-over bids for some of the smaller companies. In the latter half of 1962 and for the whole of 1963 I did not manage to write at all and so in March 1964 I wrote a final article. The portfolio begun in April 1956 now consisted of twenty-eight shares: five showed losses and twenty-three profits. £2,439 had been invested and this was now worth £8,025. Over the same period, the FT Index had risen from 190 to 337. The portfolio still contained British Home Stores, Great Portland Estates, Hickson & Welch, Rank Organisation, Shell and Thorn Electrical.

Looking through the articles recently, their innocence strikes me. I used to record my dealings in the various shares with complete frankness. There was never any problem, for one simply refrained from either buying or selling any share one wrote about for a reasonable period before and after the article appeared. I suppose Harold had simply taken it for granted that I would do this for he never raised the subject. One Friday evening when I was strap-hanging in a crowded tube, two City types standing next to me were discussing the 'Successful Investor' article which had appeared that day. One of them said that he had a friend who knew the identity of the author. 'He's a partner in one of the large broking firms. Can't remember his name for the moment!'

Very sadly, Harold died in 1969 when he was only sixty-three. He and I had had our usual monthly lunch less than three weeks before and although he had looked very tired, as he often did, I was quite unprepared for his sudden death. Shortly thereafter a small committee was formed with Lord Robbins (then Chairman of the *Financial Times*) as its Chairman to give some of Harold's many friends in the City the opportunity of subscribing to a memorial fund if they so wished. The outcome was £100,000 – a sum many times in excess of the Committee's expectations. I doubt if anything like this has occurred in the City either before or since and it came about without an atom of pressure being brought to bear on anyone. The outcome is the Wincott Foundation which every year awards prizes to a number of financial journalists who, in the opinion of the Wincott trustees, have shown exceptional ability during the year in question. There is also an annual Wincott Memorial lecture in London, given by some person of international stature, such as Milton Friedman. Harold was completely unaware of the fact that he was a unique person and if he could know about the existence of the Foundation (perhaps he does!) he would be utterly astonished.

When I joined ICFC in September 1945 I had long since ceased to value my capital resources regularly, as I used to do up to the mid-Thirties. I had, of course, given away a great deal of capital to my first family and by then I had also created two trusts for my second family and had taken care of my then elderly sister. If I had added all of this to whatever I had then left in my possession the total would have been in the region of £1½ million: all derived from the original £10 in Hampton Properties. There was not a penny of it in fixed interest securities and the equities were nearly all growth companies which I knew were well managed. I had very little time for this activity, but as I never 'played the market' trying to make quick profits (and very easily losing money in practice) this was not necessary. My investment policy was simply to back able men who were managing a soundly financed business in some industry which gave scope for growth. As part of my daily life in the City, I was meeting all sorts of people and occasionally I would come across someone whom I could see had the essential attributes that I always looked for, and which, as my experienced ripened, I learned to recognise.

One example of this was my meeting with Jules Thorn in the summer of 1950. This was, of course, wholly concerned with ICFC business but in selling Smart & Brown to him I realised that I had met a quite unusually able man. Once our deal had been completed, I asked him to lunch with me at Drapers Gardens. He was a little man, with wonderful eyes, and brim-full of mental and physical energy. His complete integrity was immediately apparent. As he talked, one realised that Thorn Electrical Industries was his whole life and that his remarkable mind was concentrated on making an outstanding success of it, taking carefully calculated risks while constructing contingency plans just in case anything went wrong. He was in every way a most cautious man and I was indeed fortunate to have his complete trust, which gradually developed as we got to know each other well. After a while, I enquired whether he would have any objection to my buying some Thorn shares, to which he replied that that was entirely up to me. While he did not object, he warned me that with the present ghastly Government (he was always critical and especially of politicians of any party) who simply did not understand industrial problems, anything could happen. If I was rash enough to buy his shares the responsibility was mine alone – was that absolutely clear? 'Perfectly clear, my dear

Jules', I said. 'I shall see if I can make a start tomorrow morning.'

I gradually built up large holdings for all my family funds as well as for myself and for many years I did not sell a single Thorn share. The company went from strength to strength and when Jules at last had to begin to think seriously of retiring, I then sold nearly all of these at a total profit which must have penetrated a long way into six figures.

Backing the right man is, in my experience, the way by which one makes big money on the Stock Exchange. 'In and out' dealing is a mug's game which, incidentally, is very time-consuming. I always listen, but seldom act on a broker's advice. Even a good broker is often too close to the market to avoid being caught up by the mood of the moment and his judgment of an individual share is unduly based on a welter of statistics (all the more so in this computerised age) whereas what really matters is a correct assessment of the character and capability of the team of men who are going to make or break the business.

I have never been able to meet as many 'new' people as I should have wished. This has proved to be quite a major mistake of mine. Except for 1941–3, until I retired at seventy from the mainstream of ICFC, I have always had to refuse nearly every invitation to any social business function or party, even if it was being held in the evening. So I missed the opportunity of getting to know people, some of whom I would almost certainly have backed. Ernest Harrison, for instance, I only met in 1979 for the first time. I respected him greatly and had this meeting been a few years earlier I would, without question, have bought a substantial holding in Racal. As it was, I felt that by the time I met Harrison the company was in full flower rather than in bud and to my shame I have never been a Racal shareholder.

Haines, the man who built up Morrison & Gibb, whom I met about the mid-Thirties was another, though lesser, example of a meeting at the right time and, of course, another shining example was Phil Belfield. When regretfully I sold all my Sterling shares to the Ross group, the profit was very substantial and, expressed as a multiple of the original cost, it slightly exceeded the Thorn equivalent. Yet in none of these cases was there any magic. The formula simply consisted of judging a man correctly, backing this judgment with a substantial investment, and then resisting the temptation to take superficially attractive profits, provided the man one was backing was unspoiled by success, continuing to grow in stature in line with the business, and in good health. These factors were more important than some temporary setback to the company or the trade in which it was engaged. In periods when the share prices were depressed for reasons such as these, I added to my existing holdings, provided my bank balance would stand it.

These were some of the successful stock exchange deals. The unsuccessful ones where I lost money (though very little overall) were really too few in number, highlighting the fact that at least one of my faults was over-caution! I undoubtedly missed some of the biggest coups, which I could have had for the asking, because of this. An example occurred in 1952 when my friend Roland W. Foad FCA, following two and a half years with ICFC as its Chief Accountant, had returned to professional life as a partner of McClelland Ker & Co. One day he told me about Radio and Television Trust (R & T) and left me a thick file to study. R & T was a quoted company where his senior partner, John Adamson (Sir Campbell's father) was financial controller appointed by the company's bankers, with the power of a receiver. R & T was a holding company owning Airmec, a quickly growing electronic manufacturing company housed in a modern factory in West Wycombe. R & T also controlled Britannic Cables, a small conventional manufacturer of electric power cables which survived on small or special orders which the large companies did not really want. John Adamson's job was to sell R & T in order to repay overdue indebtedness to the Bank.

Roland Foad, who had investigated both businesses and knew their situations in greath depth, wanted me personally to bid for Airmec. Adamson had failed to find any satisfactory buyer for R & T and Roland thought that a low price for Airmec might be accepted. I spent the whole of one Saturday with Roland in Airmec's impressive factory where I had a long and satisfactory talk with Dr Simmonds, the acting Managing Director, whom I judged to be a first rate engineer. Later, Roland took me to see the Britannic factory near Iver in Bucks which was much less impressive. I met Dr Simmonds a second time and then had a number of talks with Adamson. At the end of these, Adamson indicated that he would give serious consideration to a bid for Airmec alone at a price which I had gradually whittled down and which Roland felt was definitely in the bargain basement area. Adamson had by then found a possible buyer for Britannic so the deal was going the right way for us all. A substantial injection of additional working capital into Airmec was essential from whoever succeeded in buying it and the whole operation was going to cost between £500,000 and £600,000. At that time, I could have found that amount from my own resources but I decided it was too large an amount for me to invest in one business, essentially dependent on a single man. I also felt that although Roland, for whom I had a high regard, was ready to become a part-time Finance Director of Airmec (while continuing with his professional practice) the business needed, in addition to him, a mature semi-executive Chairman with a successful background of commercial experience. My friend Henry Drysdale CA would have been tailor-made for the job and would also have put up part of the capital required. I talked it over with him but in the end he had to decline because of lack of time (how often that happens with able people).

Nonetheless, I took matters a stage further by discussing it with Hambros (Sir Charles and Jack) one evening at dinner in the flat above their Pall Mall office. After listening to what I told them and looking at the figures they simply said 'If you decide to do this deal and would like our support on say a 50/50 basis, we should be delighted to join you'.

Roland spent most of that next Saturday at Woodmans and for the rest of the weekend I tried to think through the whole situation, going over it with Mary. I always came back to the fact that I had failed to find a part-time chairman whom I knew I could trust. On the Monday I saw John Adamson, after speaking to Hambros and, of course, to Roland and told him that with great regret I had decided not to go ahead, and why this was so. Roland, who about a year later became Director of Finance of the Iron and Steel Board (he was made a CBE when he retired from this difficult post) was bitterly disappointed, for he felt that he and Simmonds could have done all that was required, with meetings with me perhaps every second weekend. But frankly I had my doubts. The trouble was that at that period I had absolutely no free time and clearly could not take the slightest risk of anything interfering with my total responsibility to ICFC. My added responsibility to Hambros would have heightened this.

Later, a capable industrialist, whose name I believe was Prenn, bought a controlling interest and in 1955 Crompton Parkinson made a bid and acquired the whole company. Meantime, the profits had risen substantially, exceeding Roland's careful estimates and there is no doubt that had Hambros and I each put up, say £300,000 to buy and finance the business, we would all have been richly rewarded. I had 'collected' a very few R & T shares during this period and also their sinking fund certificates which one could occasionally buy in the London market. From a very small investment, I see that I made a profit of £1,692 in 1955 when the Hawker Siddeley bid for Crompton Parkinson went through. This of course, was just petty cash but had I gone ahead as I ought to have done in purely financial terms, I sometimes wonder if I would have been alive today with a happy family life. For I suspect that these fortnightly meetings were a pipe dream and that much more time would have been necessary. ICFC never entered into this saga for our basic policy was to avoid the acquisition of a controlling interest in any company with the responsibilities which this carries.

On one occasion in the early 1930s I had narrowly missed making a nasty loss when I 'sold short' a substantial number of shares in a company where the market was normally very limited in size. (Selling short means selling shares which you don't possess in the expectation of buying them back at a lower price and so making a profit). I was convinced that the price of these shares was much too high and when the annual report appeared this proved to be so. The shares dropped to about half the price at which I had sold but after I had bought only a small part of the number I needed, the market dried up. After a very worrying period, I was fortunate enough to be able to borrow the shares I had to deliver, paying a fortnightly fee for those outstanding. It took about three months to repay the shares I had borrowed. In the end I made a profit but more importantly the episode taught me a much needed lesson. Never again have I sold short and so laid myself open to unlimited liability which is, of course, what one does when one sells short or 'sells a bear' as the operation is sometimes called.

As I got older, I dealt in the Stock Exchange less frequently for myself and very seldom on a short term basis. Even so, each year when we were still having family holidays, it was a family joke that twice each weekday I would stop the car at some remote public telephone box. There I would dial 100 and make a reverse charge call to one of our London brokers whether we were in Cornwall, the Lakes or Orkney. Often I did no business but if my call coincided with the appearance of a substantial buyer or seller which suited me I would sometimes deal in five or six figure amounts.

Freddy Bodem, a partner of brokers George Henderson & Co, lived near to us during our years at Woodman's Farm and we used to commute together to the City by the excellent train service of those days, direct from Kings Langley to Broad Street with only one stop. One read without interruption and not a moment was wasted. This is now impossible thanks to 'modernisation'. Freddy was one of the best judges of the market mood I have known. He could 'smell' the future direction of the market at nearly any given time, and his diagnosis was usually uncannily accurate.

Ernest Savory, who founded E.B. Savory & Co, was the other broker whose judgment I greatly respected. I well remember meeting him by chance in Throgmorton Street one morning. This was during the period which turned out to be the last major downward plunge of the equity markets in London and New York, following the long drawn out bear market which had started with the Hatry failure. I had liquidated most of my portfolio before the end of September 1929, but as the tremendous decline in both markets continued I occasionally bought back some high quality equities at what I then thought were cheap prices. Every one of these few purchases fell further. I sold one of them after a while at a substantial loss. The rest I kept and eventually realised good profits, but this took several years rather than months.

International Nickel (a first-class share which was a prime favourite of mine) had fallen from over 70 and at 23 I had asked Savory to buy me a few, believing them to be 'bumping along the bottom'. So when I met Ernest hurrying back to his office some months later carrying his fat dealing book I said 'What are Nickels please?' '7$\frac{1}{4}$ offered' he replied. 'Good God!' I said 'how much further *can* they fall?' to which he promptly replied '7$\frac{1}{4}$ points'. I think their lowest was about 5 and in time they recovered to well over the 23 I had paid. But never since then have I witnessed the feverish slump in prices right across the market with the near panic which accompanied it.

Many people in the City and elsewhere could not disguise the alarm they clearly felt. Unlike the US, we had practically no suicides in the UK, but the strain was intense. The catastrophic slump in 1940, when invasion seemed to be imminent, was quite different. Prices certainly fell like a stone to very low levels but there were far fewer dealings for the simple reason that very few buyers existed at practically any price. Also in 1940 nearly everyone was too busy to notice very much. Ten years earlier, business had been active on most days and the general public had been heavily involved. Those who lived through both periods will assuredly never forget them.

# CHAPTER FOURTEEN

## *The Mary Kinross Charitable Trust*

Until 1953 when I was forty-nine, my life had been completely absorbed by business and, apart from my family, my only genuine interest outside that was farming, and even the farm I had been developing on largely entrepreneurial lines. However, in November 1953 I took a step which eventually had far-reaching consequences. I had always intended to repay the pension and other monies which the Royal Scottish Academy had given Mother after my Father's death. I therefore got in touch with Sir William Hutchison, then President of the Academy, and said that I would like to establish a fund, in memory of my Father, for the benefit of elderly Academicians and their widows. Sir William brought Adam Bruce Thomson, the Honorary Treasurer, into the discussion and on 15 January 1954 the John Kinross Memorial Trust was established.

As always, I started in a small way, but once I saw the real need and the meticulous way in which, under Adam's guidance, the income was used, I added substantial sums to the fund and now the capital value is in excess of £300,000. At Adam's request, I also went over the Academy's investments, and gradually made considerable changes in these. I was, however, hampered by the restrictive Charter which had last been amended in 1891, so in 1957 the Academy petitioned the Privy Council for a further supplementary Charter to provide wider investment powers, and this was granted in 1958.

On 20 March 1957, out of the blue, I received a greetings telegram which read 'Have much pleasure to inform you that at General Assembly of Royal Scottish Academy this afternoon you were elected Honorary Academician. Warmest congratulations, William MacTaggart, Secretary.' This was an unusual honour and because of the many associations which the Academy held for me, was a particularly pleasant surprise. It was also the first award given to me, and I joined a small number of distinguished men, which included Sir Winston Churchill. Later, in December 1960, Mary and I were the principal guests at the Annual Dinner of Members. Sir William MacTaggart was then President and he and Adam Bruce Thomson both spoke warmly of my

Father. Our daughter Elizabeth, then sixteen years of age, came with us and it was a great joy to have her with us on a very happy occasion. One of the most rewarding aspects of the fund is that the Trust has been able to look after the widows of Academicians who were my Father's friends. The widow of David Alison, for instance, who had ripped his picture in two for me in 1931, only died quite recently. For many years she was one of the Trust's pensioners and I used to go to see her as often as possible when I was in Edinburgh.

My interest in the non-commercial world might have been confined to the RSA had not an unexpected event occurred in 1954, some four months after I had first approached the Academy. This was a major operation for the removal of a cyst from my thyroid gland which my surgeon, Rupert Vaughan Hudson, told me was about the size of a cricket ball. This had literally appeared overnight and the first I knew of it was on 29 December 1953 when I found that I could not fasten my collar – I thought our laundry must have shrunk the collar band, I had never had an operation or been a patient in a hospital except for my wartime stay in the London Clinic, and I had always needed to summon all my courage even to go inside a hospital to visit a friend.

While my first reaction was fright, this completely changed under the influence of my three truly wonderful medical advisers; Dr George Genge-Andrews, my doctor, who I knew was incapable of telling me anything other than the whole truth; Rupert Vaughan Hudson, a superb surgeon and a man who one instinctively knew could only accept complete perfection. The third, Dr Bernard Johnson, who was the Senior Anaesthetist at the Middlesex Hospital, I only met after I had been admitted.

The operation was on Monday 22 March 1953 and when I woke up about lunchtime there was Genge who had waited to tell me – in my language – that 'everything was 100%'. After a time I started to be sick and this, of course, was really painful and lasted throughout the night. Thereafter things steadily improved. The three 'drains' became two, and then Rupert took these away and later on removed my 'necklace' of stitches. No one else ever touched me. The days went by very quickly for they were full of interest and I was very happy. On the tenth day, Rupert telephoned during the afternoon to tell me that tests had shown that the cyst was benign. I had asked about the possibility of cancer at the first consultation and although he had been confident, this was the acid test.

I left the Middlesex on Tuesday 6 April when Bill's driver took us both to the Sackville Hotel at Hove, which Rupert had recommended.

The sixteen days in hospital had been amongst the happiest in my life. The glimpse I had had of an utterly different world to the one I knew, had made an indelible impression on me which literally changed my life. I realised that for several days my whole future life had been dependent on a handful of people and that thanks to Rupert and Bernard and the others who had cared for me, I would soon be able to return to a normal life. I felt very strongly that whatever I paid in terms of money would not adequately meet my debt to Rupert and Bernard in particular. I explained to them that the only way I could settle this fairly was for me to offer them some of my time (assuming it could be put to practical use) in return for theirs and in addition to their inadequate fees.

At first they, understandably, put this down to post-operative euphoria, but on 2 June, Bernard dined with me at the Athenaeum and saw that I was very much in earnest. A little later, this led to my acting as his Treasurer when as the second Dean of the Faculty of Anaesthetists he accepted my help in raising more than £150,000 to establish a research department for Anaesthesia in the Royal College of Surgeons of England in Lincolns Inn Fields. This happened over a period of about two years and we enlisted no outside professional help. When it was over I was invited to become the first lay-member of the Finance Committee of the Faculty of Anaesthetists, and in 1961 I was elected an Honorary Fellow of the Faculty and therefore of the Royal College of Surgeons (FFARCS). I was also a member of the main Finance Committee of the Royal College for twenty three-years.

By the time the original fund-raising operation was completed during the winter of 1956–7 I had come to realise that there were many charitable projects which needed business judgment as well as money. I had many years' experience of judging the viability of business projects and I came to feel that this could be useful in the charitable field. I decided to create a family charitable trust as a means of using my surplus capital creatively. So, on 25 March 1957 the Mary Kinross Charitable Trust was registered, with an initial capital of a mere £8,000 (as always, I wanted to feel my way before committing any substantial amount). The original Trustees were Mary, Alan Pratley and Bernard Johnson and from 1959 onwards Mary Francis has not only been Secretary but has been, and is, conversant with every facet of the work which the Trust is doing. In 1980 the Trustees (all of whom have to be approved by the Charity Commissioners following a formal advertisement in *The Times* giving brief particulars of the new Trustees' background) were Mrs Mary E. Kinross MA; Mrs Fiona M. Baldwin B.Soc.Sci, Mrs Mary E. Edward-Collins, Mrs Elizabeth J. Shields, B.Sc.(Hons), all my daughters, Mr Gilbert S. Stone FCA (Rocky), Mr Peter G. Wreford. My intention was to promote whole projects and not take the lazy way of just writing cheques.

To aid Rupert Vaughan Hudson's surgical research, we did, however, help in a modest way with a research project at the Middlesex which he was directing. The work was being undertaken by Dr Deborah Doniach MD and Dr I.M. Roitt, D.Phil and our contribution was confined to the cost of additional laboratory equipment which became necessary as the work progressed. This was our first incursion into the field of medical research but it brought us beginner's luck on a mammoth scale. The subject was Hashimoto's Disease, then a thyroid condition of unknown origin, but the work led the researchers to the much wider field of auto-immunity.

On 25 September 1956 the *Lancet* published an article on the Hashimoto problem, which resulted in a breakthrough in medical knowledge in the field of auto-immunity. Deborah and Ivan, in solving 'Hashimoto', had unearthed something of immense potential and the question immediately arose as to how many other diseases could be attributed to auto-immunity. Research started on this problem all over the world (including Europe, the USA and USSR). Ivan and Deborah established a flourishing department of immunology at the Middlesex Hospital which is still investigating the scope for auto-immunity in a number of diseases that can now be successfully prevented. They have a well equipped research department with adequate staff, all paid for by the State, and are doing work recognised throughout the world as being of the highest importance. Rupert, alas, died in 1967.

Twenty-three years later, the Mary Kinross Charitable Trust has invested funds of well over £2,000,000 and has given some £300,000 to a wide variety of projects. At the present time (1980) we have forward commitments of about £150,000 and the work involved takes up a considerable amount of my time, not least in the evenings. In the intervening years we have covered a wide field. The object has been to undertake whole projects designed to fill real needs and to ensure these are managed by competent and caring men and women whom we usually help to choose. Following a running-in period, each project is designed to be self-supporting and so far all of them have been.

In some cases, where we have been fortunate enough to find someone endowed with exceptional qualities, we have created a project to provide scope for these. This was the situation at Good Companions Workshops at Rickmansworth, and Kings Langley. Mary had got to know two remarkable people – Kathy and Stanley Harrold – and one could see they possessed all the personal qualities which were required to make an outstanding success of a 'workshop' where elderly men and women (and later also psychiatric cases) could come to a happy atmosphere in a purpose-built well equipped building. There they had the choice of various types of light work and they were completely free to come for as short or as long a time as they felt able. Mary launched the project herself and for a long time, until we left Woodmans Farm, she went each week to keep in touch with the individual people and also to work with them.

A very different area in which we have been active concerns the re-settlement of men, particularly young men, leaving prison without any home to go to. In January 1968, I wrote a paper arguing the case for trying to find individual homes for these men rather than housing them together in hostels where they were bound to talk 'shop' (i.e. how to commit large-scale crime more efficiently). The outcome was that, taking as its base the offices of the National Association for Care and Re-settlement of Offenders (NACRO) in Kennington Road, SE17, the Trust engaged a first-rate experienced Social worker who succeeded in finding forty-nine landladies in SE London, each willing to have one of these young men. The Trust guaranteed the landladies against any financial loss so that if something was stolen, if the contents of the house were damaged, or if one of the men left with rent owing, we met these bills. We usually paid the ex-prisoners' first fortnight's rent to enable them to re-adjust and have time to look for work. In practice, the combination of help cost us quite a lot and I began to feel that my idea was a bit of a flop, though only two of our splendid landladies had given up. However, NACRO with all their experience took entirely the opposite view and after a few years the local Probationary Service took over the whole operation, on the basis that it had by then conclusively proved its worth.

In the same sphere, we have had a close and excellent relationship for many years with the Hertfordshire Probation and After-Care Service. There are many gaps for which council money cannot be used and where we can fill these they are able to provide a more balanced and humane service. This contact has brought home to me how humane and competent good local Government officials can be (the opposite, alas is also true, as in every walk of life).

Because of my family's long connection with Stirling, we gave the University £25,000 for resident student accommodation when it was established. We were greatly saddened by the Vice Chancellor, Professor Cotterell's untimely death and the very difficult period which the

University went through at that time.

Until recently our largest project in financial terms has been Student Homes Ltd (Bernard Johnson House in East Finchley). Bernard Johnson, Senior Anaesthetist at the Middlesex Hospital, died instantly from a coronary heart attack in 1959 when he was only fifty-four. For years he had undertaken frequent lecture tours throughout the old Commonwealth with the object of raising the standards of Anaesthesia in these countries. For some of the best of the graduates there were excellent post-graduate courses with practical clinical experience in some of the London Teaching Hospitals. There was reasonable housing accommodation for the single students but practically nothing for the married ones, and if they had children it was nearly impossible. Bernard's wife, Barbara, had for years mothered some of these students during holidays and at weekends and was obviously a natural warden. Mary and I could also see that to be absorbed in creating this new venture would be the best antidote to the shattering blow of Bernard's unexpected death.

After a long search, mostly in SW and SE London, which Barbara undertook, we bought a run-down commercial hotel in Fortis Green NW for £32,500. While plans were being prepared for gutting it and creating comfortable self-contained centrally-heated flats (sitting room, bedroom, kitchen and bathroom, with a lot of cupboard space for storage) Barbara ran it as we had taken it over – staff and all – for over six months. It was a tremendous effort but well worth doing, for all the young doctors and their families were desperate and we learned a great deal in those months. We also lost about £1,500 and never was money more productively lost!

Now we have a large purpose-built annexe and another property, Barbara Johnson House, a few minutes away and we house twenty-four medical families, of many races, colours and religions. It is heartening to see how well they settle down together. There is a library and 'quiet room' for study, a playroom for the children and a large garden used a lot by everyone. The rents, which include all the central heating (the most important single facility which we provide, for most of our tenants come from tropical countries) are rather less than half the local commercial rents for comparable accommodation. Our greatest problem is the never-ending queue of these young doctors who would like to become tenants. For this reason, our maximum lease is for eighteen months.

In the summer of 1975, I asked Roy Jenkins, then Home Secretary, if we could help by undertaking some joint project with the Home Office.

After Mary and I had discussed three alternatives with Margaret Clayton, then in charge of the Home Office Voluntary Services Unit (VSU), we agreed to provide all-the-year round accommodation for about thirty handicapped young people, to be used for fortnightly camps on the lines of the Six Circle Camps which had been so successful in Scotland. The Home Office were to provide an adequate grant for the first three years.

I anticipated no great difficulty in buying and equipping a large run-down house in a remote area of northern England but I could not have been more mistaken. After thirteen months of searching, nothing suitable had turned up. Eventually, in November 1976 I heard of a house for sale about six miles south-east of Kendal. I went with one of the committee on a bitterly cold day with thick fog, and by late afternoon I had bought Bendrigg Lodge. We have had many difficulties since then, not least over an adequate water supply, but in July 1978 the centre was opened at last, and has been fully booked ever since. The £30,000 we set aside for its total cost is now £70,000 and will reach at least £100,000 by the time everything has been finished. But we shall have a superbly equipped house and outbuilding in a beautiful position with seven acres of playing space. The project is named Northern Association for Community Care, and here again we are fortunate in having superb resident Wardens in Alan Tattersall and his wife who are on the way to making Bendrigg a unique and valuable institution.

During the formative period of the Trust, I got to know Charles Hills, then Governor of Polmont Borstal Institution, the largest of the Scottish Borstals. Charles had started the Six Circle camps and is an outstanding man from whom I have had much extremely wise advice. In May 1978, I spent a day with him at Polmont and thanks to his kindness I saw the whole operation in depth. At one stage, he picked out three boys, all about seventeen, and for half an hour I was alone with them in a small room. There were no preliminaries and so we started off from scratch – I told them my name was John and I was there because I was interested and wanted to learn. The half hour went far too quickly and although I got an extension it could only be limited. I asked them what they wanted from life and our discussion soon turned into a talk about things that mattered to them. I liked two of the boys very much and certainly did not dislike the third. As far as I could tell, they were being themselves after the first five minutes, and I left with the conviction that there was a great deal of good, certainly in two of them.

At the end of the visit I asked Charles if I might look at the files of these three. He replied 'Absolutely contrary to the rules, but I'm going to leave you with them for a quarter of an hour. Please, of course, do not make any notes and forget their names.' The result was to me absolutely horrifying. Each of them had been found guilty of at least eight serious charges, at various times. The three files together contained pretty well every crime that exists – mostly violent. The one I had been doubtful about had done some really appalling things. However, my belief that the other two were essentially decent young men – intelligent and in many ways basically kind – was not shaken.

The staff of the Borstal, most of whom I met during the day, were generally the best type of man and woman and the relationship with 'their boys' seemed to be excellent. It gave me a great deal to think about: my impressions were different from practically everything I had expected. Of course, one must remember that under Charles Hills, Polmont was an exceptional establishment. The discipline was obviously strict but the basic humanity shone through and I believe many a boy left Polmont a very different person. While so far there has been no direct outcome from our Trust as the result of this visit to Polmont, it is one of a number of contacts I have made in order to gather first-hand information about areas where we might try to help in the future.

The Trust has not done a great deal in Scotland but in 1978 to 1980 I took a fairly active, though strictly unofficial, part in helping to raise some £270,000 for an essential thirty-bed extension to St Columba's Hospice. This is the first specialist Hospice in Scotland to care for the dying and also for their immediate relatives. There is a superb home-nursing service covering Edinburgh and patients are only brought to the Hospice when home-nursing is no longer possible. The average length of stay at the Hospice is only twenty days. It is a happy and inspiring place to visit and one leaves with any conventional expectation completely reversed. Our Trust itself donated £30,000 and the fully equipped extension was opened in May 1980, free of any debt, without any professional fund raisers having been used. A unique, dedicated woman – Mrs Barbara Simpson – and several years of unremitting and intelligent work on her part achieved this result.

In Guernsey (see Chapter 16) we have felt it right to keep within the island as much as possible of the locally produced income. We have, therefore, backed several well managed local projects, including the Samaritans and the Spastics Society of which the late Ron Short (a distinguished senior official of the States) was Chairman. In 1978 we agreed to provide an additional building for Victoria Homes in St Peter Port, Guernsey in order to provide eight self-contained centrally heated flats for elderly people in need of modern, easily kept accommodation.

They can bring their own furniture and their treasures and the whole complex with its resident warden and her staff is a model of good and kindly care. We undertook to provide £70,000 but Mrs Poat who runs Victoria Homes is such a careful and efficient manager that the final cost to us was slightly less than this.

The creation of the Mary Kinross Charitable Trust in 1957 was one of the luckiest decisions I ever made. The development of the Trust's work over the past twenty-three years has brought happiness of a quality that I have not found in any other sphere, and when I shed the last of my business commitments, the Charitable Trust will absorb the whole of whatever working time I shall then be capable of. But, thereafter I hope that my daughter Fiona will be able to take over the role I have played so far. Looking beyond my children's lifetime, I greatly hope that each succeeding generation of my family will produce two or three men or women who will have the burning desire and the necessary capacity to take an active and wholly unselfish part in the work of the Trust, which should by then have a very substantial yearly income.

The Trust will, therefore, be a considerable responsibility to the Trustees but will also provide them with the means to embark on imaginative projects which, incidentally, should always be checked before proceeding with the Inland Revenue (Charitable Division) at Bootle who have invariably been exceedingly helpful to the Trust. We owe them many real kindnesses.

The Mary Kinross Charitable Trust is the principal legacy I shall leave behind me and the message I have for all my children and grandchildren and their descendants is: please cherish it and try to see that it does constructive work of genuine importance wherever there is a need which the Trust is capable of tackling. Race, colour, or creed should never be allowed to influence any decision. And the fact should never be overlooked that one can always help people best by making it possible for them to help themselves. To give anyone everything on a plate, leaving him no part to play and no need to employ his utmost resources of mind and body to help himself, is an infallible recipe for spoiling him. A century from now my descendants will undoubtedly be living in a world which I would find unrecognisable if I could return to it. Yet human nature will hardly have changed and it will still be true that to spoil a person is the surest way of ruining him.

# CHAPTER FIFTEEN

## *ICFC – General Manager: The Second Stage*

The Charitable Trust was a leisure-time activity. My work for ICFC continued. On 28 December 1953 when I came back after the Christmas break, I found that the sale of a business which I had negotiated (where ICFC had a substantial stake) had gone badly wrong during the holiday. Prior to Christmas, all that had remained to be done was for the Chairman we had appointed rather more than a year earlier, to sign the various documents. However, over the holiday, and without consulting anyone, he approached some competitors of the buyer whom he thought he knew and offered them the business at the same price. The proviso was that he was to remain Chairman, retaining his office, secretary and chauffeur.

On that Monday I found an unholy mess. Our buyers had been told by their competitors exactly what had occurred and they had withdrawn from the deal. The situation which resulted took no less than eight years to resolve and it was not until November 1961 that the business was sold to an entirely different buyer for £1.75 million. While this showed us a fair paper profit, it did not nearly compensate us for the tremendous amount of time absorbed by the affair during those eight years. We treated the man concerned extremely fairly. He remained on the Board for some time, where his knowledge of the business was useful. We appointed a new Chairman (a lawyer) and as his running-mate one of the leading accountants who was recognised as an outstanding 'business-doctor' at that time. Even after all these years I think it could be unwise to give the name of the company.

Towards the end of 1955, well before the business was sold, the man who had caused all the trouble was driving himself back to his weekend flat in one of the Sussex seaside resorts. He did this every Friday evening and therefore knew the road intimately. At a sharp bend he drove straight on at high speed and crashed into a large oak tree a few yards from the road. He was killed instantly and his Bentley was a write-off. The Coroner's verdict was accidental death and it may just be possible that he had dropped off to sleep. He left a completely insolvent estate. Bertram Ogle had known him intimately for most of his life and although this man had served a prison sentence between the two wars for misappropriation of clients' money (he was a Solicitor), Bertram had been convinced that he was the very rare exception who had behaved straightforwardly since then. Unfortunately, his private papers which came to light following his death, proved otherwise. As a result, I thereafter never accepted that a man who had committed a serious criminal act at a mature age could again be trusted, in so far as his business was concerned. It was the events of December 1953 that contributed to the cyst for which I had to undergo the operation in 1954.

On 1 April 1954, the eleventh day after the operation, I was able to write a two page memorandum for the ICFC Board proposing that we should join Hambros in a deal, to which Jack Hambro and I had put the finishing touches during the previous evening when he came to see me. This cleared up the late Alan P. Good's large holding in Associated British Engineering and Brush Electrical, and was approved by our Board a few days later. I gave this to Bill when he came to see me that evening and I must have written to him shortly after this for I have a letter from him dated Sunday 4 April: 'Thank you very much for your letter. I shall think over many times some of the things you have said. Your ideas about the future hit off very closely my own thoughts recently, especially about so organising ICFC that it shall be there for good and not in any respect as a personal tour de force. That was all right for creating it; now we want to make sure it is permanently knit into the financial structure. . . .

'I am devoutly thankful you have got over this hurdle – and so magnificently. I hope and believe that the next one or two months will be a wonderful time from which you will return greatly refreshed and strengthened.'

By the beginning of July 1954 I was again working on a full-time basis. We now had a staff of about a hundred, a portfolio of £27½ million, with more than 450 customers. We were also providing management for EDITH and guidance to Ship Mortgage. That autumn we asked Ernest Ralph to survey Bristol and several alternative areas with a view to expanding our branch network. The outcome was that in January 1955 we opened a sub-branch to Birmingham at Leicester, and a little later that year another in Leeds as a sub-branch to Manchester. In July 1955 the worst of the severe credit squeezes started, and although we fed both these branches with all the money we could lay our hands on, they had a very difficult start. However, the development of the branch system in the face of much initial opposition from our shareholders has been one of the principal factors in the long-term success of ICFC and our early expectations have been more than fulfilled.

In February 1955 in order to mark ICFC's tenth anniversary, the Board decided to hold a dinner party, possibly in July, to which the Chairmen of the Shareholding Banks and certain other persons who took a leading part in the formation of the Corporation would be invited. At the June meeting, however, Bill had to tell the Board that as several of the bank Chairmen had been unable to accept the invitation, the dinner for the shareholders had been postponed (in fact it was never held) and instead the date would be used for a dinner party for customers and others. I well remember the anger of our entire Board at this display of bad manners by the clearing banks. Bill was extremely reserved in what he said and just reported the bare facts, but the Board were in no doubt that the snub was deliberate, and that it was primarily due to Aldenham who was Chairman of the CLCB during the whole of 1955.

In spite of this deplorable happening, the Tenth Anniversary Dinner on 5 July 1955 at the Apothecaries Hall, near St Paul's, was a successful occasion. There were sixty-four people present: forty-five guests, six ICFC directors and thirteen staff. We invited many of our old customers and a wide variety of professional men. To round off the party we had a few distinguished men in various walks of life, such as Sir Henry Tizard. Not a single banker was present and two of the General Managers whom I knew later told me 'out of school' that they had been advised to find themselves otherwise engaged.

The toast of 'The Corporation' was proposed by Lord Macpherson of Dromochter, to which Bill responded. I then proposed the guests and W.H. Newton FCA (Newton & Co, Birmingham) and Denis Theed (Sir George Godfrey & Partners Ltd) responded.

On Wednesday 20 July 1955 I spent the day as the guest of Lord Macpherson on board the Port of London Authority launch on the occasion of the annual 'Down-River Inspection'. The Chairman of the PLA at that time was Viscount Waverley who in 1945 as Sir John Anderson had announced the creation of ICFC in the House of Commons. After mid-morning coffee, Waverley took me down to the cabin and there we talked together until lunch. Starting with the Macmillan Gap, he wanted to know how we had found that our function worked out in practice. He asked about the staff – their numbers and previous experience. At that time he was a director of the Midland Bank and he asked me some pointed questions about our relationship with the joint stock banks and the Bank of England. This was the last thing I wanted to discuss and I concentrated on the support we had had from Catto during our first four years, and the excellence of our relationship with Barclays during the whole of the ten years. Happily, Aldenham's name was not mentioned. In his somewhat pompous way, Waverley spoke warmly of what he felt ICFC had by then achieved.

During the summer of 1955, Bill had a number of talks with Gordon Richardson (later Governor of the Bank of England from 1973) who had then decided to retire from the Bar and come to work in the City. Bill and I had originally met Gordon in Montagu Gedge's chambers and because I had known Monty well during the previous twenty-five years, I had seen a certain amount of Gordon. I had always liked him, and Bill and I both regarded his ability as quite outstanding. On 10 August when I was on holiday in Scotland, Bill wrote to tell me that Gordon was 'definitely coming to us . . . G.R. is to come in at 3 p.m. on Monday, the 15th to discuss details, and I am hoping you will be there'.

The three of us met as arranged; the outcome being that Gordon joined us on 1 September 1955. His initial salary was £4,000 per annum, a high figure for us at that time, and his position, as minuted, was 'Personal Assistant to the General Manager'; though a more accurate title would have been unofficial Deputy Chairman. He was soon immersed in the final stages of the most difficult case we had then encountered and he negotiated the sale of Wood Bros to Readson, handling it brilliantly.

It is ironic that when our accounts for the year to 31 March 1955 were published the relationship with our shareholders was at its lowest ebb. Our profit, before tax, had risen from £854,086 to £1,291,140, while no less than 82% of the £4½ million paid out for new investments during the year came from repayments and provisions. Our shareholders by then had no longer any cause for concern, though the fact that we were now firmly established did not find favour with the die-hards amongst them.

Our main problem during much of 1956 and 1957 was again shortage of funds. We were still entirely dependent on our shareholders for cash to expand the scale of our operations, and the strains imposed on all of our senior staff in trying to bridge the gap between our inadequate funds and the demands on them from the flow of eligible businesses were never ending. We had to scrape the barrel in all sorts of ways. For example, in January 1957, taking advantage of the time lag between the approval and completion of every case, the Board agreed to our accepting 'excess' new business, provided the total of approvals did not exceed by more than £750,000 the amount of our current resources.

Thus we continued to live from hand to mouth until the 'new deal' in 1959 put an end to this way of life.

In January 1955 I had three hectic days when control of a small quoted hire purchase company, Mutual Finance Ltd (MF) in which we had built up a substantial holding in conjunction with Lord Blackford's various investment trusts, was courted by four different parties. Limerick was chairman of this company. MF was conservatively managed and towards the end of 1954 it attracted the attention of several merchant bankers who knew that Percy Livesey, the company's chief executive, was shortly due to retire. On Monday 10 January 1955 matters came to a head and I realised that we would either have to sell our minority holding, or make a take-over bid for the company, which unfortunately was impossible.

Limerick and Livesey asked me to take charge of the negotiations and during those three days all four buyers were in continuous contact with me. In a delicate way, I played each one off against the other. On Wednesday, Fitz Graham-Watson spent most of the day in my room at Drapers Gardens listening to the ebb and flow of the telephone conversations (Rowe & Pitman were MF's brokers). Lionel Fraser had demanded an option for Tillings until noon on Wednesday but this I refused. Eventually, around 5.30 p.m., it was all over with a firm bid from Tillings at 20/-, a high price on any reckoning and nearly double the recent market level. Fitz and I met Helbert Wagg the next morning and agreed a press statement which made no reference to ICFC's part in the matter. We made a substantial profit from this deal, as did Keith Blackford's trusts. I had a warm letter of thanks from him and a beautiful carriage clock as a memento of those three days, which incidentally I thoroughly enjoyed.

By early in 1957 Gordon Richardson, who had joined us in 1955, had received various attractive offers from some of the leading merchant banks and others. In the normal course of events, Gordon ought to have succeeded Bill as Chairman of ICFC. Gordon and I had discussed the future with complete frankness and I had told him that I would be most happy to work with him as Chairman, during the limited period during which I wished to continue as full-time General Manager. However, when it came down to brass tacks, Gordon found that Bill, who was then a vigorous seventy-one, had no intention of relinquishing the Chairmanship. I spent an evening with Gordon discussing the merits of the various offers he had received and it seemed to me that Schroders emerged as clearly the most attractive of these. In March 1957 he left us to go there, greatly to my regret.

This made me realise that if we were to lose Peter Wreford or Rocky we should be very thin at the top. Peter had succeeded Julian as Manager of EDITH in May 1955 and was then making an outstanding success of this key position. I wanted to promote both of them. While Bill had the highest regard for them, he felt sure neither would leave and was totally opposed to any change in the status quo until the 'new deal' had been negotiated. On this occasion my fears proved to be justified for at the end of December 1958 Peter resigned to go into business on his own account, much as I had done in 1933. Then in June 1959, Rocky resigned. Undoubtedly, he would have succeeded me in a comparatively short time but he had come to feel that he needed to have a period of complete independence as a practising chartered accountant. His departure after fourteen years of outstanding service was the most severe loss we had suffered up to that time. The bond between all three of us has, however, remained unbroken. Peter and Rocky are both trustees of The Mary Kinross Charitable Trust. These losses resulted in our having to look for my successor outside ICFC, which in turn resulted in my remaining General Manager until 30 September 1961 – two years longer than I really wanted. I had hoped to hand over to Rocky once the 'new deal' was completed and start my new life while I was still only fifty-five.

Meantime, the scope of our activities was increasing. In February 1957 and again in November 1958, in conjunction with Robert Fleming & Co, Ship Mortgage arranged the financing of a number of tankers then being built in the UK for British Petroleum. Two companies with nominal capitals were then formed as vehicles for this operation – Tanker Charter Co Ltd and Clyde Charter Co Ltd and loans totalling £52 million were raised. Their average life was about eighteen years and they were placed at rates of 6½% and 6⅜% without any Stock Exchange quotation. Flemings arranged the placings, the management of both companies remained with Ship Mortgage, and after Sir James Milne's death I took over the Chairmanship of Tanker Charter and later I became Chairman of Clyde Charter at its formation.

I had taken an active part in the negotiation of these loans with Lord Strathalmond, and Duncan Anderson, then respectively Chief Executive and Chief Accountant of BP, and a couple of redoubtable Scots. Richard Fleming also played an active part, and this led to a warm friendship between us which was only broken by his death in 1977. It also resulted in an invitation to me to become Advisor to the BP Pension Fund in January 1970 and subsequently, in May 1973, a member of the Investment Committee of the BP Pension Fund, on which I served until December 1974 – just before my seventy-first birthday. This brought me into regular contact with the top brass at BP and proved to be one of the happiest of my outside occupations.

The scheme which had been evolved for financing the new tankers was novel at that time. The real security for the loans was bare boat charters from BP designed to service the interest and capital repayments over the life of the loans. This method resulted in no charge appearing in BP's balance sheet; and not even an auditor's note in respect of these massive loans. It worked without a hitch for the next eighteen years.

On 1 March 1955 Bill had an urgent message from the then Governor of the Bank of England (Cobbold) to say that he would like to see him before the end of that day. So, breaking off a Ship Mortgage board meeting, he went over to the Bank. When he returned after a short visit he came into my room and carefully shut the door. Obviously something that pleased him had occurred. Bill then told me in absolute secrecy that he was practically certain that I was to be given a CBE. It would probably take rather more than a year to emerge from the pipeline, he said. (I imagine at that moment the Governor's formal support was necessary.)

On 27 November 1957 I had a letter from the Prime Minister's private secretary telling me that the PM had it in mind to recommend that I be given an OBE and would this be agreeable. I showed this to Bill whose face fell: clearly he was completely unprepared for this turn of events. Naturally, I accepted and nine years later my CBE arrived, due, I always felt, to Lord Sherfield who by then was Chairman of ICFC.

This resulted in my going twice to Buckingham Palace and I was fortunate in that the Queen herself presided at both Investitures. These are beautifully organised and the whole ceremony is superbly managed, taking about an hour and three quarters. When your name is called and you step forward to face the Queen, the talk you then have with her seems unhurried. In 1958, Mary brought Elizabeth and in 1967, when one was allowed to bring two children, we had my eldest daughter, Mary and our son Robin. How fortunate I have been that all my six children like each other.

ICFC's first public issue of £10 million 5½% debenture stock at 98½% took place on 23 July 1958 while I was in the Middlesex Hospital after another operation as a result of an unlucky accident in Guernsey. It was comfortably over-subscribed with a margin of some £3,650,000 and Kit Hoare was in high spirits when he came to see me in hospital afterwards. Although he was then elderly, Kit was still a force in the City and was a remarkable man.

At this time, in addition to his responsibilities at ICFC, Bill was chairman of the Kuwait Investment Board. This was an interesting assignment and on several occasions Bill went to Kuwait as the personal guest of the Ruler, Abdulla Al-Salim Al-Sabah, whom he greatly respected. On one occasion, when two of the many younger members of the Ruler's family were in London, Bill had arranged a small dinner party so that they could meet a few leading City personalities. On the day in question, Bill developed a high temperature and asked me to act as host in his place. The invitations were for 7 p.m. at a private room in the Charing Cross Hotel. The half a dozen other guests, all of whom I knew, duly arrived but no Arabs appeared. Eventually, about 8.40 p.m., I gave up and we all sat down to our meal. About an hour later, the door quietly opened and in came two rather charming young men. No explanations, and after a slightly awkward few seconds, no embarrassment. We never discovered the reason; but my belief is that it was simply due to their conception of time being on a totally different level.

At the end of June 1959 Jon Foulds joined us as a Trainee. He is now a Director and Chief Executive of our parent company, Finance for Industry Ltd. A mutual friend had introduced him to Guy Drummond who was impressed, and wrote to Rocky. I saw Jon in London on 23 March and Bill joined us for the last part of this meeting. We both greatly liked him. Jon was then twenty-six and quickly made his mark with us. After a spell as Manager of the Manchester branch he was brought to London where he had rapid and well merited promotion.

Rocky's decision to leave had been taken about the middle of March 1959. The 'new deal' had just been completed and it was obvious that with the removal of the restraints previously imposed by our shareholders, a period of rapid growth lay ahead, which was going to necessitate a much larger organisation. During my period as General Manager, I was in close touch with all that was going on, and for some twelve years this intimate management structure had proved effective. However, it seemed to me that under the new conditions which lay ahead and following Rocky's departure, the appointment of a man with different experience to that of our existing senior staff was necessary.

Once Bill accepted the fact that I wanted to hand over, things moved quickly; we agreed that we must look outside, and to my mind one person then clearly emerged. This was Larry Tindale, then thirty-eight, and the youngest of the McClelland Moore partners, one of the leading firms of accountants in Glasgow. He had worked closely with Alec Barrie, whom I had come to know intimately. Alec had the highest regard for Larry's character and ability and I found that Bill, who had met him in connection with Marchon when Larry was acting for DATAC, saw him in exactly the same light. Most happily, Larry himself responded to the idea, so with Barrie's blessing and thanks to the unselfish attitude of the other partners who certainly did not want to lose Larry, matters were arranged. He joined us as an Assistant General Manager on 1 October 1959 and this soon proved to be an outstandingly successful appointment. By March 1960 we had the necessary staff available for more branches and in less than a year three were opened in Cardiff, Bristol and Glasgow, making a total of eight.

The flow of profits from the realisation of equity stakes acquired in previous years was now accelerating and for the year to 31 March 1960 the net profit before tax was £1,843,155, a rise of £454,978. During the previous fifteen years, we had financed more than 900 companies and there were then 660 open accounts on our books. 1960 was a happy year for ICFC. The brakes were off at last and a period of rapid expansion lay ahead. Larry and I had established an excellent relationship from the start and as the months went by I curtailed my visits to branches, leaving these increasingly to him.

The last ICFC issue of which I took personal charge was the offer for sale of 1,925,000 ordinary shares of 5/- in British Belting and Asbestos Co Ltd (now the BBA Group) at 18/- per share. We had been associated with this fine Yorkshire company for several years and I had established a close relationship with Sir William Fenton, the Executive Chairman. This was obviously going to be one of the best new industrial issues of the year and I had asked Cazenoves to act as brokers. At the final meeting at Drapers Gardens when it came to the price fixing, I asked Luke Meinertzhagen if he was content with 17/6d, which we had virtually settled upon. He said that he was and to my surprise added that he was confident Cazenoves could underwrite the issue at 18/-. After a slightly awkward few moments, the price was fixed at 18/- for I felt that I could not ask Fenton to give away 6d a share, which represented £48,000.

By late Wednesday afternoon, the 29 June, it appeared that the issue was not going to be fully subscribed and Bill and I agreed that if the gap were to be only a small one, we would put in applications to cover it rather than call upon underwriters for a tiny percentage of their commitments.

At 10.30 a.m. the next morning (Thursday) the Midland gave us a figure which left only a narrow gap. I authorised applications from us to cover this and agreed a press announcement for the mid-day editions which stated that the issue had been marginally over-subscribed. Then at 1.35 p.m. the Manager of the New Issue Department of the Midland telephoned me to say they had just discovered that their 10.30 a.m. total had been overstated by 180,000 shares.

It was a devastating admission. Bill was lunching in the City and I sent him a handwritten note telling him that the shortage was then 111,200 shares – or about £100,000. I asked for his agreement to our doing another £50,000 to £60,000 adding 'Obviously there can now be no turning back'. When the messenger returned Bill had written on my note 'Yes – agree absolutely'. Luke pulled out all the stops and before long an active market at a small premium enabled all the surplus shares to be sold. This was a one off situation which luckily had a happy ending, but it could have been very different.

Our advantageous lease of 7 Drapers Gardens was due to end in September 1961 when our landlord, the Drapers' Company had decided to invite tenders for the re-development of the site (it now forms part of the tower block which is occupied by the National Westminster Bank). During the previous four or five years we had explored a number of possibilities of owning our Head Office in the City. Both Bill and I felt that because of the large number of offices then being built, we could afford to wait. In this we were mistaken and although we joined with Trollope & Colls in tendering for the Drapers Gardens site, we were considerably outbid by Harry Hyams in March 1961. By then the property boom was in full spate and our time was running out.

I talked to my friend Norman Wates, Chairman of Wates Ltd who were about to erect a five-storey office block on a site at 4–5 Copthall Avenue which they had acquired from a City livery company at a fixed ground rent of £10,000 p.a. for 99 years. Although Wates were not prepared to sell us the head lease, they were willing to give us a tenure of 42 years. The initial rental required was £2.12.6d per foot, then a high figure even for what was a choice site. However, it was by then the best prospect we had and I went to lunch with Norman and his brother Ronald at their Streatham headquarters to discuss it.

Norman and I knew each other too well and after talking for nearly two hours I had got precisely nowhere. Wates Ltd had more than one other potential tenant and when Norman took me out to my car the rent was still £2.12.6d. As we parted I said to him 'if you do nothing else you really must give us the first 21 years at the starting rent' and as we shook hands Norman assented. At the time, I felt very disappointed by this outcome, but nine years later, when we came to buy the head lease from Wates (following Norman's untimely death) and then to sell the building, what had been agreed during those few seconds accounted for several million pounds of our sale price of £15¼ million. We had invited tenders and were extraordinarily fortunate, for the timing of this sale had coincided almost exactly with the peak of the property boom and the fund which bought it from us as their 'flagship' re-sold it several years later for about half of what they had paid us for it.

## CHAPTER SIXTEEN

# *Guernsey – A Happy Diversion*

A very happy family holiday in Guernsey in August and September 1958 led to a development on the island which I could not have foreseen and which was ultimately of considerable importance to The Mary Kinross Charitable Trust. During the second week of our holiday I met Sir Ambrose Sherwill, the Bailiff, and we found that we had much in common. At that time, it was possible to buy property in the Channel Islands which at one's death could be isolated from one's UK estate, so that this part would be free of death duties. There was, however, no tax advantage from this arrangement during one's lifetime.

Sir Ambrose introduced me to several of the leading people on the Island and was in general extraordinarily kind to me and my family. The outcome was that I formed a Guernsey company – Island Properties Ltd – which bought a large derelict site in a prime position in St Peter Port for £20,000 on which a four-storey complex of offices and shops was built at a cost of over £200,000. At Mary's suggestion it was called The Albany and at that time it was the largest office building in the island.

On 1 August 1962 a Tory Chancellor (Selwyn Lloyd) scrubbed this death duty loophole: rightly I believe. My first thought was to sell out and withdraw from Guernsey. But by then I had got to know the Island and had come to feel that the democratic non-party government and the sound economy, with its balanced budget, were based on lasting values. So I decided to leave Island Properties untouched but, as it was now going to save no tax when I died, I gave the controlling interest in the company to The Mary Kinross Charitable Trust. This was a fortunate decision. Though the original motive had been to save some death duty, the Charitable Trust now possesses an exceedingly sound investment, while I have gained several close friendships in the island which I cherish.

At one of our last meetings in 1958, Sir Ambrose told me that he and some of his colleagues felt that the island needed an investment trust. There were then no local stockbrokers. Jersey had a successful trust and he assured me that the States (the Guernsey parliament) would welcome the creation of one in Guernsey. I felt grateful for the time he had unselfishly given me. So when he enquired if I could help them with the investment trust project I willingly agreed.

On 9 September 1958, at Sir Ambrose's instigation, Harry Broughton (then Senior Partner of one of the leading firms of Guernsey Chartered Accountants) came to see me in London. This successful meeting set the seal on the formation of The Investment Trust of Guernsey Ltd (ITG) which was registered on 3 January 1959 with an authorised capital of £500,000. I felt it would be prudent to have a second UK director with investment trust experience so I invited Hamish Falconer, senior partner of Martin Currie & Co (one of the leading investment trust management firms in Edinburgh) to join me and he remained on the board for twenty-one years. The original board in 1959 was H.G. Broughton FCA (Chairman), Jurat W.F. Corbet, Advocate J.E.L. Martel, Hamish and myself. The trust, whose net assets exceeded £12 million by 1980 and which had by then increased its dividend in twenty out of its twenty-one years of life, has been run with the minimum of overhead expenditure for its purpose is to provide a genuine service for Guernsey residents.

In late June 1959, Harry Broughton and I were leaving his office in Lefebvre Street in Guernsey running late in a day packed with meetings. Because I was in too much of a hurry I slipped when stepping off the pavement and fell heavily with my left leg doubled up. In falling I had completely severed my quadriceps, which are the main muscles just above the knee. The pain was worse than anything I had previously experienced and I literally lay in the gutter unable to move. A St John's Ambulance quickly arrived, and the two surgeons at the Princess Elizabeth Hospital where I was taken advised having the necessary operation in London. Two days later I was taken by Reg Blanchford (the Commandant of St John's in Guernsey) on a stretcher which was fitted into a normal BEA flight.

The next morning, Philip Newman, then Senior Orthopaedic Surgeon at the Middlesex Hospital reunited the severed muscle. My leg was then in plaster for six and a half weeks. I spent eighteen days in July in a side ward of the John Astor ward while the heat wave went on and on. When the superintendent of the Hospital – Brigadier Hardy Roberts – saw the volume of office papers I was receiving he had a direct external telephone installed for me. The side ward became known to the medical and nursing staff as 'ICFC's West End office': by no means an inaccurate description! On the 8 September after a very happy family holiday at Vitznau on the Lake of Lucerne I was back in the office, hobbling about but feeling very fit. Thanks to Philip Newman's skill I have had a normal left leg ever since.

Seven years after these events, in November 1966 the ICFC constitution was amended to allow the Corporation to operate in the British Isles instead of Great Britain and this enabled ICFC as well to do business in the Channel Islands for the first time. In January 1969 we formed a wholly-owned subsidiary in Guernsey and in September 1972 our business had grown to an extent which necessitated the formation of a second company in Jersey.

During the Seventies, the tempo of our business in the Channel Islands steadily increased. In August 1975 I heard that Rothschilds wanted to sell their 50% share of the Guernsey company which owned St Julian's Court, the large office they and Hambros had built to high standards on a prime site in St Peter Port. The other 50% of the capital was owned by Hambros Bank. I went to see Michael Cominos who was Chairman of Rothschilds' Guernsey company, and whom I knew well. After several friendly meetings I bought their shares in St Julian's Properties in September at what seemed to be a very reasonable price and has indeed proved to be so with the passage of time.

During 1980, our ICFC Channel Island portfolio crossed the £10 million mark, while The Investment Trust of Guernsey Ltd, now with some 900 shareholders, continues to set up new records. More than thirty shareholders usually come to ITG's annual general meetings which we try to make as interesting and informative as possible. They last for fully an hour-and-a-half ending with tea and biscuits and a general exchange of views. The goodwill generated by all this is, I believe, of inestimable value.

## CHAPTER SEVENTEEN

# *ICFC – Executive Director*

I formally retired as General Manager of ICFC on 30 September 1961, being succeeded by Larry Tindale and Arthur English as joint General Managers. However, in October 1964 Arthur retired and Larry became sole General Manager. I had already been elected an Executive Director of ICFC on 25 July 1961 to fill the vacancy caused by the retirement of Lord Dudley Gordon. This established a precedent, as it was the first time that a member of staff had been invited to join the board. So far as directorships outside ICFC were concerned, I confined myself entirely to investment trusts at that time. In July 1961 I became a director of Scottish Ontario Investment Co at the invitation of Hamish Falconer, its chairman, and a director of several other investment trusts. Then in March 1962 Hamish and I revived a dormant Martin Currie company, North British Canadian Investment Co as a specialist trust managed by ICFC to invest in the shares of small UK companies. I joined this board at the outset, and these two appointments resulted in my going back to Edinburgh ten times in each year for the next eighteen years.

In March 1962 I also joined the board of ICFC's own London Atlantic Investment Trust, succeeding Bill Piercy as chairman on his death in 1966. Later in 1962 when Michael Bucks of Rothschilds invited me to join the original board of Equity Income Trust, a Rothschild trust formed in July of that year, I accepted and so began an association with Rothschilds which still continues. In August 1967 when a sister company, Equity Consort Investment Trust, was created I also became a director of that company. Years before I had come to feel that the good Jew and the Scot have many common traits. Neither ever gives up if he believes in the rightness of what he is trying to achieve. Both want absolute value for their money. But if what they want is rare and of supreme quality both will be prepared to pay a high price – the Jew probably outbidding the Scot. Both can be extremely generous on occasions, as well as mean. Once the intense bargaining is over the deal will go through with a minimum of trouble for mutual integrity rules both their actions.

Dealing with a first-class Jew is utterly different from dealing with a

Celt whether Scottish, Irish, or Welsh. There is a streak of treachery in the Celtic character and although there are obviously many exceptions the fact that 'I've been welshed' (meaning I have been cheated) has become part of our language is significant. For a Celt to cheat an Englishman or any non-Celt is usually regarded by them as smart, not dishonest.

At one time the Rothschilds invited me to fill a vacant place on an advisory committee to some of the Lowson Trusts. By then this was a burden to them and they were completely frank about it. Leopold de Rothschild took the meetings, which discussed investment policy and focused attention on some of the least desirable holdings. Michael Bucks and I were the other two members of the Committee. Then there was the Lowson contingent, and quite often Denys Lowson would come himself. Some of the meetings generated a good deal of heat and it was remarkable that Lowson ever agreed to my appointment barely twenty years after the Texas Land affair. By then I knew Michael Bucks well and the most rewarding outcome of these meetings was my getting to know Leopold de Rothschild who to my mind is the most delightful member of the present generation of the family.

It is not surprising that when the Bank of England wanted to have a Rothschild as a member of its Court, they invited Leopold. He is incidentally, a keen bird-watcher and, although I am not, we share a love of the far North-West of Sutherland and some of the inns he frequents, which are also known to me, are perfect examples of basic simplicity.

Evelyn de Rothschild I hardly know. We once tried to do some business when the sensible thing would have been to have amalgamated the two Glasgow evening papers. He was on the board of the *Daily Express* which owned one of these while I was then a member of the 'SUITS' board which owned the other. But the two conversations we had came to nothing.

With Jacob Rothschild I have had a fruitful relationship which has given me unalloyed pleasure. Jacob is one of those rare beings capable of original thought. His financial flair and sense of timing are superb. Though, like everyone else, he has made his mistakes, the proof of his flair is the outstanding success of RIT. He and I were until recently the two honorary financial advisers to the Royal College of Surgeons of England.

In March 1965 Richard Fleming, then the head of Robert Fleming & Co, invited me to join him on the board of the newly created Imperial Investments, the wholly-owned investment trust of the Imperial

Tobacco Group, and in size by far the largest investment company in the UK. He had been appointed Chairman of this company and wanted to have one colleague from the City, the rest of the Board being all Imps men. In practice, these outside activities have worked extremely well. Rothschilds and Imperial Investments (where I succeeded Richard as Chairman when he died in 1977) have asked me to continue, although I am now seventy-seven.

During the past nineteen years, I have seen at first hand the varied investment techniques of these four groups (Flemings, Martin Currie, Rothschilds and ICFC) and I believe the cross-fertilisation of ideas is valuable to everyone.

Meanwhile, I had been branching out in other directions, too. During the autumn of 1961 I devoted a lot of time to discussions with Sir John Benn, Chairman and Managing Director of UK Provident Institution, which led to the formation of Technical Development Capital Ltd on 9 January 1962, with a capital of £2 million. On 1 February 1962 a prospectus for TDC was issued and thanks to Cazenove's placing power and to Benn's enthusiasm and hard work, all the shares were subscribed by institutional investors, ICFC taking a 5% stake. The gist of the prospectus was contained in two sentences: 'The company has been formed because there is a good deal of evidence that, whereas this country is second to none in inventiveness, we are slower than some of our foreign competitors in applying this to everyday industry. One reason is the present lack of finance for bringing technical developments and inventions, which have passed the initial research stage, into commercial production and on to the market.' As this was obviously an area which concerned ICFC, Bill Piercy urged me to fall in with Benn's wish that I should join the TDC board and also become a member of the board committee which was the equivalent of ICFC's Cases Committee.

TDC's board of seven consisted of Benn as non-executive Chairman; Professor Sir John Baker, the Head of the Department of Engineering, University of Cambridge; Lord Catto of Morgan Grenfell; Edward Hawthorn, a highly qualified engineer and the only whole time director; myself; Lord McCorquodale of Newton, a colleague of John Benn's on UK Provident Institution; and Jeremy Smith of Smith St Aubyn, the Discount House. The 'Cases' Committee was composed of Benn, Hawthorn, Smith and myself.

As any newly formed company with money to lend discovers, there was a rush of applications in the early stages and the weekly 'Cases' Committee took a lot of time. I was the only one of us with practical experience of the type of applications we were receiving, and these early cases were of very poor quality. After three months we had done no business and Benn was becoming restive. I wanted us to give ourselves six months to get our eye in before doing any business, unless a really good case was offered, which unfortunately never materialised. Benn unwillingly agreed to this but by the winter of 1963/64 relationships within the board were strained. Catto, Jeremy Smith and I saw most of our problems in much the same light. Hawthorn, who was an able man, had a pretty impossible role and Benn, who was an idealist, was frankly out of his depth.

After two years, I felt that we had not achieved anything meaningful. We had just had a stormy board meeting where I had greatly annoyed Benn and McCorquodale by opposing a proposal which they both wanted to follow up. I felt strongly that it was only a question of a short time before the proposed company would be in deep water. We struggled on at TDC for the rest of 1964 but by the end of that year I again had far too much on my plate. Hugh Weeks most unselfishly agreed to take my place in TDC and on 2 February 1965 I resigned. Hugh had been a director of ICFC since 1960 and also a director of FCI since 1956 (he was the only person who was ever on the boards of both corporations at the same time). He was a particularly pleasant and able person and he and I have remained firm friends to this day. A distinguished economist, he was deservedly knighted in 1966.

Hugh's experience in TDC was much the same as mine. A year later TDC's losses were rising and the institutional shareholders were becoming restive. The obvious solution was for ICFC to take over TDC, and on 28 June 1966 an offer at a price agreed by the auditors of both concerns of 6/9d per £1 share, 10/- paid, I was made and in due course ICFC acquired 100% of the TDC shares. Had we not resisted the temptation in our early period at TDC of doing some business simply for the purpose of getting TDC airborne, the loss to the original shareholders would have been much greater.

Since then a great deal of effort has been devoted to TDC and by 31 March 1978 some £17 million had been invested in about 150 cases. ICFC feels – absolutely rightly I believe – that it must try to fulfil TDC's original purpose, but sadly I have to say that if TDC had been a separate organisation with normal overheads it would have been 'in the red' for at least the first fourteen years of its existence.

It was also during 1962, in the summer, that my friend L.J. Williams, then Chairman of City of London Real Property Company (CLRP), asked me to join this board. I was doubtful about my suitability, for I knew practically nothing about property, but after meeting the board and hearing the warm invitation repeated, I accepted. This was a fine company which owned some of the best office property in London and I learned much about the property world as a result. In March 1969, the Land Securities Investment Trust Ltd (LS) and two other property companies made competitive take-over bids for CLRP. With Sir John Mellor of the Pru, I was a member of a small committee of the board which dealt with these. Eventually, LS won the battle while we secured good terms for our shareholders.

I had been Bill Piercy's alternate Director in Ship Mortgage Finance since it was formed and in October 1963 I was elected to the board and remained a director until I retired in 1975 when I was seventy. With the advent in June 1967 of the Government scheme to guarantee loans to facilitate new building in UK yards, Ship Mortgage's normal business was killed, but we were asked to undertake the vetting of these applications as agents for the Department of Industry. During the last six years of my service with Ship Mortgage, I was a member of the committee of three people who did this; the others being Lord Sherfield, then Chairman of Ship Mortgage, and Sir Michael Wilson of Lloyds Bank, who followed Jeremy Smith. We had applications from all over the world, from Hong Kong to Athens, which by 1973 had reached a total of £100 million. The outcome was a large volume of work for British shipyards during those years which would otherwise have gone abroad.

In my last years as General Manager of ICFC, and for some time thereafter, I continued to do a certain amount of speaking; for instance, at various conferences of the British Institute of Management. From the earlier days I remember particularly the National Conference in Brighton in November 1958. Much of what I then forecast about the likely future course of inflation, the rise in importance of the institutional investor, and the deterioration of the jobbing system, has now come to pass. I had suggested at that November 1958 conference that the then popular conglomerates would prove to be a passing fashion, saying to the 500 people present 'It behoves the shoemaker to stick to his last. Few financiers make good industrialists, and equally few chemists or engineers can feel at home in, say, a chain store. Thus the specious arguments put forth about the advantages of diversification lack real conviction.'

By 1964 ICFC had invested £100 million pounds. On 30 January 1964 there was a short ceremony in Piercy House, our then headquarters, when Bill presented a new customer with his cheque, which took us up to the magic figure. After the lunch which followed, I made a presentation to Bill on behalf of the senior staff. But our horizons were still broadening. In July 1964, Robert Gray of Parsons and Gordon Simpson of Bell Lawrie Robertson, both of whom I knew well, came to tell me it had been decided to sell Glasgow Industrial Finance Ltd. This was a company formed by a number of investment trusts (mainly in Glasgow) in 1946 to create a Scottish issuing house. The company had done some £26 million of business during the eighteen years of its existence but it had not in itself been very profitable, and it had been decided either to dispose of the business or wind it up.

I felt it was genuinely important to Scotland that the business should be continued, with its ownership in neutral hands independent of any of the London merchant bankers, and ICFC seemed well suited for the role of owner. The purchase price was about £25,000 and with some difficulty we then changed the name of the company to Scottish Industrial Finance Ltd (SIF) and increased the capital to £250,000. We also registered two companies in order to protect the names of Glasgow Industrial Finance and Edinburgh Industrial Finance.

The press announcement on 4 August 1964 emphasised that while all three companies would be housed in ICFC's offices in Glasgow and Edinburgh, their business would be separately conducted from that of ICFC. W.B. Kirkpatrick and H.G. Usher were appointed Managers in Glasgow and Edinburgh respectively. The boards of the three companies consisted of myself as Chairman, Alec Mackenzie CA of Glasgow, then a director of ICFC, and Sir Hugh Watson LLD, DKS of Edinburgh, one of the senior partners of Dundas & Wilson CS and the Deputy Governor of the British Linen Bank.

The original Glasgow Industrial Finance had been managed by Sir Alistair Murray and his brother Jim and had done very little business for some time. I went to Scotland immediately, determined to put SIF on the map. It was akin to starting from scratch but I had two first rate managers and we formed an effective team. Harry Usher resigned after a while in order to start his own manufacturing business (of which he made a great success) and Bill then became sole Manager of SIF.

For the rest of 1964 my diary is strewn with visits to Scotland. I combed Edinburgh and Glasgow and then went to Aberdeen, Inverness, Dundee and even to places such as Arbroath. While there were enough professional men in Scotland possessing the necessary specialised knowledge for issue work, there was no printer who could produce overnight proofs of a prospectus with the speed and accuracy which is vital. During 1964, Outrams with Bill Kirkpatrick's help, created a department in Glasgow which was able to provide this service. I wanted all the work involved in a public issue to be carried through in Scotland and by the autumn of 1964, for the first time, this became possible. Before long, potential issue business began to be brought to us. It was very reminiscent of the early days of the Cheviot Trust. It was also the focus of one of the most interesting take-over battles of my life. On Monday evening 7 September 1964 I had a telephone call at about 9.30 p.m. from Sir Hugh Fraser (later Lord Fraser of Allander). I was just back from a family holiday in Orkney and five days before this call the Thomson Organisation had made a take-over bid for George Outram & Co Ltd, of which Sir Hugh was then Deputy Chairman and which owned a number of Scottish papers including the *Glasgow Herald*. Sir Hugh had decided to fight the bid and the purpose of his call was to invite me to act as his advisor. I accepted straight away, seeing this as a remarkable opportunity for SIF which could handle the defence or a counterbid for Outrams on behalf of one of Sir Hugh's other companies.

What then followed remains unique in the entire history of take-over battles. The struggle for Outram went on for fifty-two days, and we beat off five bids. In the latter stages, Lord Thomson engaged Warburgs, a merchant bank which up to then had never lost a take-over battle. Their fifth and final offer of 31/7½d in cash for each Outram share valued the company at £8,294,383 compared with our offer on behalf of Scottish & Universal Investments Ltd (SUITS) of £7,343,644, largely in paper and £950,739 less than the Thomson cash offer. But Warburgs and Thomson were too late and we won the final round, though by a very narrow margin. After it was all over, I wrote a detailed account of the operation at the suggestion of Professor S.G. Checkland, Professor of Economic History in the University of Glasgow which now has this document.

Two matters described in this memorandum proved of great significance in determining the outcome of the battle. The first was that in the early stages I compiled a short list of brokers in Scotland whom we had reason to believe had clients holding Outram shares. From this list I eliminated the firms whom, after the most careful enquiry, I knew, or suspected, were in touch with Thomson. I then had a new direct telephone line installed on my desk in London which was constantly manned during and after Stock Exchange dealing hours, and whose number was known only to these 'safe' brokers. Whenever any of them received a selling order in Outrams he telephoned this number and we dealt direct at the middle market price. In this way the Broker got a slightly better price for his client, we got the shares, and the market was unaware of any transaction. We succeeded in keeping this secret throughout the whole operation. On one day towards the end I had bought over 100,000 Outram shares in this way. By then my intelligence network was letting me estimate pretty accurately the number of shares Thomson had bought by about 3 p.m. each day. On this particular day my estimate of his purchases was slightly under 5,000 shares and I decided to feed into his brokers' lap 6,000 of our own precious shares. A day's 'bag' that put him into the five figure bracket would, I hoped, reduce the risk of Warburgs trying to find out if there was any reason for the dearth of shares trading in the market and possibly discovering the extent of our purchases.

The second matter was sheer luck. On 12 October, Patrick Sergeant, the eminent City Editor of the *Daily Mail*, telephoned to say he would like to come to see me, and, as was always my custom, I readily agreed to this. After we had gone over the state of play, he came to the real point of his visit: he asked me directly what percentage of the Outram capital we then held. I said at once that, while I was anxious to be as helpful as I could, this was obviously something I could not discuss. Turning on his considerable charm, Sergeant then said, 'Perhaps it isn't necessary – I have good reason to believe you now have around 30%.'

I have – unfortunately – always blushed too easily when embarrassed and, at that moment, I certainly felt so. This figure, the holy of holies, was known only to Sir Hugh, myself and two or three people. At that moment, the true figure was fully 40% but the question was so near the bone that I felt my colour rising. Sergeant saw it too, and drew the understandable conclusion that he had scored a bull's eye. He smiled broadly and got up to go. Realising what was happening, I said absolutely nothing, sitting quite still, and ceasing to attempt to control my face – it had suddenly become an asset in those few seconds!

The next day, Sergeant in his *Daily Mail* column told his readers, 'Sir Hugh has accumulated 30% of Outram' and such was his reputation that this was widely accepted as being accurate and it influenced Warburgs and Thomson who believed they had a greater margin of time than in fact they possessed. By the time they made their fifth offer on Saturday 17 October we were so near to the vital 50.1% that they had missed what would otherwise have been a certain victory. The strain of all this has to be experienced to be fully understood. On Friday evening, 9 October I thought I saw a lull for the weekend and Mary and I went for a break to the Dudley Court Hotel at Brighton. Before we had been there for ten minutes a Glasgow call came through and when after lunch on Sunday we left for home my telephone charges amounted to more than half the entire bill.

When at 6.50 p.m. on Monday 19 October 1964 Sir Hugh and I told the waiting press men at the Savoy Hotel that SUITS controlled over 50% of the capital of Outram there was widespread amazement. It was a tremendous moment that I shall never forget, and after we had been photographed together I went home and slept until tea-time the next day! Hugh and I were then sixty-one and sixty respectively and during the latter part of the period, we started each day at 7.15 a.m., when we planned the tactics for the day, which ended just before 2.30 a.m., when I had taken the last press calls before the final editions were put to bed. Hugh lacked my robust constitution and I have always felt that the intense strain of those fifty-two days was in part responsible for his fatal heart attack two years later. Under the present take-over code, the outcome would without any doubt have been reversed. That I believe would have been a pity for, as *The Times* said in a leading article at the time: 'It cannot be right that, so long as there are two leading papers in Scotland, they should be in the same hands'.

As a result of the close contact during that period, Hugh Fraser and I had got to know each other intimately and from then until his sudden death, I saw a great deal of him. Although very different characters, we were on the same wavelength. In many ways he, too, was a shy man and the more I got to know him the more I liked and respected him. He was an inveterate chain smoker and although I have never smoked he said to me just before the Christmas of 1964, 'I want you to be a member of the Fraser club. This is your badge of office.' When I opened the box there was a beautiful 18-carat gold cigarette case and inside was a message engraved in his handwriting. 'But I don't smoke' I said. 'It doesn't matter', he chuckled, 'it's the badge of a club with a very limited membership.' A little later, unknown to me, he had asked the Editor of the *Glasgow Herald* to write a feature article concerning my career in the City and this appeared on 19 April 1965. In the section concerning Outram, Hugh had written the following sentence which had been printed verbatim. It read – 'I could have fought the battle alone but I could not have won it without John Kinross.' This way of saying thank you was typical of Hugh's generous nature.

In the autumn of 1966 when I think he felt that he might not have very long to live, he said to me one evening after dinner 'My greatest concern is the immense burden I'm leaving for my son. Will you help him through the first year or two and if he asks you to join the House of Fraser board, may I hope you'll do this?"

'Young Hugh' whom I knew only slightly, came to see me shortly after his father's death and eleven days after this sad event, I joined the House of Fraser board and a month later became a director of SUITS, which was then controlled by the Fraser family interests and in turn owned a substantial minority interest in House of Fraser. The understanding was that this would not be for more than about two years. Actually, I was there for over five years.

Walter Keymer was in charge of the accounts and J.C. Stewart, the recently retired Senior Partner of Wilson Stirling & Co CA was the excellent Finance Director of both companies. The whole of the financial side of the group was, therefore, in apple pie order. Soon after I joined, one of the leading American store groups made a take-over approach through Warburgs and the vital meetings were held in Geneva to ensure secrecy. Bill Kirkpatrick and I acted for House of Fraser, my opposite number being Sir Siegmund Warburg, whom I greatly respected. The Americans made what I felt was a fair opening offer and I was in favour of making a counter proposal at a somewhat higher level which, had it been accepted by the Americans, would have resulted in a bid for the whole of the capital at what I felt would have been an acceptable price. But at the last moment Hugh felt that he did not want to do this; Elson Gamble, his Deputy Chairman, supported him and so the discussions which had lasted for three days proved abortive. I never had the close relationship with Hugh that I had with his father, but over these five years we got along well together and I appreciated his unfailing courtesy and personal kindness. He was essentially a straightforward person who, as his father had forseen, carried a burden which made any real private life impossible.

Our board meetings were usually held in Glasgow in the extremely modest executive offices in which Lord Fraser had worked for many years. During that period, I was the one 'outside' director on these two boards. Much has been written about the usefulness or otherwise of 'outside' directors. While some of our most successful companies, such as Thorn Electrical have (until recently at least) been entirely composed of Executive Directors, I have come to feel that there is wisdom in having a sprinkling of directors who are not involved in the day-to-day management of the business. Without this, there is always a danger of the board becoming too inbred. But I think it is essential for every outside director to be available at all reasonable times, for informal discussions. The 'professional director' who only attends monthly board meetings and the Christmas office party is useless. In the Twenties, dubious company promoters such as Clarence Hatry had what amounted to a scale of fees for outside directors they employed on their boards, largely linked to the titles of the individuals. I am in favour of promoting a limited number of 'workers' to become directors of their company provided they are appointed on their genuine merits, and I hope to live to see this much more widely practised.

Recently, the many new restrictive rules for directors aimed at preventing 'inside dealing' have hampered financial companies from dealing in the shares of any company where one of their own directors is also a director of the company in whose shares they wish to deal. This may be the inevitable penalty we have to pay for the past excesses of stupid people, but I am afraid it may result in some good men refusing invitations to join boards of listed companies, where they could have made a useful contribution. It is now questionable whether it is wise to accept a non-executive directorship of any listed company if one is also a director of an actively managed financial company.

During my lifetime the ethics of 'making money' has, quite rightly, been questioned. For myself, I am convinced that provided money is made with complete moral and legal honesty, it should be encouraged and not derided. The heart of the problem is how to dispose wisely of the money so made, and I would suggest that far more thought should be given to this.

In 1955 a business organisation with whom I was personally in close touch, received about £750,000 out of the blue. The much-needed project for which it was intended lay several years ahead and was going to cost about £2 million. I was asked to invest the £750,000 during the preparatory period with the object of maximum capital appreciation. Over the next nine years the realised net profits before tax of the small finance company created for this purpose totalled £2,246,789, the annual amounts ranging from a high of £371,824 to a low of £154,203, all derived from Stock Exchange dealing.

Obviously there are people who would say that I made an indecent amount of money: but I firmly believe the only thing which matters is that this operation made possible something which was well worth doing. My friends did all the donkey work. I merely dealt (without reference to anyone). This was mostly planned each morning in bed when the *Financial Times* arrived at 7 a.m. When we had reached our target I stopped, with mixed feelings! The cynics will wonder how much I made out of all this for myself. The answer is absolutely nothing. My reward was to enable a project in which I deeply believed to become possible.

# CHAPTER EIGHTEEN

# *ICFC – Deputy Chairman*

On 7 April 1964 Bill Piercy sent the following note to all members of the ICFC staff:

> The following notice will appear in the press tomorrow:
>
> 'Sir Roger Makins GCB GCMG, has been appointed Director and Deputy Chairman of Industrial and Commercial Finance Corporation Ltd. He will succeed Lord Piercy as Chairman of the Corporation upon Lord Piercy relinquishing this office at the Annual General Meeting to be held on 9 July next.
>
> Mr John Blythe Kinross OBE will then become Deputy Chairman.
>
> Lord Piercy will remain on the Board.'
>
> I am naturally sad to relinquish the Chair after twenty happy and constructive years in which I have throughout had the support and encouragement of all of you. I should like to thank you for this.
>
> I have every belief that Sir Roger Makins, who succeeds me in the Chair on the 9 July, will command your full confidence and respect, and that you will give him the loyalty which I have always had.
>
> I know too, that you will continue to give Mr Kinross, who already has your affection, your full support in his new position.

Bill was then seventy-eight and quite recently he had begun to show his age. He presided for the last time at the Board meeting on Tuesday 7 July 1964 when all the Directors were present. By then the only remaining members of the original board were Blackford and Limerick. The other six were Alec Mackenzie, Sir Michael Milne-Watson, Dudley Robinson, Sir Roger Makins (later Lord Sherfield), Hugh Weeks and myself.

Bill had told me a little while before his announcement appeared that the Clearing Bankers had decided that the second Chairman in ICFC's history should be an independent man, unconnected with ICFC in the past. I sensed that he feared I might be disappointed at this decision. But

I was able to tell him, to his evident relief, that this was most certainly not so. I was absolutely content with my niche in the City and I greatly valued the wide variety of my activities. I was unwilling to alter my way of life, as I should inevitably have had to do in undertaking the many social and public obligations involved in the Chairmanship, and in my heart I knew perfectly well that I should not have made a good Chairman of ICFC.

On 2 July 1964, we had a dinner party for Bill at the Athenaeum. There were eighteen of the ICFC senior staff present, also the two original directors and Hugh Weeks; with Bill and myself that made a party of twenty-three. It was a happy evening with just a few informal speeches. Writing to me afterwards from Merano, Bill said 'I shall always remember the dinner party, which brought together so large a part of our joint comradeship and efforts since 1945. It will always be remembered too, I am sure, by all those who were present. I have a strong conviction that things are turning out well for the future. But it is important that *you* should not (I won't say overwork) but overdo the overworking. . . .'

Bill retained an office in our Copthall Avenue building (Piercy House) to which we had moved in January 1963. He retired from the ICFC board on 4 July 1966 while remaining Chairman of EDITH and Ship Mortgage. Three days later, on Thursday 7 July 1966, while attending a meeting of the Kuwait International Advisory Committee in Stockholm, he had a heart attack and died instantly. He had said to me more than once that he hoped to die with his boots on and that was exactly what he did. He was buried at Burford where he had bought 'The Great House' in 1934 (for £1,500). On 26 July there was a Memorial Service for Bill at St Michael's Church, Cornhill. The church was full and it was a moving occasion for many of us. Sir Douglas Logan, the Principal of the University of London, gave the address. I read the lesson.

For the rest of the Sixties, my work load was quite as high as it had been in the last few years of my whole-time service at ICFC. In the first two years especially, Scottish Industrial Finance absorbed a great deal of time. I was Deputy Chairman of ICFC for ten years (1964–1974) and in addition I was a Director of thirty-one companies, of which I was Chairman of eight. The pressure did not compare with the Fifties, but it is a sobering experience re-reading my office diaries covering that period.

Until the end of 1966 I frequently spent at least a week of each month in Scotland. Thanks to stockbrokers Rowe & Pitman, SIF started off by acting for G. & J. Weir Holdings Ltd in a placing of £2,500,000 6½% Debenture at 97½% in November 1964. This was followed in March 1965 by the flotation of F.J.C. Lilley, the specialist public works contractors. Lord Fraser had introduced me to Frank Lilley and this issue was the eventual outcome. In the same month we made four issues in all, the other three being George Gibson the Edinburgh shipowners, John G. Stein (refractories) and A.G. Barr the well-known soft drink manufacturers. Stein was the largest of these (£1,365,000) and in this case some of the board wanted to employ one of the London merchant banks. I had several meetings with Colin Stein, the Chairman, and then I met the whole board, who agreed that we should act for them. Colin was a man of outstanding ability whom I greatly respected. In the autumn of 1965, SIF floated the Fraser Westfield Motor Group which is now part of the Appleyard Group. The starting point in this case was my friendship with Lord Strathalmond, the Chairman of British Petroleum. Fraser Westfield was his family business in Scotland; the Chief Executive was his nephew. We also acted for Blackwood Hodge where we placed 1,500,000 7½% Preference shares at 21/- and a little later there was the flotation of Hunting Associated Industries. In 1966 and 1967 the number of issues was quite small but we were well employed on advisory work. We also acted for Dalmore Whyte & MacKay, the whisky distillers, in a placing of £500,000 7½% Debentures where J.C. Stewart CA, my colleague on the House of Fraser Board, was Chairman.

Sir Hugh Watson had died on 16 October 1966 and through Sherfield's good offices, we were fortunate in persuading Viscount Muirshiel to take his place on the SIF board. As J.S. Maclay, he had been Secretary of State for Scotland from 1957 to 1962 and was one of the most respected public figures in the West of Scotland where he lived.

In 1968 and 1969 there was another spate of issues. We floated Hart Builders, an Edinburgh firm, Ayrshire Metal Products, Hewden-Stewart Plant Ltd, which is now a leading firm in the plant hiring field, and Watson and Philip Ltd, the food distributors. We also acted for the House of Fraser when they purchased J.J. Allen Ltd in November 1969. By then SIF was involved in a number of take-over situations, and Bill Kirkpatrick handled the large volume of work which this entailed with great competence. He and I had built up a first-class relationship and SIF was flourishing.

In 1971, Reo Stakis asked SIF to undertake the flotation of his business and in June 1972 we made a successful Offer for Sale of seven million Ordinary shares of 10p at 36p (£2,520,000).

Bill had spent well over a year in winning Stakis' confidence and after a while I met him, liked him very much, and finally we secured the business for SIF in the face of considerable competition. Stakis who originally came to Glasgow from Cyprus, is a remarkable man and his hotel and leisure company has gone from strength to strength since we made the original issue.

But the toughest negotiation I had during this period was the take-over bid by General Refractories Ltd (GR) for John G. Stein & Co Ltd. The Stein family had retained a substantial interest in the company, and GR could not succeed without their consent, but unfortunately the Stein family was not always united in its views. Schroders acted for GR and Charles Villiers headed their team in the initial stages. He was an able and experienced Merchant banker and a formidable opponent in a negotiation such as this. But I can only feel that a blunder was committed when he was appointed Chairman of British Steel for in my opinion he was not an industrialist in any sense. The negotiations over J.G. Stein & Co, mostly held at Schroders' Cheapside offices, lasted rather more than a month during the spring of 1967. Roger Plant, then the Head of ICFC's Investment Department, came with me to all the meetings. GR eventually paid a full price, but on the other hand, it acquired a first-class business with some exceedingly able people among the senior management.

In 1967 I gradually devoted less time to SIF. Bill Kirkpatrick had deservedly built up a first class reputation in Scotland where his head-quarters were in our Blythswood Square office in Glasgow. I was, of course, in Glasgow nearly every month with Fraser's and I invariably saw Bill during these visits, after which I went to Edinburgh for the two Investment Trust Boards at Martin Currie & Co.

At the end of 1969 on one of these visits, Hamish Falconer told me that the Bute Trustees, who had been seeking a tenant for the family's town house at 8 Charlotte Square were now prepared to sell the freehold. This was not generally known, as the property had been advertised for letting only. We had been on the look-out for larger premises for ICFC in Edinburgh and I realised this was an opportunity we must not miss. We bought this superb house for £55,000, subsequently restoring the interior to its original state and making a small flat on the top floor – where I have stayed ever since on my visits to Edinburgh. In architectural terms, this office is unique among our eighteen branches. In 1980 its current value is assessed at £750,000.

After Bill Piercy's death, I was asked to take his place on two organisations. These were the White Ensign Association (created to help naval personnel of all ranks to prepare for their retirement by directing them to experienced specialised advice for their particular needs) and the National Federation of Women's Institutes where there were two Honorary Financial Advisers, the Hon. Alexander Hood of Schroders and myself. In this second case we were primarily concerned with the management of their invested funds.

The White Ensign absorbed quite a bit of time and the senior naval officers concerned reciprocated most generously by entertaining the lay members of the committee from time to time. At the beginning of July 1971, Lewis Whyte (Chairman of London & Manchester Assurance) and I went together to a dinner in the magnificent painted hall of the Royal Naval Academy at Greenwich. The menu was over-generous and the roast duck was especially rich. During the night I developed violent stomach pains, and, after an uneasy weekend, the pain flared up during the Monday night and reached such intensity that Mary telephoned John Hunt (Lord Hunt of Fawley since 1973) who was then my doctor and at 4 a.m. on Tuesday morning Elizabeth drove me to the Middlesex Hospital where I was admitted to Prince Arthur Ward. For a while I was treated as a suspected heart case but a gall bladder X-ray showed that mine was full of large stones. Cecil Murray, who was a friend as well as being the senior Surgeon at the Middlesex for anything of this nature, decided that it was too 'hot' to operate and so I went home after a few days. Later, on 3 August, Cecil did the job in an hour and fifty minutes. I was in Athlone Ward for thirteen days in all and after the first couple of days, once again I was really enjoying being in the Middlesex. There was a remarkable spirit in the ward; everyone who was over the worst tried to help the others. Losing my gall bladder has done me nothing but good ever since.

When Woodmans Farm was sold in the summer of 1968, we had kept Little Hyde, the best of the farm cottages, which we made into a pleasant week-end home and it was there that I convalesced. Earlier in 1968, Mary and I had explored St Johns Wood one Sunday, already realising that Woodmans had become too big for us with the children mostly away from home. As we moved on to Regents Park, we turned at random into Cumberland Terrace and stopped to admire the beautiful Nash façade. These terraces are all Crown property and one of the porters told us that the lease of a second floor flat was for sale. Cooper Brothers, the chartered accountants, were acting for the vendor and the next day I got in touch with the partner concerned. Coopers were asking £18,000 for the twenty-three year lease of the flat which had five bedrooms and two bathrooms and was in a bit of a mess internally. I felt this short lease was a poor investment and so I did not need to put on an act – I just exuded natural gloom over the proposition. We were about to leave for a fortnight's holiday in Portugal and I said I would come and see Coopers again once we were back. However, the flat had by then been on the market for some time and the partner concerned told me they would appreciate an earlier decision. So I said I would pay £13,000 and if they refused this I would be relieved, which was perfectly true. But my offer was accepted and I left for Portugal feeling that I had paid a ridiculous price. I could not have been more mistaken, for the current value of the lease in 1980, with only thirteen years left to run, was far in excess of what I had paid in 1968.

The expansion of my range of business interests also brought some enjoyable by-products. On 16 May 1969 Mary and I went with a small Ship Mortgage party to Liverpool and she launched the m.v. *Silverhawk* at Cammell Lairds. This was a 9,760 ton tanker designed to carry a range of liquid chemicals for the Australian coastal trade. It was built at a cost of about £2 million for Nile Steamship Co Ltd, an ICFC subsidiary. Unfortunately, at that time a strike was affecting part of Cammell's work-force and Geoffrey Moss, the Managing Director, told us that instead of the normal method of launching, the crude process of knocking out the 'chucks' until the ship responded to gravity was to be used.

That was the theory. But as we walked to the berth a man came running towards us calling out 'We couldn't hold her. She's away!' A few minutes later we saw the ship afloat in the dock. Lack of any recent experience had resulted in too many chucks being removed too soon and she had launched herself. The band on the launching platform was still in full swing: no one had told them to stop. Fortunately, no one had been injured and after Geoffrey Moss had stopped the band and arranged for the ship to be towed to another berth, we went back to the office and drank champagne for about an hour. By then, the *Silverhawk* was tied up and the band re-assembled. A tripod had been rigged up and the traditional bottle of champagne was hung from it. Nothing like this had occurred in Cammell Laird's 130 year history, so by now there were several hundred people waiting to see what would happen. Geoffrey Moss took Mary to the extreme edge of the berth, holding her round the waist. Mary then said in a voice which was clearly audible 'I name this ship, *Silverhawk*. God bless her and all who sail in her' and using all the force she could command she literally hurled the champagne bottle at the bow. It reached its mark and broke, to everyone's delight.

At the lunch party afterwards, Sir Leonard Owen, Cammel's Chairman, abandoned his set speech and spoke impromptu. The manner in which the mishap had ended had made the day for all of us and Mary's wit put the finishing touch to what became a hilarious party. Cammell's had asked her to choose the traditional present at Garrards and the diamond brooch and bracelet which she was given are beautiful examples of contemporary craftsmanship. But what she treasured every bit as much was a large pineapple which one of the waitresses gave her just as we were leaving. She said to Mary 'We all thought you were such a sport, so we wanted to give you this'.

When I look through my diaries of the Sixties and early Seventies, I realise that nearly all my lunches during this period were a vehicle for talking 'shop'. Harold Wincott's name occurs frequently, until just before his untimely death. There was a real bond between us and to me he was a totally unique person in the curious world of financial journalism. I also respected Francis Whitmore (*Daily Telegraph*) and Maurice Green (*The Times*) both of whom came from time to time. Among the merchant bankers, I saw most of Richard Fleming, but other names which crop up are Kit Garnett and John Lloyd of John Govett & Co, Mark Turner of Kleinworts, Bob Clark of Hill Samuel, Lord Poole of Lazards and, occasionally, one or other of the Rothschilds.

Lord Strathalmond used to come to lunch until he retired from BP and later I saw Eric Drake, Alastair Down (now Chairman of Burmah Oil) and Geoffrey Searle. Among the joint stock bankers, there was H.U. Lambert, now a Deputy Chairman of Barclays Bank and Norman Butler of Martins, an exceedingly pleasant man. The close relationship with Hambros was never quite the same after Jack's death but now and again I would lunch with Jocelyn Hambro. Isaac Wolfson came once or twice a year.

Eric Weiss, the creator and Chairman of Foseco Minsep was a delightful man whom I also saw regularly during that period. Long ago he had decided that to have more than about 500 people in any one factory would be counter-productive, for the personal touch would be lost. So, whenever any of the Foseco plants reached this limit, another factory in a different location was started, even though this was quite uneconomic in its early stages.

There are many other names but through the whole of this period I think Ronnie Leach, senior partner of Peat, Marwick, Mitchell & Co, perhaps occurs more frequently than any other, unless it is Alan Pratley. Alan had been the youngest partner of Davie Parsons & Co CA in 1928, when I got to know him well. He was possessed of excellent judgment, was unselfish to an unusual degree, and became my closest business friend, and also did a great deal of valuable work for ICFC. As well as being an original Trustee of The Mary Kinross Charitable Trust, he knew all about my personal affairs and those of the children. He was a year older than me, but he always looked so young and fit that I never gave this a thought. On 6 June 1968 driving home to Banstead, he pulled in to the side of the road and died before he could get out of his car. He was only sixty-five and so far as I am concerned no one has ever filled his place.

Roy Jenkins and I kept in touch after he left ICFC. This developed into a warm mutual relationship and I also greatly liked his wife, Jennifer. When he was Chancellor in February 1970, I went to lunch with them at 11 Downing Street and thanks to Jennifer's kindness I saw a number of the beautiful rooms which the house contains.

Many other names crop up and there are a number of Americans and Australians and a few from Eire. In May 1964, Mary and I had had a week's holiday in Dublin and also saw something of the beautiful countryside nearby. I returned in later years on several business visits and then Bill and I went over to explore the possibility of EDITH doing business in Eire. To this day, the Investment Trust of Guernsey has a number of Irish investments which have done us proud.

After the traumatic experience of the ICFC tenth anniversary dinner, nothing on similar lines was attempted until September 1966 when our twenty-first anniversary was marked by a dinner at the Mansion House, with 249 guests. Lord Sherfield proposed the Toast to the Lord Mayor and replied to the Toast to ICFC proposed by Sir Maurice Parsons, the Deputy Governor of the Bank of England. I proposed the guests and Sir John Mellor replied to this. On this occasion, most of the bank Chairmen were present and the evening went well. Bill had died only two and a half months previously. Roger Sherfield naturally referred to this in his speech and there was a general sadness that he had not lived to be present on this occasion.

Then on Thursday 5 November 1970 we gave a twenty-fifth anniversary dinner for ICFC, again at the Mansion House. This time the party numbered 291 and the guests were a distinguished gathering of the many professions associated with ICFC plus the Civil Service and a representative section of our customers. Roger Sherfield proposed the Toast to Her Majesty's Ministers and our principal guest, the Rt. Hon. John Davies, Secretary of State for Trade and Industry, then proposed the Toast to ICFC in which he touched on the reasons for the Heath Government's decision to abolish the Industrial Re-organisation Corporation. He then went on to ask whether the City of London had sufficiently modernised its structure to meet the present day needs of industry. It was a largely political speech which did not go down very well.

Davies had to leave immediately after speaking in order to be in time for a division in the House of Commons. When he had left I responded to the speech. I spoke of the 'adventure of building ICFC' and touched on some of the highlights of the first twenty-five years. Hugh Weeks then proposed the guests, and Leslie O'Brien, Governor of the Bank of England, replied. In spite of Davies' somewhat controversial speech, this was a successful occasion and the beautiful rooms of the Mansion House made a perfect background. It was an especial pleasure that Lord Blackford, by that time the last member of the original board of ICFC, was able to be with us. Although he was then eighty-three, Keith's mind was as acute as ever, while his interest in everything was undiminished. Little more than two years later, on 31 December 1972, he and his wife, who had been a courageous invalid for a long time, died very suddenly within a few hours of each other. Keith was eighty-five and I have missed him ever since. The last letter which he wrote me is dated 11 December 1972:

Dear John,

A line of Xmas greetings to you and may 1973 bring you all the best that you can wish. £13 million for Piercy House is a colossally good start. [It was in fact £15¼ million]. How much will each clerk cost the buyer for office space before he starts paying his salary? But I fear you will have to stand a v.big Capital Gains Tax. The political scene is more than usually interesting. I believe that Heath is gaining ground in spite of Sutton and Cheam. His greatest enemy has always been the TU leaders. Give my love to the ICFC boys, Tindale, Hugh Weeks and Co.

Yours ever,
Keith

The joys of travelling were something I discovered comparatively late in life. Until 1971, apart from visits to the USA in 1938, 1947 and 1950, I had not been abroad on business. So it marked a new departure when, on 3 March 1971 Mary and I left for a business trip to Australia. I had been investing in Australia since 1947 and it seemed sensible to have a first hand look at the country in which The Investment Trust of Guernsey had 8% of its portfolio. We flew by Qantas to Sydney, spending four days in San Francisco en route. During our ten days in Sydney I met a wide variety of interesting people and made contact with the management of most of the firms whose shares we held. Stafford Fox, then Chairman of BP Australia, was particularly helpful. Later we flew to Perth (where the shade temperature was 94 degrees F). We spent a day on the large BP launch going as far as Fremantle, and the Swan river was at its loveliest in the bright sunshine. We had a week in Perth, which we both loved. Again, I met many of the local business community, and Ron Kyle, the creator of Coventry Motor Replacements Ltd, made a particular impression on me. I started to build up a holding in these shares, none of which I have ever sold.

On Saturday 27 March we went on to Melbourne. This time, the people I met included some of the mining fraternity. I had interesting talks with Sir Maurice Mawby, chairman of CRA and his colleague, Rod Carnegie. John Baillieu, one of the leading stockbrokers, was another outstanding man whom I liked, but I took especially to Sir Lindesay Clark, then chairman of Western Mining. After we had talked for a bit, he rang the bell and asked his assistant for 'my map of Kampbalda'. He then covered the boardroom table with this and for over half an hour he brought to life the various stages of this unique discovery of nickel ore, where he had named all the individual workings after the men who had originally located them. I have seen him on each of my two subsequent visits to Australia and also in London.

I also got to know and respect Campbell Johnston, senior partner of J.B. Were. I had useful talks with Charles Rennie of the ANZ Bank and Charles Bell, the chief executive of the National Bank. I met Kenneth Myer, then chairman of Myers, Australia's leading department store company, and as I was then still a director of the House of Fraser, this talk became something of a two-way exchange. On my last day, I squeezed in a meeting with Dick McCrossin, the Head of Australian Resources Development Bank. He made an instant impression on me which has grown over the succeeding years. Here I felt was a really first-rate private sector operation.

At this time, Australian mining shares, and in particular the rubbish, were in a ferment. I had seen enough in Sydney to recognise the warning signs of a rigged market in many of the recently introduced shares, with fraud somewhere in the background. I had witnessed much the same thing in Canada, and also in the London market in 1928, though it was then artificial silk and other 'new' industries rather than mining. In all three booms, the fundamentals were similar and the Stock Exchanges concerned had all been guilty of allowing their facilities to be misused. Although this put me off the Sydney Stock Exchange, I liked Sydney itself. I saw it as a much more internationally minded city than Melbourne which reminded me of Edinburgh, with some of the same introspection, petty snobbery and a background of self satisfaction which, as seen from the outside, was difficult to justify. We, therefore, cut our stay there by three days and flew back to Sydney. This enabled me to see several people whom I had missed and, in particular, I had two meetings with Sir Robert Norman, Chief General Manager of the Bank of New South Wales. We clearly saw the mining boom in similar terms and in general I detected a kindred spirit.

On Thursday 8 April, we left for Fiji, reaching Nandi at 5 a.m. local time, from where we were driven to the Fijian Hotel, about two hours along the coast. It was the first time either of us had been in a tropical climate and the tremendous contrast between our air-conditioned room and the high humidity and heat outside was troublesome. However, we had a much needed rest.

Our plane for New York left Nandi at 1.35 a.m. on Monday 12 April. When we woke on the Sunday morning it was to the accompaniment of tropical rain such as we had never seen. This continued all day long, sometimes accompanied by violent thunderstorms. After various conflicting reports of the state of the gravel road to Nandi, we were advised to leave much earlier than our scheduled time and after tea we set off in a hired car with an Indian driver. As we left, the rain stopped, water lay everywhere and numerous streams were flooding across the road. However, by taking it all very carefully our excellent driver made slow but steady progress. Then, after it was quite dark, we came to the edge of a deep valley at the foot of which was a large river, crossed by a bridge normally high above the river. Up to that point we had barely seen another car but now we were at the tail end of a long line of halted vehicles and far ahead on the other side of the river was a similar line of cars with their headlights facing us.

Our driver stopped and after a while he returned to tell us that while the level of the river was now falling fast it was still more than five feet above the bridge which was, of course, impassable. We waited in the dark car listening to the noise of the flood waters and talking to the driver who from time to time went to inspect the road ahead. A lot of time passed and no car moved. Our driver seemed confident that if we could get across this bridge there would be no more major hold ups. About ten minutes before his estimate for our deadline, one Land Rover from the opposite bank succeeded in crossing the bridge and our driver said to me 'I try – yes?' . . . So we set off down the hill past all the stationary cars. He changed down to bottom gear and then we were on the bridge, which was trembling violently.

We had removed all our hand luggage from the floor and sat holding this, with our feet on the back of the front seats. The water swirled into the car just below the level of our seats. The car was a then current standard Ford model and only once did the engine splutter. When we reached the other side our driver stopped and inspected the engine. We had indeed been fortunate. We got to the airport eighteen minutes before take-off, and after an affectionate farewell to our staunch driver, we were on board the Boeing 707 and airborne exactly on time. Mary, as always, had been completely unflappable. Apart from the strain of the wait of nearly three hours before we crossed the bridge, the drive had been exhilarating.

We then spent six memorable days in New York, a city which we both love. Mary had not been back since 1939 and on the afternoon of the day we arrived we walked down to the foot of Fifth Avenue and sat for a while in Washington Square. That end of Fifth Avenue was very shabby and the pavement was so rough in many places that we had to walk with great care. At the far side of Washington Square the plate glass windows of a closed shop had been smashed and the broken glass was lying on the pavement, which had been roped off. We wondered if the authorities had deliberately left the mess to serve as an object lesson. Nearby, a speaker was addressing a practically non-existent audience. We listened for a while to a distinctly boring recital of the virtues of communism with thinly veiled calls to overthrow the elected government of the USA. A solitary policeman was making notes; the scene was one of complete calm!

I spent a good deal of time in the Wall Street area where I saw several old friends. Charles Rosenthal took me on to the trading floor of the New York Stock Exchange and I had an interesting talk with one 'specialist' in particular. At the weekend, we spent most of one day with Les Warner, then President of General Telephone and a Director of Thorns, and his wife at their home in Darien, Connecticut. He sent his car to collect us and I noticed that his chauffeur locked all the doors before we left. He told us that when one was held up at traffic lights there was the possibility of someone forcing his way into the car.

Our departure date – Sunday 18 April – came all too quickly. From every point of view, the six and a half week trip had been a success. I had made some good friends in Australia and came back feeling that it was right to be relatively heavily invested there.

In 1976 I returned to Australia and this time went on to New Zealand.

Lord Porritt, whom I knew well when he was President of the Royal College of Surgeons, and his wife had invited us in 1971 to stay with them at Government House (he was then Governor-General of New Zealand) and I had always regretted that we did not take up this typically kind invitation. By 1976 Arthur Porritt was back in London and though I met many of the leaders of the financial community it would obviously have been different with Government House as a base.

Amongst other things, I was exploring the possibility of setting up an EDITH type of organisation. In Wellington I had a useful talk with the formidable Prime Minister (Robert Muldoon) and spent most of the Sunday with Sir John Marshall, a former Prime Minister, and his wife (a truly marvellous couple) at their farm. I developed an affection for the New Zealanders to an extent that I did not for most Australians (with some notable exceptions). I spent some time with John Hunn and his excellent team who are in charge of the state owned NZ equivalent of ICFC (Development Finance Corporation) and it seemed infinitely better organised than anything I had seen in Australia (except for the Resources Bank). AIDC in Canberra, set up by Sir John McEwan in order to tackle very much the same problems, appeared to me to be an almighty mess. The man I immensely respected was Harry Knight the Governor of the Reserve Bank whom I saw several times at the Bank's headquarters in Sydney. I felt able to talk to him without reserve. He would be an outstanding man in any part of the western world.

A year later, April 1977 – I accepted an invitation to take part in a seminar sponsored by two Australian State agencies dealing with the finance of small businesses. There were four speakers, from the USA, Canada and Australia. I was asked to speak of the UK experience. I therefore enjoyed an interesting two days in Sydney and Melbourne and then I again spent some time with the Sydney bankers and with Harry Knight. The attitude of the older men at the head of the commercial banks was in contrast to Harry Knight's vision and was practically identical with Sir Charles Lidbury's in the UK in 1944. Sir Robert Norman was particularly kind, as he has always been, but I failed to convince him that any Australian equivalent of ICFC was necessary. The only ray of hope for the future was that several of the younger bankers, who as I write this in 1981 are now the chief executives of their banks, were more responsive and in general terms recognised that there was a genuine need for a new institution. I went to New Zealand again at the invitation of John Hunn and spent three exciting days with him inside DFC.

On this trip my friend Peter Wright (the 'Wright' of Hancock & Wright) took me in his plane for a three-day trip to the Pilbarra about 1,000 miles north of Perth. Hancock & Wright discovered most of the iron ore in this huge and savagely beautiful area and they receive royalties on a large part of the ore which is produced. We had Air Marshal Sir Val Hancock as co-pilot who, having retired as C in C of the Royal Australian Air Force, liked to keep his hand in at the controls. We landed at camps hundreds of miles from any ordinary route where iron ore deposits were being systematically investigated and I met people from all over the world of a type I had never come across before. They were – like Peter – the true salt of the earth.

In 1976, and again a year later, I spent six days in Hong Kong, which I regard as the most efficient and exciting city I have ever seen and perhaps the last hunting ground of the true entrepreneur – it even beats the New York of 1938. Thanks to Rob Norman's introducing me to Guy Sayer, then the Executive Chairman of the Hong Kong Bank, I was able to meet the heads of every business I wanted to see and I came back with the conviction that Hong Kong was in practical terms one of the safest places in the world in which to invest. In March 1980 Jon Foulds (Chief Executive of FFI) came with me for a third visit lasting a packed week. We saw many fascinating people including the Governor (Sir Murray MacLehose) and spent most of our last day – Sunday – with Sir Laurence Kadoorie at his weekend home. A measure of Hong Kong's explosive business activity: there are now more than a thousand Chinese families in Hong Kong worth over a hundred million pounds sterling each. The Investment Trust of Guernsey, as I write, has over 18% of its total portfolio of about £14 million invested in Hong Kong, which I believe will continue to grow and prosper because of the character and intelligence of the hard-working population of over five million Chinese and the presence of a sensible Government, which has the sense not to over-govern, combined with ample capital freely available.

To return to 1971. At the end of October I was able to resign from the board of SUITS and in January 1972 from House of Fraser. Our ICFC business in the Channel Islands was then growing apace. So I continued to work at full stretch in the early Seventies and in 1973, when I was sixty-nine, I succeeded Roger Sherfield as Chairman of EDITH. I had been a Director of the company since June 1967 and from its formation I had been closely concerned with practically every aspect of its affairs. I had been in daily touch with Roger Plant the recently appointed Manager of EDITH during the period when he was Head of the Investment Department and during the three years when I was Chairman of EDITH once again we worked together very easily.

The most important event during my Chairmanship was that I succeeded in raising ICFC's share of EDITH's equity capital from 26% to 41%. Although ICFC was then receiving substantial management fees from EDITH, these did not nearly compensate for the effort of the ICFC staff, especially in the branches. This caused a certain amount of internal strain and I decided that if the ICFC stake in EDITH could properly be increased this would be right for everyone. EDITH's business was prospering and it was fairly soon going to be necessary to increase its capital resources. In June 1974 I killed two birds with one stone by providing EDITH with further capital and increasing ICFC's stake at the same time. I designed the terms of a large rights issue, putting a high price on the new shares. The underwriting was unattractive so there was no difficulty in ICFC retaining the whole of it. In due course, therefore, ICFC had to take up nearly all the issue. At the cost of ICFC paying a full price, therefore, a much better balance of shareholding was established. The whole operation had been completed less than a fortnight before the new 'take over' rules were introduced, under which ICFC would have been obliged to bid for the whole of the company having acquired a stake of this size!

During the period of my chairmanship, Roger Plant and I visited all the principal ICFC branches each year. I addressed meetings of local professional people, through whom the great bulk of our business will always arise, and we also visited a number of the EDITH customers in each area. During the latter Sixties and early Seventies, I usually went to Norwich each year to lunch with the Norwich Union board. ICFC had had an excellent relationship with them from our early days. Desmond Longe was President of the Society during this period and these lunches, and the talks which followed, were occasions to which I always looked forward. Norwich to me is one of the most attractive of English cities, not least because of its beautiful cathedral.

At the seamier end of the business world, and especially during the 1970–72 period, I met a number of the new breed of 'secondary' bankers who were then expanding their empires all too rapidly. It was not exactly 1928 over again, for the methods were more sophisticated and on the whole the businesses they were buying into bore no relationship to the rubbish of the Twenties. The trouble mainly lay in the enormous degree of pyramiding which was used to create these 'banking' empires, by methods which were bound to lead to trouble in the end. However, while the going was good, it was not difficult for these young Turks to create the illusion that they had found new methods of creating wealth, and those who doubted this were dubbed out of date. At the time, the popular press was uncritical to say the least, and I feel it must shoulder some of the blame for what subsequently happened.

While I have been lucky in having a strong constitution, one shock occurred in 1973. Saturday 7 April was a bitterly cold day. As usual, we were at 'Little Hyde' and I had come in about 1 p.m. after a morning's gardening with Jim Stent. About 1.50 p.m. when Mary and I had finished lunch, a concentrated and violent pain developed in my chest and spread up my arms. I thought at first it was acute indigestion and lay down on my bed; but it became blinding and it was impossible to lie still. After about an hour-and-three-quarters the pain subsided, but by then I was pretty sure that I had had a heart attack. So I dialled the home number of my friend, Dr Walter Somerville, one of the leading cardiac consultants in the UK. He answered the telephone (what luck!) and told me that I had diagnosed what had happened correctly. We agreed that I would come at once to the Middlesex to be a patient in his ward (Meyerstein). John Wilson, my faithful office driver, came for me and by 9 p.m. when I got to the Middlesex, Walter was waiting. I was in Meyerstein for four and a half weeks and at times I felt in far worse physical shape than I have ever done either before or since. Some of the powerful drugs I was given had considerable side effects and this time, unlike all my previous periods in hospital, I did not enjoy my stay.

Eventually, on Friday evening, 11 May, thanks to the wonderful kindess of our friends Sir Alex Spearman and his wife, Diana, I was taken to their lovely home near Sarratt, only about a mile from Woodmans. Mary and I had been due to go to Menagio on Lake Como and Walter Somerville felt confident that I would be able to follow a week later. With some difficulty, I persuaded Mary to keep our booked dates taking Barbara Johnson, Bernard's widow who was then warden of Bernard Johnson House, in my place. Then on Tuesday 15 May I was taken to Heathrow, put in a wheelchair, and lifted on to the Milan plane, where I was met on arrival by Mary and Barbara. Barbara went home after a further week and Mary and I came home on 29 May, by which time I was a different person. I was back at the office again early in June but it took six months to get back to my normal routine and about a year before I felt completely well again. Since then I have undoubtedly been fitter than for years past.

On 30 November 1973 the merger of FCI with ICFC took place. This had taken over four and a half years to negotiate and it was almost entirely due to Roger Sherfield's diplomatic skill and determination that it eventually came about. I believe it will remain the outstanding achievement of his ten years as Chairman of ICFC. The first attempt at a merger had been made in a series of talks between Sherfield, the Governor of the Bank of England (Sir Leslie O'Brien) and Sir Humphrey Mynors (Chairman of FCI) in January–May 1969 which explored the possibility of an amalgamation of ICFC and FCI but eventually these came to nothing. This was primarily because Sir Archibald Forbes, Chairman of the Midland Bank, felt that a merger would let the insurance companies and investment trusts who held FCI's partly paid share capital off the hook (the uncalled capital was the banks' principal security).

In July 1970, Roger returned to the attack following the Heath election victory in June 1970. Sir Archibald who was then Chairman of the Committee of London Clearing Bankers was still strongly opposed to the idea and once again he killed it. (Archie, who was a nice yet formidable character, had never really liked ICFC, which he believed had taken business away from the banks.) In the autumn of 1972 a new phase opened, largely due to the fact that Eric Faulkner of Lloyds was then Chairman of the CLCB with John Prideaux of National Westminster as his Deputy. Throughout the four and a half year period, Roger had usually gone by himself to the numerous meetings, but on 23 November 1972 he asked me to accompany him to a meeting at Lloyds Bank with Faulkner and Prideaux, which proved to be crucial.

On this occasion three alternatives for the future ownership of ICFC were discussed:

(1) that ICFC should continue more or less as it then was;
(2) that some part of its equity should be made available to the public;
(3) that the ownership should cease to be collective and should pass into the single ownership of one of the banks.

In the discussion which followed, it was clear to both of us that the decision was likely to be a continuation of the status quo, but the two bankers undertook within six months to give us the official view of the CLCB about this and also about the future Chairmanship, which it was agreed were inter-related problems. In due course our shareholders chose the first alternative, and also decided that the Chairman should continue to be an eminent man from outside ICFC. Shortly thereafter, Freddie Seebohm, then Chairman of Barclays International, was invited to succeed Roger. It was not until the end of June 1973 that nearly everything had been agreed on the FCI front. Even then, the differences which remained proved quite difficult and it was November 1973 before the merger was implemented. In fact, the operation was a take-over of FCI by ICFC but in order to ensure a smooth passage a new holding company – Finance for Industry (FFI) – was formed to acquire *both* ICFC and FCI. In the process, the Bank of England's stake in ICFC rose from 3% to 15% with 85% remaining in the hands of the English and Scottish banks. In all FFI started life with resources of £482.75 million, some £186 million above the combined resources of the two constituents.

It was unfortunate that throughout the most vital part of these protracted negotiations, Larry Tindale was on secondment to the Department of Trade and Industry and, therefore, could take no direct part. He had been invited in terms which made it impossible to refuse and in April 1972 he started his two year stint in Whitehall as Director of Industrial Development and Paul Hildesley took over as General Manager of ICFC.

With Larry away, I was more involved in the details of these negotiations than would otherwise have been the case. On 27 November 1973, for instance, I sent Roger Sherfield a handwritten confidential note as follows: 'Thinking over our talk yesterday re composition of the FFI Board: I would be concerned if you and Freddie were to take the view that a majority of "ICFC directors" on this board was not vital during your Chairmanship and his. I see FFI as a piece of mechanics; useful so long as we control it. If we don't do so then instead of taking over FCI we should have sold ICFC to a Board controlled by people who know very little about us. If Michael Milne-Watson were appointed to the FFI board I think the point would be met'.

He acknowledged this saying – 'Thank you. I have taken the point about MMW.' Three weeks later, the FFI board appointments were in line with what I had wanted to see and Paul Hildesley was nominated as its first General Manager with Donald Clarke as Secretary-Treasurer.

The following year, at the Annual General Meeting of ICFC on 6 August 1974, four members of the Board who had reached the age of seventy retired. (After Bill's death, Roger Sherfield had wisely instituted a convention that in future everyone should retire at seventy.) The four were Lord Sherfield, Sir Hugh Weeks, Sir Charles Goodeve and myself. There was a farewell dinner party at the Brewers Hall on 31 July 1974 when I replied on behalf of the retiring Directors and of Arthur English, who was retiring as our Chief Tax Consultant. I followed Roger, who had of course replied for himself to Freddie Seebohm's speech. I had given a lot of thought to what I wanted to say and having uttered the necessary platitudes, I went on to speak directly to the younger members of the senior staff, thus:

> . . . You will inherit a unique institution which will then have taken rather more than a third of a century to build up. In all you do, I hope you will always keep before you as a first priority the maintenance of the special position which ICFC occupies in the financial structure of the United Kingdom.
>
> Let me explain. When ICFC was created in 1945 it was the outcome of thirteen years of intermittent debate between the City, the Civil Service and their political masters. As long ago as 1934, the efforts of Governor Montagu Norman very nearly launched us. Yet, so formidable were the difficulties of our birth that we were not delivered, a small but determined infant, into a somewhat sceptical world until eleven years later. Even then, this might not have been achieved without the pressures generated by the war.
>
> You must never forget that we were not just another institution. We were designed as something entirely different from anything then existing and we remain so to this day. Prior to our creation, the small businessman had absolutely no organisation to which he could turn for his long-term capital needs. This in a word, was the 'Macmillan gap' which we were designed to fill with resources of £45 million, unprecedented at that time. Now, twenty-nine years later, I believe we have proved conclusively that this gap was a fact and that it has been successfully filled by ICFC – a Corporation in the private sector, be it noted – which is profitable in its own right. Yet in 1945, many people in the City doubted the existence of the 'Macmillan gap' and few believed that it was capable of being profitably filled.
>
> During these twenty-nine years, our standards of service to small and medium-sized business have been our first consideration. The long-term profitability of our operations has, of course, been a close second, and the supreme art has always been and always will be to hold a wise balance between these two major objectives.
>
> We are still prepared to lend a suitable man £5,000 and we do many things which in the short term at least are unprofitable. We could so easily increase our profitability almost overnight by changing much of this approach. There is always, therefore, likely to be this temptation and how easy and how profitable it would be to succumb to it. I hope that when your time comes you younger people will never allow yourselves to forget this point. If ever you were to be tempted

to lower our standards of service, the old gap would gradually re-emerge.

In the process, we might have become one of the largest merchant banks, profitable to a high degree, but the gap created would be of such political importance that it would have to be filled and so the end of this sequence I believe would be the creation of a new institution to fill the gap which ICFC would then have left behind. I do not fear that you will ever allow this to happen, but you must be on your guard and see to it that we remain the unique institution that we are.

My last word is this – financial success alone may have been enough to satisfy the generation which preceded mine. My generation, I think, were not completely satisfied by it and I am confident that your generation certainly are not. You rightly want to feel that in your life-span you are making some contribution, however modest, to the improvement of the social and economic well-being of the country. As you get older this feeling will increase and I believe you will find this element in your working life essential.

So it is my greatest wish for all of you that in the future you will experience in this unique Corporation the contentment that only such satisfaction can bring to your working life.

Although from that day onwards I have scrupulously kept away from all current ICFC affairs, I can truthfully say that never once have I had to look for something to do. Knowing that plenty of activity lay ahead, I took pains to ensure that no leaving present would appear on my 'retirement', and I got my way!

Roger Sherfield was succeeded in the Chair by Freddie Seebohm while Larry followed me as Deputy Chairman. These were, of course, excellent appointments which have been outstandingly successful. Freddie had seen a good deal of ICFC and EDITH ever since the 1950s when he was the Barclays local Director in Birmingham and ICFC again had the advantage of having a Chairman who possessed a professional understanding of its business. Yet ICFC was extremely fortunate to have had Roger Sherfield as its Chairman for the ten vital years following Bill Piercy. Roger's knowledge of men and affairs was profound, and his understanding of how best to approach the leading figures both in the financial and political worlds, as well as his old stamping ground in Whitehall, was crucial. He was a strong character who commanded universal respect and, unlike Bill who was undoubtedly devious in some ways, Roger invariably said exactly what he thought with complete clarity and brevity. He was a man with great force of character who treated one of our messengers exactly as he would have behaved to the Chairman of a clearing bank.

Roger's sense of duty was immensely high. For example, on one occasion when we had a dinner for the senior staff he had spent the day in bed with a sudden attack of gastric 'flu. Yet he presided at the dinner, eating nothing and drinking only soda water. He looked quite ill and probably had a high temperature, yet his after dinner speech was, as always, first rate and his wit as sharp as ever. On more than one occasion, Roger went out of his way to do kind things for me, for which I shall always be grateful. Our relationship was nothing like so close as the one I enjoyed with Bill, but it worked well and happily during those ten years.

Although by August 1974 I was seventy and a half years of age, I was asked to remain as Chairman of EDITH and Scottish Industrial Finance until I came up for re-election, which in EDITH's case was in two years' time. I also continued to be a semi-Executive Director of ICFC (Guernsey) Ltd and ICFC (Jersey) Ltd, as well as retaining my Directorships of London Atlantic and North British Canadian Investment Trust, both of which we managed. However, I retired from the boards of all our subsidiary and some associated companies, such as Industrial Mergers, Income Investments etc., ten in all. I had been Chairman of Industrial Mergers Ltd since its formation in January 1967. Eric Izod was its Manager and, thanks to him, Industrial Mergers became the fastest growing division in ICFC and for a period it was doing more merger business than any of its competitors. More important, it maintained a high standard of conduct.

Early in 1972, the Chairman and General Management of ICFC had suggested that I should write an account of the events within ICFC from September 1945 to 1961 when I retired as General Manager. I felt considerable doubt about my fitness for this task, and so before agreeing to it I consulted Keith Blackford. In a letter dated 26 February 1972 he said, 'More credit is due to you than to anyone for the outstanding success of ICFC so you are just the man to write about it. . .'

Roger Sherfield arranged for me to have access to the relevant files in the Bank of England and thanks to Sir John Thomson, Chairman of Barclays Bank, I was given the same facility at 54 Lombard Street. Largely due to Arthur Chesterfield and Ralph Elliot, the Westminster Bank files were also made available. These were fascinating, not least because of the notes in the margin which Charles Lidbury was in the habit of making. Understandably, the Treasury felt unable to open their files, but I was able to see most of what was needed in the Bank of England and I had the great advantage of first-hand knowledge of most of what had occurred from September 1945 onwards.

I asked Dr Alan Butt-Philip, then on our staff, to help me. He was in his early thirties and had read history at Oxford. He and I spent many days in the library of the Bank of England and later at Barclays head office. Among the mass of correspondence which we read, Sir Otto Niemeyer's remarkable letters to Lidbury in 1944, on the one hand and to the Treasury on the other, were outstanding, Niemeyer who employed both wit and irony, seemed to us to be more than a match for the redoubtable Lidbury and he certainly held his own with the Treasury mandarins. ICFC owes much to him. It took us more than a year to assemble all the data we needed. Alan spent some time in the Public Record Office, and we acted only just in time to prevent many ICFC files, invaluable for our purpose, from being destroyed.

I had asked Alan to write all the pre-natal part of ICFC's history, starting with the Macmillan Committee in 1931. This he did so well that I asked him to add a chapter dealing with our relationship with our banker shareholders between 1945 and 1959. I felt that I had been too intimately concerned with this to write a completely unbiased account. The excellent chapter which he has written, therefore, entirely derives from what the files reveal.

I finished the draft in the early part of 1976 (in all there are twenty-two chapters, of which Alan was entirely responsible for three). I found it difficult to write and the draft, as it stands, needs some further work to tidy it up. It was always intended to be a record for the archives, not for publication, so the whole project has had a low timing priority. However, great care has been taken to ensure that everything contained in the twenty-two chapters is strictly accurate. It is simply intended to form part of the raw material for a professional historian when ICFC attains its first half century, or at some other appropriate period.

## CHAPTER NINETEEN

# *To Sum Up*

As I have explained, this account, primarily of my business life, was initially written for my grandchildren – fourteen in number, to date – in the hope that at some time in their lives it would prove of interest to some of them.

I had originally intended to call my narative 'What Fun It's Been' but I was dissuaded from this on the grounds that the title might suggest a show business autobiography. But those four words sum up the whole of my business life, though they do not imply it is over yet. My varied business interests still keep me very busy indeed.

In a world which is changing with increasing speed my grandchildren are inevitably going to live their lives in very different conditions to those which I encountered. So I had to decide at the outset whether the considerable amount of time which would be involved (writing this has taken nearly three years of my spare time) made it worth attempting. In deciding to write it I was influenced by the fact that, although the scene that I have tried to describe has already changed, human nature isn't very different. I felt that if I could accurately recount what I have taken part in, it might be some value to some of these fourteen young people. In every situation it is people who matter, and in essence the people my grandchildren will encounter will have much the same characteristics as those with whom I dealt. Kind Mr Jones of Turners Asbestos (pages 31 and 32) will continue to exist, though he may become still rarer.

I have come to feel that most people hope for much the same things whatever their race, religion or colour. Fundamentally, everyone wants a happy and secure home with someone to share it, which usually includes children in order to form a family. Men and women everywhere want to be given an opportunity to develop whatever talents they may possess and so to fulfil themselves. Self-fulfilment may take the form of creating business enterprises and making money in the process. When the money becomes the sole object and dominates rather than serves the man who makes it, self-fulfilment begins to recede. The more materialistic societies are the least happy – of that I am certain.

I have come to believe that life is not in fact so subject to either 'good luck' or 'bad luck' as is often supposed. Of course, there are occasions when for no apparent reason one meets the right person at the right time – be it one's future wife or business partner. But I believe that we are all given these opportunities and that the difference is that some people are able to recognise the potential significance of what is happening while others are not. I believe it is possible to develop an internal early-warning system, alerting one to seize an opportunity when one genuinely occurs, and equally to recognise the need for caution when a dangerous temptation presents itself. In the latter case, one is conscious of a signal which warns that one is about to overstep the mark in some direction.

Instinct, in essence, is the product of experience stored up over the years in one's subconscious mind. Anyone who leads a full and active life gains in experience all the time, so his instinct gradually becomes more reliable. I believe that one should treat instinct with the utmost respect. Nearly all the mistaken business decisions I have made at various times in my life have been due to 'second thoughts' where I have disregarded my original instinct.

In the long run, I believe we all get pretty much what we deserve. The principal exception is health. If you are lucky enough to possess a sound constitution, even though life may sometimes be unfair in the short term, you have it largely in your own hands to make a success of it in the end. On the other hand, if you have fundamentally bad health – which you can do little or nothing to rectify, then this indeed is 'bad luck'. It is true that there are many examples of heroic people who have triumphed in spite of this but it is an appalling handicap.

By 1936, when I was thirty-two, I had reached my goal of financial independence so that ever since then I have been able to choose my work without regard to its financial reward. This has given me invaluable independence of choice; in a sense I have been self-employed for the last forty-five years. The greatest handicap I have encountered has been shortage of time. I have never had enough of this since I was sixteen and even now this is the case. I can recall many occasions when I would have given a great deal for even ten minutes more.

Like Bill Piercy, I hope to die 'with my boots on'. In ICFC we all retire at seventy at the latest and thereafter, of course, one keeps completely away from the areas of all one's previous responsibilities. If one is fortunate enough still to be physically and mentally fit, a sudden transition from intense activity to an idle life could literally be a sentence of death. People who have long-established hobbies or alternative interests are fortunate; in my own case, work has always been my hobby and for long periods of my life I have never had time for anything else. I do, therefore, consider myself fortunate in having enough outside directorships and some regular work on the periphery of ICFC (in particular our two Channel Island companies) which give me a busy four-day week, even now.

For some time past, it has been my aim to end my life as I began it – with nothing in financial terms. But in the Seventies it has been virtually impossible to live in any relatively quiet area of Central London on one's pension and 'unearned' income, however large the latter may have been (a top rate of tax at 98% saw to that). It has, therefore, been essential to retain rather more capital than I would otherwise have done to supplement my net income. I have already lived five years beyond the Biblical span of life, and on the basis of my present medical prognosis it is possible that I still have a fair life span ahead of me.

I should like to end by saying how blessed I have been in my relationship with the various women who have taken some vital part in my life. The debt I owe to my Mother is incalculable, but I also owe a debt that I shall never be able to match to both my former and my present wife. In addition, since business has played such a large part in the whole of my life, I am very conscious of what I owe to my various secretaries, two of whom became my business partners. In this respect, my wife Mary herself was totally unique. But I have been incredibly lucky to have had Mary Francis as a helpmate for the past twenty years. We all regard her as one of the family, playing a vital part in nearly everything that has happened and latterly, among many other things, making a supremely good Warden for Bernard Johnson House in East Finchley, one of the principal projects of the Mary Kinross Charitable Trust.

I have no doubt that whatever time is left to me will continue to be of absorbing interest. How lucky I am that this should be so. What fun it's been, and continues to be with each day that is always too short.

# INDEX